ALL THE WAY HOME

Cover illustration: Donna Kae Nelson

Text Illustrations: Philip Chalk

Second printing, 1989

Printed in the United States of America

Library of Congress Catalog Card Number 87-71897

ISBN 0-89107-465-1

ALL THE WAY HOME

*Power for Your Family
to Be Its Best*

Mary Pride

CROSSWAY BOOKS • WESTCHESTER, ILLINOIS
A DIVISION OF GOOD NEWS PUBLISHERS

OTHER CROSSWAY BOOKS
BY MARY PRIDE

The Child Abuse Industry
The New Big Book of Home Learning
The Next Book of Home Learning
Schoolproof
Unholy Sacrifices of the New Age
The Way Home

Contents

Acknowledgments

This book could not possibly have been written without the help of the following people:

- Five members of the Crossway Books staff: Jan Dennis, a father of six, who edited the book with honesty and encouragement; Lane Dennis, a father of eight, including two adopted children, who contributed invaluable suggestions to the section on adoption; Mark Schramm, who designed the splendid format; Lila Bishop, who was always delightful and helpful, even late on Friday afternoons; and Ted Griffin, whose keen eye spared the book from many flaws.
- Three friends who read through and criticized the manuscript: Prudence Barker, a deacon's wife and home-schooling mother of five, and Phil and Pam Lancaster, our pastor and his wife, home-schooling parents of five. I might add that Pru and Pam between them are two of the best examples of hospitality, organization, and family management I know, and that someday I hope to be like them!
- The wonderful readers of my newsletter *HELP* who shared so much with me, especially those quoted in this book: Tammy Alger, M. B. from Washington, Pamela Boswell, Garland Brock, Arlene Dryden, Liz Ensley, Joanie Etter, C .F. from California, L. G. from California, Susan Gaddis, Les and Penny Gioja, Judy Goshorn, R. H., Kim Jeffery, Marcia Jones, A. K. from Wisconsin, Elizabeth Kendal, Mary Jane Kestner, Nancy Krumreich, Lauri Lienhard, Donnajean Meahl, Diane Moos, D. M. from Iowa, Liz Messick, Lynn Nobles, Martha Pugacz, Judy Pickens, Karen Rhodes, Marsha Riben, Linda Rivas, Charlotte Siems, Beryl Singer, Laurie Sleeper, Diane Stearns-Smith, D. T. from New York, Sandy Teall, Kathy von Duyke,

and Chaire Whitmire. Among the readers quoted you would find (if you totted it up) over 500 years of practical mothering and marital experience.

Our six children have been chock-full of life and clever ideas while I was writing this book, some of which contributed to the book and others of which provided pressing incentives for immediate spiritual growth! They are sweethearts, each and every one of them, and so is my husband Bill, who ran herd on them for the last weeks while I was finishing this book, in his spare time when he wasn't taking care of our home business. I thank God for them all, and for you, to whom this book is dedicated with hopes and prayers. May God bless you and bring you *all the way home!*

Introduction

This book has a long and motley history.

It all started as one sentence in a footnote in my first book, *The Way Home*. I had an innocent little idea, mentioned in the footnote, that it would be nice to follow up that book with a second volume, in which I could present resources and ideas to help readers put the suggestions of the first book into practice.

The idea grew. It prospered. It leafed out into a book contract. I happily started researching resources, writing away to all manner of odd organizations, and reading books until the wee hours.

But, unknown to me, a time bomb was ticking away in my neat little outline—a chapter on Home Education Resources.

For behold, the chapter grew into a section. The section grew into a book. Before I knew it, I had not written *this* book—the one you are now reading—but *The Big Book of Home Learning*. And even that book divided and grew into two books, *The New Big Book of Home Learning* and *The Next Book of Home Learning*, both bulging at the seams and anxious to divide into even *more* books if I would let them.

Every year or so, I would go to my publisher and get a contract to do this book, which then before my wondering eyes would cheerfully change into something entirely different. This book has, at various times, turned into *The Child Abuse Industry* (a book on the failures of our bureaucratic child abuse system) and *Schoolproof* (a look at how to make teaching more fun and effective), neither of which bears the remotest resemblance to my original, humble little project.

It got to the point where I was embarrassed to try bringing this project up. I envisioned the raised brow, the touch of delicate disbelief in the voice on the other end of the phone line: "Really? You want to try writing that follow-up to *The Way Home* again? What book are you actually planning to write *this* time?"

Obviously, enough was enough. I had to take myself firmly in hand and finish the project as advertised.

This long delay had meanwhile produced some unexpected assets. In God's providence our family had started a quarterly newsletter/magazine called *HELP*. Ever lazy and always willing to learn something new, I had set *HELP* up as a reader forum. This meant that most of the insight, resources, ideas, and other neat stuff we published did not come from Bill or me, but from thousands of other families as they shared how they were making their daily lives more Christ-centered and joyous.

In other words, here was a ton of marvelously creative stuff just begging to be mined for the benefit of us all.

So now, even though this book is, as usual, wriggling in its bonds and pleading to be turned into four or five different projects, I have no intention of letting it get away. How could I bear to let you miss out on Beryl Singer's hilarious "Postpartum Guide for Fourth-Time Mommies" or the true story of how God cured a husband's TV addiction by frying his TV set, to name only a few of the wild, wacky, and wonderful stories hundreds of others have shared with me?

In this book you will hear from women surprised by infertility and women surprised by babies. You will be inspired by other families who have started home businesses, planted home ministries, and made waves in their communities. My own family is engaged in these activities, and the book also draws on our years of research and practice.

All the Way Home is not a bulletin launched from an ivory tower, but a real get-down, hands-on manual. It was written in the midst of home schooling our older children, making up ads for our home business, getting refreshments together for our church, helping out in a state representative's campaign, answering letters, nursing the baby, reading to the toddler, and cleaning the house.

Not that anybody here expects you to start 100 new activities all at once! After the initial chapters on how to relax and enjoy your marriage and children, a good part of the book is devoted to management strategies to help you settle in your own mind which activities are top priority at this season of your family's life, and organization strategies to help you accomplish your goals. The rest of the book then outlines how to start up a home business, how to develop as a church leader, how to develop a family ministry, and how to influence your community for Jesus.

The only Biblical road to revival is through preparing our families to serve God in the way He intended. So much has been said about "strengthening the family"—now it's time for the family to strengthen itself. God has given us the way and the tools. All we have to do is use them.

Throughout this book, I take the position that certain things are good: permanent marriage, sexual purity, babies, parents raising their own children, personalized charity, and family financial independence, to name a few. If you have any question about any of these positions, read *The Way Home*. It makes the Biblical case for family-based living as a total lifestyle. *The Way Home* is the "what to" book; *All the Way Home* is the "how to" book.

I must say that I have really enjoyed living this book, even more so than writing it! As I look around at our six children studying, playing, and helping around the house; our home office and basement warehouse; our shelves lined with books full of ideas for future projects; our garden-to-be, full of beautiful dreams; and my dear husband who has worked so hard with me—my heart overflows with thanksgiving to God. He is really the best part of the story, even more than what He has done for us. We have seen so much of His tenderness, faithfulness, and care. It happened one day at a time, as we went from a childless couple who still in many ways were children ourselves to the parents of half a dozen, from living hand-to-mouth in a succession of run-down apartments and mobile homes to having something to share.

We started the journey detailed in this book with just a mustard seed of faith and hope, and I am glad, because now I can report that God blesses those who are faithful in even tiny things. Wherever you are, you can come all the way home the same way we have—one step at a time!

How to Use This Book

Each chapter in this book was designed to open up an avenue of family fruitfulness.

- The text leads you through the main idea.
- In the side columns you will also find quotable quotes, tips, ideas, and stories from a host of sources: books, magazines, newsletters, other homeworkers, and the Bible.
- To make the fullest use of this book, please take the time to look through the Resources. I have compiled, for each chapter in this book, information about the best books, magazines, organizations, and suppliers to help your family grow further in that area. These are ranked in terms of their usefulness to a beginner; so if you are new to a given subject you won't be overwhelmed with too many options at once.
- And of course the index, compiled by my loving husband Bill, will help you find the information you need *fast!*

I would love for this book to become the "friend" who helps you get connected to dozens of new areas of family productivity.

Enjoy it. Read the text like a regular book, and browse through the margins for more insights and ideas, or just for fun.

Then choose one area you would like to venture out into, turn to the Resources for that chapter, pick a few books to read or organizations to write away to, and amaze the rest of us! "Do you see a man skilled in his work? He will serve before kings; he will not serve before obscure men" (Proverbs 22:29).

More power to you!

Marriage for Mortals

*G*rowing up in the sixties, I learned many important things about marriage from the covers of popular women's magazines. I learned that marriage was for pleasure and romance. I also learned, from thousands of desperate articles with titles like "How to Hold on to Your Man," that men typically wanted *out* of marriage and it was a woman's job to keep hers *in*. This was to be accomplished by being

(1) Prettier
(2) Sexier
(3) And More Fun to Be With

than all other women in the world.

Not surprisingly, with such a view of marriage I decided early on to opt out of the entire picture. As the apostles said to Jesus in another context, "If this is the situation between a husband and a wife, it is better not to marry" (Matthew 19:10).

The apostles had been alarmed by Jesus' pronouncement that men were supposed to stick with their wives until death did them part. I was alarmed by our society's message that men and women were only supposed to stick together until debt did them part, or sexual frustrations, or wandering eyeballs, or any of the other myriad excuses for unfaithfulness promoted by Madison Avenue and our friends in the media. A little thought proves that no amount of expensive makeup or aerobic exercises can make a fifty-year-old mother of four resemble a fresh-faced twenty-year-old. So why should any woman enter that competition, only to lose it as she inevitably gets older? As one cad on the prowl for younger women put it recently, "I don't care if my wife gets a face-lift, loses 30 pounds, and buys a new wardrobe, she'd just be a 50-year-old woman who looks great for her age."[1]

Events have since vindicated my skepticism. The divorce rate is hovering around fifty percent,[2] and that doesn't even include the vast number of men

> Restoration of a culture will be marked by restoration of marriage as a source of joy and a cause for celebration.... This renewal must be heralded, as divine renewal has always been, by "the voice of bride and bridegroom." The church cannot experience a full or valid renewal unless it once again embraces the biblical pattern of marriage.
>
> —Derek Prince
> *Charisma*, August 1986

My husband Henry read parts of *The Way Home* and the first result was that we relaxed about marriage and began to get along even better. We had been striving for romance and communication, etc., and finally realized that we just needed to be committed and work together. The funny thing was that as soon as we did this, the romance and communication began to happen.

—Charlotte Siems, OK

who temporarily use and then abandon women without bothering with the ritual of matrimony. Not that women are any slouches at chopping the ties that bind, either—seventy percent of divorces are initiated by women. Apparently the guys aren't any better at staying pretty, sexy, and fun to be with than the gals.

So much for the bad news. The good news is that there is a way to stay married that the people who write for women's magazines never knew about. It does not depend on you discovering the Fountain of Eternal Youth or wowing the world with your cosmopolitan charm. No false eyelashes or Fredericks of Hollywood lingerie is required. No muscle-building sessions with the hulks down at the health club are needed, either (if you happen to be a man reading this!).

In *The Way Home* I talked about some different models of marriage. Three types of "Me" marriage are popular now: companionship, intimacy, and the fifty-fifty contract. If you want to find out what's wrong with these, read that book! Now we are going to talk about the right kind of marriage—the productive marriage—and how it works.

In Whom We Trust

An elementary physics principle says that you can't hold two things together that are being tugged apart by outside forces unless there is another, stronger force binding them together. We all know about the outside forces pulling your husband or wife away from you. Now let's look at the *inner* force that holds a marriage together.

Is it (check as many as needed):

- ☐ Sex?
- ☐ Affection?
- ☐ Sheer force of willpower?
- ☐ Clever tricks?
- ☐ Always giving in to your spouse's demands?
- ☐ Good cooking?
- ☐ Economic necessity?

The inner force that holds marriage together is not any item on that list. Some may contribute to a marriage, some do not, but none of them gives you what it takes to consistently slog on through rough and stormy weather.

The little-known truth is that *God* provides the force that holds marriages together. This is true for non-Christians as well as Christians. Just as God physically holds the atoms in our bodies together, whether we are saved or unsaved (Colossians 1:16, 17), He is the power, whether recognized or not, behind every successful marital union, whether of believers or unbelievers. Conversely, men and women only begin abandoning normal committed heterosexual relationships when God "gives over" a people as punishment for their idolatry (Romans 1:21-25).

Our marriages are like popcorn kernels. Sin heats up the kernels and starts them ricocheting around the pot. For a while, God holds down the lid. Once He takes off the lid—giving over a people—the marriages start flying every which way.

Point One about marriage, then, is that *God holds it together.* For Christians, as husband and wife orbit together around the Sun of Righteousness (as Christ is called in Malachi 4:2), the Lord provides the "gravity force" to keep us from flying off into space! But when husband or wife, or both, take their eyes off serving God and start thinking of serving themselves, you have trouble. You alone don't have enough "gravity" to keep your husband in orbit around you, or vice versa.

Hundreds of other books talk about what happens when one of the marriage partners flies off into space. For now, let's talk about what marriage *should* be like. This is not being idealistic. You aim at a target in order to hit it. Vague wishes for romance and an occasional dinner date do not provide reasons for staying married when the going gets tough.

The reason God is willing to go to the trouble of establishing your marriage and holding it together is that He has a purpose in mind for it. You're going to

Definition: Marriage is a covenant designed by God to show forth God's image and carry out God's plan.

☐ Christian parents see that
the Bible says we are supposed to spank disobedi-
ent and rebellious chil-
dren (Proverbs 13:24,
23:13-14, and 29:15 for
starters). We use force (not
violence) to punish their
bad behavior. Families
that ignore God's rules
about swiftly punishing
sin get wild, unruly children.

☐ God's laws for civil government say that rulers
are supposed to punish
criminals and violent rev-
olutionaries. Rulers are
meant to use force (not
police-state uncontrolled
violence) to punish criminals' bad behavior. Gov-
ernments that ignore
God's rules about swiftly
punishing crime get wild,
unruly neighborhoods
where nobody dares am-
ble to the corner without a
can of Mace and an attack
dog.

hear this several times during this book; here it is the
first time: *God loves His people and has a wonderful plan
for their lives.* He has a plan for your marriage.

Marriage is not just R&R from the world or a way
to have legal sex. Marriage is supposed to be *productive,* or as the Bible puts it, *fruitful.* You are supposed to
be able to look back at your years together and say,
"Look what we did!"

Four Kinds of Fruitfulness

Part of what you do in marriage is have children,
if God enables you to conceive and bear them. This is
one kind of fruitfulness: *physical* fruitfulness.

Marriage is also intended to be a little picture of
the relationship between Christ and the church (Ephesians 5:22-32), and so far as yours is, you are being
spiritually fruitful.

Thirdly, not only does God-centered marriage prevent your family from causing social problems, it also
is like a little laboratory for developing *socially* fruitful approaches to human relationships. The rule that
works (or doesn't work) in your family works (or
doesn't work) in the state. So we don't need to try
massive social experiments to see what will happen if
governments become permissive or tyrannical; just
look at a permissive or tyrannical family. Contrari-
wise, the skills and example learned in a productive
family ideally equip children, when they grow up, to
become community leaders. More on this in a future
chapter!

Marriage is also intended to be an *economic* part-
nership. By this I do not mean that Mom and Dad are
supposed to both abandon the kids and trek out to office jobs in some multinational corporation. That's
living like roommates, not financial partners. Couples
are intended by God to work *together* economically:
one contributing raw goods and the other finishing
the products, one operating as Chairman of the Board
and the other as Plant Manager. The ideal is not side-
by-side enslavement to megalithic monopolies, but
each man "under his own vine and and under his

own fig tree" (Micah 4:4)—in a word, independent family businesses that direct the talents of all family members to a common goal. We will see in detail how this works out in future chapters.

So God designed marriage to be physically, spiritually, socially, and economically fruitful. These kinds of fruitfulness are all closely connected. Children, our physical fruit, should be brought up as Christians, thus becoming part of our spiritual fruit. We become socially fruitful through the process of training them, and economically fruitful as the whole family learns to work productively as a team. Other kinds of spiritual fruit—an increase in one family member's Christian virtues, for example—also often brings forth fruit in the other areas, just as simply having children provides an opportunity for growth in many other areas.

We may not necessarily be able to produce all the desired results. We may not be physically able to bear children, or our home business might go down the tubes. But we ought at least to aim in the right direction. The contraceptive mentality that sees kids as a burden, holiness as impossible, personal responsibility as undesirable, civic liberty as outmoded, and small business as uneconomical has got to go. These are the glory of the family, and no small part of the reason why God designed it in the first place.

Why It's Worth It

You see what a difference this outlook makes. "Staying married for the sake of the kids" is not a laughable reason for hanging tough when your spouse is hauling you over the rocks. More to the point, being allowed to have joy in the legitimate fruit of your marriage keeps you off the rocks in the first place.

If you've ever given birth to a baby—you've accomplished something.

If you've ever had a really cutting remark all loaded and ready to fire, and stuffed it back in the silo instead of launching it at your mate—you've accomplished something.

> The point is not that the family is perfect but that there is no substitute for it.
>
> —Joseph Sobran

A seminary we know received a gift from a denominational women's organization designated for services to seminary wives. Here are the "benefits" to be provided as listed on the sheet publicizing the gift:

☐ Marriage Seminar/Testing
☐ Professional Christian Counseling
☐ Mother's Mornings Out
☐ Wives' Support Group
☐ Quality Babysitting Services
☐ Wives' Tuition Supplements
☐ Senior Year Couples' Follow-Up
☐ Senior Wives' Mini-Course
☐ Annual On-Campus WIC Seminar

Note the assumption that children are problems to be removed and that couples need *paid* counseling, instruction, and testing.

If you've ever helped out a fellow human being instead of sending him to a government agency for relief—you've accomplished something.

If you've ever baked cookies, or done your own laundry, or *not* lobbied for a Federal Department of Housework to take care of your dirty dishes—you've accomplished something.

If you've ever sat down together and planned a budget, or sat down together and planned a business—you know you have accomplished something!

You can accomplish some of these things solo. God intended, however, for most of this work to be done by productive marital partnerships. Any of you raising a child alone know why. There's safety in numbers, not to mention that a husband can spell r-e-l-i-e-f after a wife's day chasing toddlers! More importantly, society can't take its character from the God-designed male-and-female team if one-half is perpetually missing. Each sex is mystically different. Fitted together they show the whole picture of God's character: His protection and His nurture, His justice and His love. Torn apart, they show more of Satan's character: his bitter griping and envy, his destructiveness and irresponsibility.

Every sphere of life, from civil government to business, and not forgetting child-rearing, needs both male and female sexually bonded together to keep it sane. It's not enough to hire women into the business and sign up men to work in the day-care center. Without this special bond and its concommitant permanent responsibility for projects set in motion, strange things start happening. Take a look at the 25th Precinct of Harlem or the burned-out South Bronx.

Your mission, Mr. and Mrs. Smith, should you decide to accept it, is to keep this home, church, business, world, and nation on course.

The Sickness Model v. the Growth Model

Speaking of keeping on course, it's about time someone looked critically at all those courses on marriage. You hire a sitter, purchase tickets, and spend a weekend learning how to get in touch with yourself and your feelings and your spouse and his or her feelings. Mmm, it feels good, having your feelings massaged. Forget your blushes when the jolly seminar leader forced you to tell twenty total strangers about your most embarrassing sexual moment. This is *real!* And so are the hugs in the encounter group!

After all this, you get homework. Special chats with the loved one about your relationship. Note-taking and journals. "What We Should Have Done on Our Summer Vacation." More books to read, oh my! Getting in touch with yourself is a lot more work than you thought it would be. Apparently you are a pretty slippery character. It is fun, though, to learn to psych out your better half. "You are just a Placater," sounds so fine tripping off the old tongue when it looks like you are losing an argument. Get in there and learn to twist some dials before your mate starts twisting yours!

It's not entirely pleasurable, of course, to find out about all these *problems* your marriage has. But then, you couldn't honestly say things were perfect, and that is why you went to that seminar or bought that book in the first place, isn't it? Looks like a lot of hard work is needed to patch up the holes and shore up the walls. Great things are promised, though, if you heroically follow every bit of advice bought and paid for. Peace. Love. Joy. Ten minutes with nobody screaming at you. But now this other fellow over here sees that bid and raises it. He'll give you peace, love, joy, no screaming, *and* tender intimacy. Better check that one out. Oops, now we have found out even *more* problems! You are immature and I am verbally abusive. You are in the throes of the Peter Pan Syndrome and I like to play power games. You are a nogood Type A Personality and I am a not-much-better Brand X. Much more work is needed . . . more uncovering of our innermost selves . . . more tearful latenight personality-probing . . . more attempts to patch up the holes and rents in our marriage. Yes, indeedy, this marriage is *sick!*

Of the several friends who have gone to and recommended that we go to marriage weekends, *all* are divorced.

Human nature *sees* and *concentrates* on what the mate "was to have learned at that seminar and is now ignoring." "He's not doing what he learned he should."

What we need is to consider the other as more important than ourselves, and marriage becomes amazingly smooth!

Marriage weekends concentrate attention on us instead of on God, where, as you point out, it belongs.

—A Missouri mom

I used to read a lot of books on marriage before our children came along, and Wayne would say, "Just forget what some author said, it's *me* you married, not him, and I'm the only one you have to please."

My favorite times alone with Wayne weren't planned, they just happened in the normal course of family life. . . . Not that planned time together isn't good, but too much introspection about your marriage can be counter-productive. Just enjoy living together. Don't give yourself grades in marriage.

—Beryl Singer, MA

As Jesus said, "It is not those who are well who call a physician, but those who are sick." So one good way for a physician to build up his practice is to convince a lot of well people that they are sick.

The old-time hucksters of snake oil remedies used to promise to cure people's actual ailments. The new ones invent ailments to cure. I'm not saying that all of us are great husbands and wives. I'm saying that, though we may not act the best at all times, that does not mean our marriages are "sick" or "have problems" in the usual sense. Sickness implies a lack of health, and health seems to be defined nowadays as sinless perfection, not to mention a total absence of all pressures or stresses from outside.

I've Got You, Babe

Look at a baby. Any baby. Do you see someone who can balance a checkbook and drive a car? Of course not. Does that mean the baby is sick? Does he have problems? Of course not. The baby is a baby. When he grows up, he will do these things.

Most of us today get married when we are still social babies. We don't know how to share our toys. We cry. We have tantrums. We can therefore expect a certain number of collisions between irresistible forces and immovable objects when we first wed. This is normal for our stage of development, and does not require anxious experts poking around our innards to resolve. What happens, given the proper conditions which I will describe in a minute, is that we begin to grow up.

Growing up is a natural, healthy process. The baby does not introspect about whether he will learn to crawl. He wants to crawl; he keeps on trying; eventually he does it. He learns to talk by listening to and babbling to the grownups, and he does this much more successfully than he later will learn to read in school where the experts have planned carefully sequenced lessons for him.

New theories of marriage have turned marriage into a three-ring circus of pleasure, personhood, and parenthood. You can't perform in all three rings at once, but you are told you must. You are further told your marriage is ill unless you can not only perform in all three rings, but do it with a smile. Having set up this impossible standard, the experts now order you to meet it immediately, and label you a failure if you don't.

If you fight, if you yell, if you have trouble deciding who should do what when, if you hurt each other's feelings, if you can't always control the kids, you are normal human beings. This doesn't mean you should keep on doing these things forever. You should grow up. But this means taking a long-term view, not expecting Instant Marital Satisfaction to be dished up with your Wheaties.

Comparison Shopping

Let's look at a few of the other important differences between what I call the Sickness Model and the Growth Model of marriage.

The Sickness Model posits that the life of your marriage is artificially sustained only by continual infusions of expert advice and assistance. You are running on batteries that need constant replacement.

The Growth Model recognizes that your marriage has its own inner principle of life, supplied by God. Your marriage is organically alive and does not need transfusions or a heart-lung machine to keep it going.

The Sickness Model asserts that experts are the proper trainers of married couples. Their institutional training is their credential. You will be trained through lectures and indoctrinated in theories.

The Growth Model says that older couples should teach the younger. Their experience and righteousness are their credentials. You will learn through these older people's example, their stories, and the Word of God.

The Sickness Model says your marriage needs constant intervention: you are not alive, just animated by electric current.

The Growth Model says you are alive and need only to be fed: your marriage needs nurture and support.

SICKNESS	GROWTH
1 Artificially sustained	1. Alive
2. Experts	2. Older couples and Bible
3 Constan intervention	3. Nurture
4. Replace husband's and parents' authority	4. Respect husbands and parents
5. Technique	5. Righteousness

11

The Sickness Model attempts to replace the husband's authority with that of the expert. The Dr. Spock generation saw how Dad's desire to discipline his erring offspring was often overruled by The Book (meaning Dr. Spock's *Baby and Child Care*, not the Bible).

The Growth Model respects the family's authority, and does not try to help the wife or the children by sidewinding around the husband or parents.

The Sickness Model concentrates on technique: doing it right.

The Growth Model emphasizes righteousness: being right with God.

Therefore, Some Practical Suggestions to Improve Your Marriage

(1) Quit reading mass-market women's, parents', and baby magazines. Especially the "authoritative" ones like *Parents* and the yuppie three-ring-circus ones like *Parenting*. Rules of thumb: (a) If the ratio of reader input to expert input is less than fifty-fifty, skip it. You can learn something from other people's experiences; their theories will only mislead you. (b) If the writer has not *personally* raised righteous children, pass up that article.

(2) Ask your mother, your friends, your next-door-neighbor, and the old ladies at church when you have a problem. (Remember: A problem is just a riddle looking for a solution.) Don't trot off to professional counselors or write to Christian leaders. "Better a neighbor nearby than a brother far away" (Proverbs 27:10). Trap: Going for advice to a member of the opposite sex. This is how pastor-elopes-with-elder's-wife scandals are born.

(3) Try to cultivate a "team" feeling between your spouse and yourself. Avoid the this-is-mine-and-this-is-yours syndrome like the plague.

(4) Bloom where you're planted. Don't try to change partners. Look forward with hope and faithfulness, rather than back with vain regrets and wishes. And thank God for what you have. It could be worse!

For at least 25 years I've received offers for free subscriptions to women's magazines. My reply was, "Why should I subscribe to magazines that try to tell me that I'm not enjoying being a wife and mother?"

—Martha Pugacz, OH

Holy Sex

2

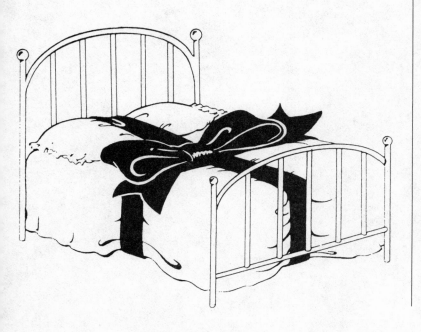

*T*a-dah! It's the Total Woman! Rose in teeth, draped in sexy black lingerie, she perches by the front door waiting to seduce her man as he comes home from work. Always ready for action, she knows how to twist her hubby around her little manicured finger.

Ta-dah! It's the Total Man! He has read every sex manual on the market and can follow all the directions in the little diagrams. He knows all about his wife's erogenous zones and his own as well. Always ready for action, he maintains his youthful physique with regular workouts down at the health club.

So much for Hollywood.

Now here come Actual Man and Actual Woman. He is sloppy around the middle. She has varicose veins. He gets tired sometimes. So does she. He does not always operate at the pinnacle of peak excitement. At 2 A.M., she sometimes has no excitement at all. They both have worries on their minds and kids around the house who would hoot and howl if they ever saw Mommy staking out the front door with a rose in her teeth.

All the same, this Actual Couple might very well have a far better sex life than the Total Couple. Handsome or energetic or not, they still have the power to be their best sexually, because sex is *not* what the Total Couple thinks it is.

God Invented It

In *The Way Home* there is a chapter called "The Joy of Unkinky Sex." I got more response from that chapter than from any other in the book. Briefly, it makes the case for not deliberately separating sex from fruitfulness. Sex, you see, is much more than climax. Like any other God-ordained human endeavor, sex is an opportunity to glorify God and build up His kingdom.

The real problem is that sexual freedom has meant, for millions of people, a cluster of debasing addictions. We are offering human beings the kind of freedom appropriate to dogs.

—Joseph Sobran
National Review

Today it would be fair to say that most of us don't understand sex. I'm not saying we don't do it, just that we don't do it right. The very word "sexy" means the opposite of "wholesome." We have this attitude that here is a totally self-indulgent pleasure that will be even more fun if we can come up with some way of doing it that will make us feel slightly wicked.

Doubt what I'm saying? Let me ask you this. When was the last time you prayed to God while making love? I don't mean high-faluting prayers about the church's evangelistic outreach while your mind wandered all over the landscape—just some prayer about your sexual act itself.

Is Only the Forbidden Thrilling? I don't have any hard data to support this, but I do have a definite feeling from what I see and hear that nine out of ten Christian couples never think to pray to God when difficulties crop up during sex, or to thank Him afterwards. Even worse, if they tried it, it would squash all the excitement they had been feeling.

The reason is that, subconsciously or not, we think sex is the devil's gift, not God's. Women talk about how they "gave up" adultery when they got saved, not about how they discovered true sexual satisfaction in the bonds of marriage. Men are proud of themselves for passing up porn magazines and prostitutes, because deep down they think they'd have more fun if they used such things. We have this idea that we could achieve more delight in sex if only we weren't constrained by all these Biblical rules and regulations. How noble of us to settle for evangelical boredom rather than go for the gusto!

Even the evangelical sex manuals suffer from this underlying attitude. Their focus seems to be on encouraging Christian couples to indulge in all sorts of formerly forbidden techniques, so that we won't feel deprived from not getting to follow the world all the way. We are supposed to search for the Perfect Climax even more fervently than non-believers. Hence, the Total Woman and all her kin.

Some might object here that I'm being unfair. Some Christian sex books do insist on our obligation to pleasure our partners, not just ourselves. *The Total Woman* itself is very strong on making hubby happy. What could be wrong with that?

I'll tell you what's wrong! Sex is not just star-studded climax—yours or anyone else's. It is how new life is brought into the world and how husband and wife are knit together in the bonds of love.

The church today is losing its sense of sex as *sacred* (something that unmarried people and people of the same sex should not do) because we don't know how to make it *holy*.

So much for the sermon. Now let's talk about how to take a typical married sex life—one strongly influenced by our cultural view of sex—and turn it into Holy Sex.

What Is Sex For? To start, it might be more accurate for us to talk about sexuality than sex. Sexuality includes the totality of your sexual being as a man or a woman: the female cycle and reproduction, the male begetting of life. It also includes your togetherness as a couple: becoming one flesh in that mystical union that represents the closeness of Christ and the church.

This, of course, is not what you learned in public school. There you learned that sex was for feeling good and babies were hazards to be avoided. (There even is a book by the name *Babies and Other Hazards of Sex!*) In school and from your peers, with a big assist from the media, you learned a short-circuited view of sex. For many, this has led to a serious problem I am about to describe.

See if this is you: In order to excite yourself for love-making, you fantasize. You think of porn movies you have seen, or imagine your husband or wife doing things to you that he or she never actually does.

> The truth is that typical sex education courses are almost perfect recipes for producing personality problems and even perversions later in life.
>
> —Psychiatrist Melvin Anchell
> *National Review*

You have heard that it was
said, "Do not commit adultery." But I tell you that anyone who looks at a woman
lustfully has already committed adultery with her in his
heart.
   —Our Lord Jesus Christ
   Matthew 5:27, 28

You imagine yourself with a movie star, or maybe
with some low-down dirty character. You may even
do this during intercourse, responding not so much
to your spouse as to your dream lover.

Some do this only when they feel their sexual excitement sagging; others do it all the time. Some do it
in their literal dreams; others in their daydreams. An
increasing number get so caught in its grip that they
start actually acting out their wicked fantasies in real
life, leading to broken families and horrible social
problems. It is a tremendously common habit, now
even promoted by "experts" (see the sidebar), and
one I have never seen addressed by any Christian
book. Which is why we are going to tackle breaking
that habit right here.

The Devil Makes You Rue It

You already know where this habit comes from. It
comes from public school sex education classes, from
peer-group huddles, from professional marriage
counselors, and from the media. All these encourage
a fantasy view of sex that has nothing to do with
fruitfulness or even with marital unity. When even
some so-called Christian books encourage physical
masturbation, it's not surprising that few of us have
ever been taught how to avoid mental masturbation.

Now how do we conquer what can, for some of
us, be the habit of years? How can we "bring every
thought captive" to the Lordship of Christ? How can
we not only be sexually pure in our physical actions
(avoiding adultery), but in our heads (avoiding spiritual adultery)?

How God Sees It. First, we have to be solid about
how God sees this. The reason why few couples are
able to both pray and remain sexually aroused at the
same time is that we are locking God out of our sex
lives. We have to know what pleases Him and what
doesn't. Then we can both delight in God and in our
spouse.

We know what God doesn't like: adultery, sexual perversions, and so on. Now let's finally acknowledge that God is pleased when a Christian couple makes love trusting in Him. I mean trusting in Him for both the means and the result. It's like any other area of life: we have to be submitted enough to the will of God to admit He controls that area.

Getting down to cases: You will never have climax or conceive a child unless God wants it to happen. You don't have the power to produce your own sexual satisfaction or physical fruitfulness. This means that climax (yes, even Hugh Hefner's) is a gift from God—an almost universally unacknowledged gift. Children are a slightly more acknowledged gift, though even here our society is schizoid, thanking God for children at certain times (the first child of a wealthy young couple) and not at others (the fourth child of a poor black woman).

I wouldn't be at all surprised to discover that those who have trouble trusting God for their sexual satisfaction also are unwilling to trust God with their reproduction. It's hard to relax in the hands of God when you don't trust Him physically enough to let Him plan your family. In fact, one of the constantly-cited reasons for female frigidity and unresponsiveness is "fear of becoming pregnant."

Be that as it may, Step One in recovering a holy sex life is conceding control to God.

Step Two, praying to God, follows automatically. If the only person who can give you sexual satisfaction is not your spouse or yourself, but God, it makes sense to ask Him for it. Of course, if you want His blessing you will have to follow His terms.

Which brings us to Step Three: cutting out the fantasies. Feel free to skip ahead to the next section if you don't have this problem, thanking God all the way! But if you *do* fantasize, here is some help on shaking that sin.

WHAT THE "EXPERTS" ARE SAYING ABOUT SEX

Throughout the meeting [of marriage therapists], little was said about love and commitment. In fact, not all that much was said about marriage. . . . Since sex was for fun, one developed the impression that it did not make much difference whether one masturbated or had intercourse. However it was thought that intercourse might be a bit more pleasurable.

—John Quesnell
The CCL News

It happened in stages, gradually. It didn't necessarily, not to me at least, happen overnight. My experience with pornography . . . is once you become addicted to it—and I look at this as a kind of addiction like other kinds of addiction—I would keep looking for more potent, more explicit, more graphic kinds of material. . . . You reach that jumping-off point where you begin to wonder if actually doing it will give you that which is beyond just reading about it or looking at it.

—Ted Bundy, notorious serial
rapist and murderer
Interview with
Dr. James Dobson

Romance novels are our society's acceptable pornography for women. I speak from experience here as I became addicted to them about fifteen years ago when they were probably a little tamer. That addiction lasted for two to three years until one day I woke up and realized my marital discontent was a direct result of this sinful input. I stopped reading them immediately and have not picked up one since, though the mental pictures from all those books still come back to haunt me and, yes, even tempt me.

—Pam Lancaster, MO

Cleaning Up Your Sex Life

This is going to hurt. Don't say I didn't warn you! You are going to be sorely tempted to fall back into the old ways of arousing yourself. Here are some tips that may help:

(1) First you will be tempted to believe that you never will have climax again unless you fantasize. You will fear living the rest of your life in a permanent state of unsatisfied arousal.

This is a common fear for women, but it can't happen. If you are aroused enough to be frustrated, this builds up a "charge" that will make you more quickly aroused next time. Sooner or later, if you are faithful not to discharge your charge by foul means, God will enable you to get sufficiently excited in the way He ordained to find relief in His appointed way.

(2) Tell your spouse what you are going through. When you feel a fantasy coming on, ask him or her to hold off for a bit while you calm down and fight it off. Use this time to concentrate on the person to whom you are trying to make love.

(3) Learn to stop looking at other people as objects. Making other people into sex objects is not *the* root of the problem—forgetting God is the root of the problem—but it certainly contributes to it.

Who's Afraid of Virginia Slims?

Point #3 is a "heavy" point. We are brought up from babyhood with sexual images of people. Everything from blue jeans to cigarettes is sold by some lad or lassie with tight clothes and a come-hither look. The advertisers want us to concentrate on the product, not the person, so the model has his or her personhood reduced to a slick visual image. Who *is* the Marlboro Man or the Virginia Slims cigarette girl? We don't know and we don't care. We see these people as images, not as flesh-and-blood human beings who sweat, cry, and have rent payments to meet.

Men look at a pornographic picture and are tempted—because they are not looking at a person they know or care about, but an offer of sex that just happens to be attached to a particular female body. Because the girl is not a human being in his eyes, but an *object*, a man is aroused by the spectacle of her offering herself. If it was his sister or his mother in the picture, he would not be aroused but ashamed and humiliated for her.

I found out about this law of nature—that sexual sin depends on seeing other people as objects—when Bill and I were cleaning out a neighbor's apartment some years ago in Alabama. The apartment building was not very clean or in a very nice neighborhood, but the rent was cheap. Since we always paid the rent on time, our landlord liked us. So he magnanimously offered to give us the paid job of cleaning the neighbor's apartment when the neighbor skipped town without paying his rent.

Never in my life had I seen a living-room floor completely covered with porn magazines before. And so was the kitchen. And the bedroom. We had to pick them up, and there was no way to do so without seeing them.

After a hurried discussion about how we were going to dispose of these unexpected riches of raunchiness (the paper bags we had brought wouldn't do—someone might see the magazines and take them), Bill wisely reassigned himself to another job. I started picking up porn and stuffing it into black plastic trash bags. The magazines were sprawled all over, rather like the girls inside, so a lot more was displayed than the cigarette and booze ads on the covers.

I had seen *Playboy* and *Penthouse* in my pre-Christian days. But never had I seen any really get-down girlie magazines before. I didn't want to see them now, either. I prayed to the Lord that I would not be tempted to any unseemly thoughts, and kept on shoveling. You couldn't just shut your eyes and stuff it in a bag, because our cleaning kept turning up new stashes: under the couch and the kitchen sink, under the cushions on the chair. So those girls kept staring out at me, try as I might to avoid them.

TRENDS TO REVERSE

☐ The average urban teenage girl sees 1,500 sexual acts or references to sex acts on TV each year, according to a study by Michigan State University. Sexual content in the 25 or more R-rated films she sees is far more explicit, say researchers.

☐ About six percent of people in the USA are sexual addicts so obsessed with sex that they have allowed it to be the "governing principle" of their lives, family therapist Patrick Carnes of Minnesota told seven hundred psychologists, sociologists, and family counselors at the National Council of Family Relations in Philadelphia.

☐ The November issue of *Spin* magazine's cover advertises a free condom inside.

—*National and International Religion Report*
October 24, 1988

After a while, something strange happened. I started noticing the girls' faces. Here one was smiling—but her smile looked insecure. She didn't look too bright, or even too pretty. I started to wonder how she fell into this life of posing for such magazines. What dreams of hers as a little girl had been destroyed? What lies had been told her? No little girl grows up wishing to appear in some pitsy 'zine like this.

Perhaps it was because these lowlife magazines weren't as slick as their "respectable" counterparts, but I began to see the women behind the bodies. They all looked so sad (underneath the grimacing smiles) and pathetic. In ten years nobody would want them even for this. What then? Alcoholism? Suicide?

The Lord taught me a lesson that day. He showed me that I had been letting Madison Avenue "sell" me people as images. From that time forward, I would make the effort to see people—even advertising models—as people.

It's the Real Thing: Duty and Delight

Sexual fantasies depend on the person fantasized about not being real. No pimples, no sweat, no bad breath, no crumpled morning face, no runny-nosed flu, no hemorrhoids, no razor-stubbled legs, no nothing! No fantasy lover ever feels depressed, has a headache, or burps. If this happened, it would destroy the stimulation of the fantasy. He or she is an unreal slave, living only in your mind, existing only for your pleasure.

Real life, as we all know, is far different. In real life you have to deny yourself in order to serve your lover. A good husband hears his pregnant wife throwing up in the bathroom (not exactly the stuff of fantasy) and loves her nonetheless. A good wife notices her middle-aged hubby starting to sprout head where hair used to grow, and kisses him on the bald spot. In fantasyland, the world revolves around us; in real life, we have to forget ourselves for the sake of others.

The husband should fulfill his marital duty to his wife, and likewise the wife to her husband. The wife's body does not belong to her alone but also to her husband. In the same way, the husband's body does not belong to him alone but also to his wife.

Do not deprive each other except by mutual consent and for a time, so that you may devote yourselves to prayer. Then come together again so that Satan will not tempt you because of your lack of self-control.

—The Apostle Paul
1 Corinthians 7:3-5

Let's explore this a bit more. The truth is that worldly sex tends to be selfish, whereas holy sex is unselfish. Naturally, you hope for physical satisfaction yourself, but in holy sex you are willing to submit your desires to the needs of your spouse and the will of God. This attitude reduces frustration tremendously.

Do as You Would Be Done By. Take, for example, Jerry and Sue Jones. Jerry has been having difficulty sexually lately. Tonight he manages to get Sue aroused, and then once again poops out.

Now what?

This very common situation typically leads to Sue ticking Jerry off for being a lousy lover. She may order him to engage in non-genital sex so she can relieve her sexual frustration, or perform some other un-Biblical sex act. Meanwhile, Jerry is already beset with fears that he is losing his masculinity. Next time he is going to be even more nervous. Whether or not anything physical was wrong with him, his anxiety surely won't help him or Sue. More: in today's social climate, he may fear Sue searching for sexual satisfaction elsewhere. She surely hasn't relieved his worries on this score!

Let's run this scene again, this time with Jerry and Sue practicing holy sex. Sue is disappointed when Jerry is unable to keep going. She prays for him silently. Tonight her prayer is not immediately answered. So Sue accepts that, for some unknown reason, God has not seen fit to bless them with physical satisfaction this time. It's not Jerry's fault: male ability is not something anyone can control. She wants to reassure Jerry, so she cuddles up to him and tells him she loves him and that she enjoyed just being together and trying. If Jerry starts kissing her back, I'll give you fifty-fifty odds that if nothing is organically wrong with him, the evening will end up on a higher note than anticipated. Even if it doesn't, both Sue and Jerry feel loved and appreciated and are enjoying their closeness.

Women can be strongly tempted to let sex degenerate into a wicked system of punishment and rewards. Making the old man sleep on the couch because he displeases the queen can be a comical situation for a TV program, but it can destroy a marriage in real life.

A woman cannot justly complain about her husband's spinelessness if she humiliates him in the bedroom. She cannot undercut his masculinity and still wonder why he refuses to take his place as head of the house. A man should *never* be made to feel that he is degrading his wife because he desires her. His desire was given him by God and in its appointed place it is like all other things God created, "very good." The Bible says that a woman who brings her husband shame is like "rottenness in his bones" (Prov. 12:4).

—Elizabeth Baker
The Happy Housewife

Let him kiss me with the
kisses of his mouth—
for your love is more delightful than wife.
Pleasing is the fragrance of
your perfumes;
your name is like perfume
poured out. . . .
His left arm is under my
head,
and his right arm embraces
me. . . .

—Song of Songs 1:2, 3; 2:6

Is This Sex or Tennis? Speaking of closeness, no-body has to tell today's couples to fondle each other. Again, though, we aren't necessarily doing it right. For one thing, consider that distressing word "fore-play." Totally aside from the strong feeling it gives that you are about to play tennis rather than make love, the word "foreplay" insinuates that you are just fooling around warming up to the main event.

The Bible takes a different view. Read through the Song of Solomon again, if you haven't recently. See what great emphasis the married couple in this Bible book place on looking at, touching, caressing, and even becoming aware of each other's aroma. See, also, that the genitals are not even mentioned, al-though face, neck, shoulders, breasts, torso, and legs all are.

Could it be that we today are rushing to get to a Main Event and not taking enough time to smell the roses? Have we put sex on a freeway when it should be more like a ramble down a country lane?

One of the great benefits of not using your spouse as a sex object is that you can stop and notice him or her. Everyone loves to be noticed. Everyone likes to feel wanted and special. Wives may campaign for it more loudly than husbands, but no husband is smart who pits his entire sexual identity on always being ready to perform. It's kind of nice to feel desirable for your own sake, not just for your technique. Anyway, the Bible shows both sexes noticing and delighting in each other, so this must be good for us!

"He who finds a wife finds what is good, and re-ceives favor from the Lord" (Proverbs 18:22). The se-cret of contentment is to value what you have. God didn't *have* to give you a wife or husband at all! So take time to enjoy physical intimacy, without feeling like every second must be spent in chasing climax.

You don't know what you're missing until you fi-nally relax and trust God to take care of your body. Once you do, knowing you *might* conceive adds real spice to sex. What a relief not to be constantly worry-ing about "protecting" yourself from the aggressions of a tiny little fertilized egg. How different to be actually excited about maybe, this time, giving life to a whole new little person! Where else can you actually help to perform a miracle?

Holy sex means sharing God's creative joy. We will look at one terrific outcome of holy sex—babies!—in the next chapter.

Bring on the Babies!

You and your husband are drifting ecstatically in a rubber raft on a rolling blue sea. Nestled in each other's arms, you are dreamily nuzzling each other when your husband suddenly tenses.

"There they are! I saw one!"

You peer over his sun-warmed shoulder. Nothing. All you see are the waves rolling by.

"What did you see, dear?"

He is not paying attention. Slowly he reaches for a wooden paddle and hefts it, staring over the water.

Suddenly you see them too! Leaping out of the water, a whole school of them is swarming around your raft!

You grab a paddle and help your husband smack them back into the sea. Even so, a particularly bold one slips by your defenses. It plops in the raft, rolls over on its back, and says its first word: "Mommy!"

This is the public school view of sexual intercourse: you and your partner in a rubber raft, beating off the swarms of babies who attempt to leap on board. If you don't protect yourself, one of the little tykes will break through your defenses. Hence all the talk about "unprotected" intercourse and women "at risk" of pregnancy.

We grow up taking our fertility for granted, which is not a good idea. In real life fertility is a special gift, like musical talent. Almost 50 percent of married couples this very minute are infertile.[1] And the fertility rate is decreasing. In 1965, 73 percent of couples in the childbearing years were able to have children; in 1985, it was only 52.7 percent and dropping.[2]

Some of this sterility is self-inflicted, but a good chunk of it is not. Even in countries where virtually every woman wants children, a large percentage will never be able to have them. As feminist Germaine Greer admits, what Third World women really want is fertility, not birth control pills.[3]

If being productive is acting in the image of God and a source of happiness, it's no wonder that the "creativity" involved in conceiving new life is a source of great joy and happiness as well. Generally, children love babies, parents love babies, and a new child born into a loving family is the most joyous of all occasions.

—Congressman Ron Paul
Abortion and Liberty

What I would primarily like to relate is my experience with infertility caused by endometriosis. What a shock it was, after having two children, to learn I had infertility problems. . . .

I have since become aware than *many* women suffer from endo (some unaware of it). One of the primary reasons that endometriosis develops is because women postpone childbearing until their late twenties, not realizing the price. I've seen very few media articles written on this medical fact. (I wish I had known about this sooner).

—Sandy Teall, OR

Cherishing Your Fertility

God has set things up so the unrighteous can eat their cake but not bake any new ones. "They will engage in prostitution but not increase, because they have deserted the Lord to give themselves to prostitution, to old wine and new, which take away the understanding of my people" (Hosea 4:10). This presents an incredible opportunity for Christians who are willing to follow the Lord's never-repealed command to increase and multiply (Genesis 1:28, 8:17, 9:1, 9:7, 35:11, 48:4, 48:16, Leviticus 26:9, Deuteronomy 6:3, 7:13, 8:1, 13:17, 28:11, and Jeremiah 29:6 for starters). The effect of us building up our households by having children is magnified when the general fertility rate drops.

A number of readers of *The Way Home* have written to me wondering about why, even though they breastfeed, they are having children so close together. My theory is that God is making up for lost time with many of us who are still willing to have children. He is giving Christians in this generation a chance for revival instead of just shutting the door on us. If the faithful make the most of this opportunity to "increase greatly," we can raise up a large group of extremely high-quality disciples—our own children—in a relatively short time. We can spiritually recapitalize the church!

Let me say right now that this does not mean that any individual infertile Christian couple is necessarily being cursed by God for personal unfaithfulness. "Time and chance happen to all," as Ecclesiastes 9:11 puts it. God may have reasons for permitting your infertility—we will look at some such reasons later in this chapter. Still, if the church *as a whole* is infertile, this is a sign of God's displeasure with the church *as a whole*. If the nation *as a whole* is infertile, you may be sure God is displeased with that nation. Fertility and infertility are among the God-given "signs of the times" that the righteous are supposed to read.

As ever, God's sovereignty and man's responsibility go together. If you cherish your fertility, God is more likely to bless it. If you squander it (on waiting forever to have kids) or wound it (through sterilization or drugs), God is likely to let you have your own way—which turns out not to be so great when you get there.

With this introduction, let me give you some sisterly advice on how to preserve your fertility, including some information you very likely have never seen before.

First, if you use the Pill you strongly increase your chances of developing diabetes, a disease that can harm your children, blind you, kill you, and even raise your insurance premiums. This is not to mention the Pill's more commonly-known risks, such as yeast infections and heart attacks. Doctors hardly ever tell you about the diabetes threat when writing your prescription. Nor do they tell you that they will refuse to continue to prescribe the Pill because of health risks after you reach age thirty-five or so. This is totally aside from the Pill's known abortifacient qualities, which I detailed in *The Way Home*.

Second, there is *no* artificial contraception that doesn't somehow increase your risk of future barrenness. Even just waiting to have children increases your risk of infertility. Endometriosis, which leads to infertility, often strikes couples who are waiting for the "right" time to conceive.

Third, promiscuity leads to disease and infertility as night follows day.

Fourth, "safe, legal" abortion dramatically increases your chances of miscarriage and sterility, including ectopic pregnancy.

When you look at the list of actions connected to infertility, it's pretty clear that infertility really is a judgment on a society that rejects holy sex and God's gift of children. Just like God's other gifts, you can't count on the offer remaining open forever (Hebrews 3:7). The best way to preserve your fertility is to *use* it—and thank God for it!

Three years into our marriage the verdict came—"You will never bear children." It is impossible to explain the pain that followed that declaration. Some thought we were lucky, few could figure out why we were so devastated. All I knew was that I needed to be a mother! Being very stubborn, determined, and resourceful people, it was not long before we were pursuing that marvelous *other* method of building a family: adoption. Now almost eight years after the "verdict" was handed down, we are the parents of three beautiful Blessings— not "flesh of my flesh," nor "bone of my bone," yet marvelously my own. And we hope to add more.

The point I wish to make is this. There is no guarantee that anyone will conceive "at will." And those who plan to have children later may find that "later" brings them "unplanned barrenhood." How thankful I am that we learned of our infertility so early in our marriage, and that we were able to pursue adoption and build the family we had always dreamed of.

P.S. Anytime *we* add a new child to the family, people cannot console themselves by thinking, "Surely this child was an accident." Nobody adopts by accident. My . . . how some people react!! ("You want MORE!??!")

—Claire Whitmire, PA

Having the size of family you are able to "handle" is an interesting theory, but you never know what you can handle until you try. I am handling five children now much better than I ever handled one, two, or three!

The passage of time and acquisition of experience makes a big difference here. When other mothers wonder how I "do it" and talk about how they can barely manage with the two children they have, I always tell them that I felt the same way when I only had two children. By nature I am a rather selfish and impatient person. Only through having children have I been able to overcome this. It still takes effort at times, but as I've matured and cared for my children I've learned to be patient most of the time. Over the years I've also become very efficient at what I do and have gained more confidence in my ability to do things that have to be done.

It's also important to define what the "it" is that you are doing. I'm not doing anything that is unnecessary or adding to my stress level. I try to keep my priorities straight and do the most important things first. I train my children to work around the house and to help each other when they can. So, my fifth baby has actually been the easiest one so far.

—Pamela Boswell, CA

What Happens When You Trust God to Plan Your Family?

Picture this dialog:

You: "OK, Lord, we've decided that You know more than we do about how our family should grow or not grow. So we're going to trash our birth control devices and trust in You."

God: "Aha! Now I've got you! I've just been waiting for you to trust Me, so I could zap your family with all kinds of horrible problems."

Is this good theology?

Is this even real life?

In *The Way Home*, I presented the Biblical case for trusting God to plan your family. Since then, I have heard from hundreds of couples who are doing just that. Not one had a horror story. In fact, many had stories like the following inspiring true tale of God's provision.

A True Story. Pamela Boswell of California has a lovely story to tell about how God cared for her family.

"Some wonderful things have happened since Michael decided to let God plan our family.

"When our fifth child was born, Michael was a title officer putting in a lot of overtime, and we didn't get to see him very often, at least not as much as we wanted to. Our house was very old, in constant need of repair and was pretty small—originally two bedrooms and one bathroom, we had enclosed the back porch to make a third bedroom. It was a half-hour drive to my husband's office, which added to his away time.

"Now, I don't want to imply that we weren't happy with what we had, but there were times when I wished we'd had more room, weren't always at the edge financially and that Dad could be home more.

"When the baby was six months old, Michael got a promotion and a $3,000-a-year raise. Three months later he was promoted to title department manager and got an additional $5,000 raise. Three months after that he was transferred to a neighboring county, was promoted to county manager and got another $5,000 raise.

"Our youngest daughter is now nineteen months old, and we are living only ten miles from my husband's office. We were blessed with being able to purchase a newer home in the country with five bedrooms, three bathrooms, and both a living room and a family room. Since Michael is now 'the boss' his working time is more flexible and he is home much more than before.

"I think it is very interesting that all of this happened so suddenly and in such quick succession after he decided to leave our family planning to the Lord."

The Cutest Miracle. Isn't that wonderful! Many, many women have stories like this to share. But, to tell you the truth, God providing for a couple who conceive in difficult circumstances isn't nearly as big a miracle as having the chance to conceive in *any* circumstances.

Consider what needs to happen for a baby to be born. First, a husband's healthy sperm has to encounter a healthy egg in the very short time period during which the egg is ripe. Then the fertilized egg—which is just a single cell—begins to divide. It finds its way to the uterine wall and implants itself. It starts to develop specialized cells which will become the heart and eyes and lungs and skin and bones. Each organ has to grow perfectly, at breakneck pace, for nine months. The placenta, which nourishes the baby, has to connect properly to the mother. And somehow, if nothing at all goes wrong of the ten billion things that *can* go wrong, you will have a healthy baby.

Really, if you stop to think about it, babies are a literal miracle. They are against nature. All of creation except for living creatures runs downhill all the time. But pregnancy runs *up!* You get more out than you put in!

It's unbelievable that a sperm and an egg can, over time, turn into a new human being with ideas of his or her own. If the Lord had created the whole human race at once, and then just one woman out of all

I gave birth to a thirteen-week-old baby boy. . . . I lost the baby on Tuesday—the following Sunday was Sanctity of Life Sunday—I don't know how my husband made it through his sermon.

I have had to draw some important conclusions from this ordeal:

1. I have a child that is existing in a reality far greater than mine and I will someday see this child. For now he beholds the Father's face.

2. I now know what it feels like to have empty arms and can weep with those who can't have children or who have lost them.

3. I must (and I hope others will too) face each pregnancy with the understanding that a "miscarriage" (I prefer "early birth") could happen. . . . I will greet each pregnancy understanding the honor I carry in conceiving a child and I will love that child even if I only know him a few short months in my womb.

4. A child that is only carried a few short months is still a person and I can love and talk to him in the womb. Though his mind is underdeveloped, his spirit is fully there, given by God at conception. . . .

5. This conviction of children as blessings and gifts is no fad. I no longer take the privilege of pregnancy lightly.

—Susan Gaddis, CA

We "tried" to get pregnant with our third child as soon as my periods started when our second was a year old. It all seemed so mechanical because we were "trying" almost every day and there was very little spontaneity or romance. The reason we were trying so hard was because our second child's birthday was December 3, and we didn't want the inconvenience of another birthday at holiday time.

Well, our third was due in October, but wasn't born until November, so now we have three birthdays during the holidays (including my husband's). So, from this experience I think it's rather foolish to try too hard to conceive and plan when your child should arrive. . . .

My conclusion is that it is just as important not to rush God's timing as it is not to try to delay it. . . . Right now I very much want to have another baby (as does the whole family), but even though the current baby is nineteen months old, God still hasn't provided one. I really don't think He would want me to wean my nineteen-month-old in hopes of forcing fertility to return. I believe the spacing provided through breastfeeding is God's way of preparing our bodies and hearts for a new baby. Just as we decide to accept however many babies God wants to give us, we also need to accept it when he decides not to give us one when we want one. Eventually the time will come when He will not give us any more.

—Pamela Boswell, CA

the millions had become pregnant and given birth, we would all be down on our knees with awe of that miracle. Even when you have seen it happen before, it is hard to believe!

Today we take this miracle for granted. I blame Planned Parenthood and its various front groups for this. If you believe their view of sex, pregnancy is almost automatic for any "unprotected" couple. What a shock to discover you can't really conceive on command! It's a tremendous letdown, like trying to start your new Porsche and discovering the engine has been stolen.

I have had some experience of barrenness myself. During that time, I was disappointed to see that Christian books about sex dwelt at great length on contraception, but had only a pinch of space to spare for advice on how to improve your chances of conceiving.

We're not going to make that mistake! First, we will look at godly methods of fertility improvement. Then we will scrutinize some ungodly ways babies are sought nowadays, so you can avoid the temptation of trying to build your house without God's blessing.

What You Can Do to Improve Your Fertility

(1) Pray. God really does open and shut the womb. Fertility is not a matter of random chance. A personal aside: we have *never* conceived a baby until we prayed for that baby.

(2) Avoid tight clothing (men). Underwear and pants that strangle the scrotum fry all those little sperm. The solution is boxer shorts and looser pants.

(3) Diet (prepare for pregnancy). Obesity and scrawniness both hinder your ability to conceive. A well-balanced diet keeps you in the middle ground and enables your liver to start detoxifying *before* you get pregnant—meaning less nausea when you are pregnant! It helps to make and grow as much of your own food as possible. Start using whole grains instead of processed flours, eating lots of fruits and raw

veggies, and skipping gloppy sauces. Steam veggies lightly instead of frying them. Roast or broil meat instead of frying it. Try to eat regular meals and a light wholesome snack when you are hungry in between. This keeps your system running smoothly and prevents binging and diabetes. The Brewers' book *What Every Pregnant Woman Should Know* is actually a wonderful workbook for diet planning for not-yet-pregnant women as well.

(4) Avoid excessive exercise (women). Too much exercise prevents conception. God must not want mothers to be lean and mean!

(5) Cut out the coffee, tea, and caffeinated soda. Some evidence has just come to light (see sidebar) that caffeine use is correlated with infertility.

(6) Sleep. Men can become sterile by burning too much midnight oil. I haven't seen any studies correlating lack of sleep and infertility in women, but common sense tells us that getting exhausted is not a good way to start off your pregnancy even if you do conceive.

(7) Time of the month. Now we come to Natural Family Planning. In its various modes, this can include simply observing your vaginal mucous and your energy level, or it can become a complicated matter of taking temperatures and charting graphs. I can see some value in becoming aware of your cycles, provided this knowledge is not (a) used to rob sex of all spontaneity or (b) take the place of trusting in God's ability to grant or withhold babies. The Couple to Couple League provides both books and training via classes or a home study course for the most scientific methods.

(8) Abstinence. Bill Gothard's Institute on Basic Youth Conflicts has taken a very pro-conception position. Their materials go farther than others' in stressing a return to the Levitical law requiring abstinence during a woman's period. Their interpretation requires abstinence for fourteen days starting at the beginning of flow. My reading of the passage indicates that the Old Testament Jews actually practiced seven

A team of North Carolina researchers surveyed 104 infertile women, about half of whom were heavy caffeine users—one cup of coffee or its equivalent in tea or soda a day. They were half as likely per menstrual cycle as women who drank less than one coffee-cup's equivalent in caffeine per day. Women who drank two or more cups of coffee a day were one-fourth as likely to get pregnant, and after a year were five times less likely than the other women in the study to conceive.

—*Insight*
February 13, 1989

Just recently a friend who had four children (before I knew her) had her husband have a vasectomy. Then their three-year-old was called home with leukemia. At age thirty-nine she called me about having this reversed. . . . Well, they had it done. I told her I didn't have children after I was thirty-eight, so her chances were not great. OH THE MERCY OF GOD—this year in June she had a seven pound ten ounce boy. . . . She is forty-two!

—Martha Pugacz, OH

days of monthly abstinence, which seems more livable. Some today practice abstinence only during the period itself, which seems the bare minimum Scripture requires (see Leviticus 15:9, 18:19, 20:18, and Ezekiel 18:6). Either way, a period of abstinence before a wife's fertile time seems to enhance your opportunity of conceiving, possibly because it concentrates the sperm or (again) possibly because this is the way God likes us to do things.

(9) Position. Weird sexual positions often minimize the sperm's chance of traveling to its chosen destination. And of course certain types of sexual activities make conception impossible (I talked about those in *The Way Home*). What works best is the wife on her back with her fanny propped on some pillows during lovemaking, and remaining in that position for at least fifteen minutes afterwards to give the little wigglers a chance to get where they want to go.

(10) Reversals. A growing number of Christian couples are regretting their hasty decision to get sterilized. Of that number, one-half look at the cost of a surgical reversal and wonder if God will heal them miraculously, and the other half gets busy saving the money. I have heard of some miraculous healings, but never where the family was just sitting around praying for one without trying to save. I would also like to encourage you with the news that, of subscribers to my newsletter, a much higher percentage have successful reversals than statistics would predict. This indicates to me that God smiles on Christians who have the faith to seek reversals.

What's So Awful About Handicapped Babies?

Many couples anxious to have a baby lose all their appetite for parenthood when it appears that their babies might be born with problems. Our society seems to take it for granted that giving birth to a handicapped child is a major disaster, and that we should be miserable instead of rejoicing over such children. In the case where parental foolishness has exposed a healthy unborn baby to unnecessary risk—such as by taking illegal drugs—of course the child's handicaps are a cause for mourning. But is the child herself a cause for mourning? And what about the very frequent case where it seems likely that genetic problems could crop up? Is it better to be childless than to give birth to such a child? Are handicapped children "problems" to be prevented, or are they gifts of God?

We have had to face this issue, as our first son was born with severe problems that first cost him five weeks in a neonatal ICU, and then caused such severe muscular weakness that one nationally-known neurologist said his chances of either dying or being crippled for life were ninety-eight percent. By God's grace, the neurologist was wrong, but we didn't know what would happen next. Doctors were advising us to avoid future pregnancies.

The fundamental issue, I feel, is "Is the body more important than the soul?" Frankly, I believe we are affected by our society's disdain for the physically unfashionable and non-perfect. God has no such value system. When we decide that we are doing a child a favor by denying him the chance of life because he might, or even *will*, have physical or mental problems, we are unconsciously repeating the lie that such children are not worthy of life. I seriously doubt if, in Heaven, one of these children will come up to us and say, "Wish I'd never been born."

Parents also worry that their handicapped child will feel rejected by society, making his or her life not worth living. But you can be as thoroughly rejected and despised for your bulk, skin color, pimples, lack of wealth, social class, or ethnic group as for any physical deformity. Physically perfect people kill themselves every year because of such rejection. The rate of suicide among those handicapped from birth, though, is actually *lower* than that of the general population! The worst rejection occurs among schoolkids, anyway. You can solve that problem by home schooling. And as for the future . . . I know lots of physically perfect people who can't seem to get married, but paraplegic Joni Eareckson Tada has a husband!

SOME COMMENTS FROM PEOPLE BORN WITH LETHAL BIRTH DEFECTS

Because the start was a little abnormal, it doesn't mean you're going to finish that way. I'm a normal, functioning human being, capable of doing anything anyone else can. . . .

If anything, I think I've had an added quality to my life—an appreciation of life. I look forward to every single morning. . . .

Most of the problems are what my parents went through with the surgery. I've been teaching high school for eight years and it's a great joy. . . .

—From *Whatever Happened to the Human Race?* by Francis Schaeffer and C. Everett Koop, M.D.

When I was born, the first thing my dad said to my mom was that "this one needs our love more."

—Craig Vick, a "Thalidomide baby" whom Bill and I met when he was a Covenant Seminary student. Quoted from *Whatever Happened to the Human Race?*

Enclosed is the birth announcement of our last child which I thought you would enjoy. How I shudder when I think how close I came to a tubal ligation because the doctors told me that the survival possibilities for subsequent pregnancies (after the death of our second baby due to rH problem) was basically zero. How I thank God that He did not let me carry through with that idea and that He continued to give us hope that a miracle would take place and I would be able to have a healthy baby. Circumstances can and do change. I am sick to think that if I had rendered myself sterile, we would not have our precious little Isaac. . . .

            —Joanie Etter, OR

Parents also worry that they won't have the time, energy, and money for a child with special needs. I've heard this a lot, and even thought it in the past, and it seems to me that the idea of us having limited resources that we must carefully hoard and dole out is another modern lie. "My God shall supply *all* your needs according to his riches in glory by Christ Jesus" (Philippians 4:19 KJV)! Several times in my mothering career I have felt that I absolutely had no more to give—and then God gave me *abundantly* more than I had to begin with!

God is not limited! Since He doesn't ask us to limit our welcome to children, it's *His* business to provide the resources—not ours to see them in place in advance. Money, in particular, should be the least of our worries, as God has promised to provide as much of *that* as we truly need. (I must say that my own experience, which includes years of living financially by faith rather than by sight, bears this out.)

It doesn't bother me at all to contemplate sacrificing myself for our children, including any handicapped children we might have. Frankly, I *admire* Mother Teresa's work, and it would be an *honor* to be chosen to do this kind of work in my own home! In any case, people like you and me have the resources to deal with this situation—experience as parents, experience as teachers of our children, a God who stands by us. There are support groups for parents of children with every conceivable kind of handicap, too. You can find them all at the library in the Gale Research Company's *Encyclopedia of Associations*.

Hold the Test Tubes, Please

But what if you just can't conceive and give birth to a child, no matter what?

Here is the problem. Lots of childbearing-age couples are now unwillingly infertile—more than 12 percent.[4] In 1982 around 4.4 million American women were infertile,[5] and that doesn't even count the additional four million who were sterilized for "medical" reasons. Many are barren as a result of their previous evil decisions (e.g., abortion[6] and sexually-transmitted diseases, especially gonorrhea and chlamydia[7]). Others have wasted their early childbearing years confidently expecting they could have a baby later, at their own convenience. The national Centers for Disease Control blame the rage for delayed childbearing for more than doubling the number of couples consulting with infertility specialists in just one four-year period (1981-1985).[8] These people discover, now that it's too late, that they want a baby. God won't give them one, so they try to *make* one.

With all the fanfare about "new" reproductive technology, the fact is that it is anything but new. Take a look at this list:

Surrogate Motherhood. The "surrogate" is made pregnant by the sperm of a man to whom she is not married. On giving birth, she hands her baby over to him to be raised by him and his wife. Look at the Bible story of Sarah and Hagar, or the duel between Rachel and Leah in which each gave her handmaid to Jacob as a wife, to see this exact same setup. The bottom line is that the handmaid's child belongs to the wife, not to his own mother. The only new wrinkle here is that the operation has been sanitized by separating fertilization from intercourse. But according to the Bible, sex is not just the act of intercourse, but the whole process of conception and birth as well. God ordained marriage not only so couples could be "one flesh," but so they would "increase and multiply." Since the so-called surrogate mother is never married to the man, what we are looking at here is a combination of adultery and slavery.

The surrogate, being the child's real mother in spite of the media's sleight-of-hand insistence that she is just a caretaker of another couple's child, may become emotionally attached to her own child and refuse to give him up. Then the contracting couple, who supplied nothing but sperm and money, fight for their right to keep the child they bought and paid for. The Mary Beth Whitehead case is perhaps the most

> A mother is a mother is a mother. . . . These are surrogate wives, not surrogate mothers. He is hiring himself an extra wife.
>
> —Barbara Katz Rothman
> *The Tentative Pregnancy*

39

In a 1983 study of 125 surrogate candidates, Michigan psychiatrist Philip J. Parker described three major motivations—money, a desire to be pregnant and an interest in reconciling some past birth-related trauma. About a third of the women had aborted a fetus or given up a baby for adoption.

—*Newsweek*
January 19, 1987

If separation of procreation from the conjugal act is permitted, conception becomes a question of mere technical reproduction, and terms such as conjugal love, maternity, and procreation become meaningless.

—*L'Osservatore Romano*
Quoted in *National and International Religion Report*
November 7, 1988

notorious example of how judges simply cannot tell that the surrogate mother *is* the mother. In what other instance would a husband get any kind of custody of his mistress's child?

Advocates of mothers-for-hire claim that Mary, the mother of Jesus, was a surrogate mother. Baloney! That would imply that God had a wife, for whom Mary bore Jesus. Mary raised Jesus herself. She never gave Him up to another woman.

This does not mean I do not feel sorry for the vaguely hopeful, gullible women who have been persuaded that handing over their own flesh and blood is some kind of perverse charitable act. They really are getting a raw deal. Old Testament concubines were entitled to their man's financial support for the rest of their lives; today's "surrogates" are offered less than a half-year's wages, making it clear that their status is more that of slaves than wives. Not surprisingly, Mary Beth Whitehead complained that, while she was pregnant with her daughter, "Elizabeth Stern was trying to take over her life."[9]

Artificial Insemination by Donor. Some medical student is given a copy of *Playboy*. He then goes into a private room and masturbates into a receptacle designed for the purpose. That sperm is frozen and placed in a sperm bank, labeled with a code identifying the donor (who is paid for his services). Prospective parents then pick out a father for their child by his identifying characteristics—e.g., "Blond, blue-eyed, 5' 11", an athlete, above-average IQ, sociable." The wife, if all goes "well," is then inseminated, gets pregnant, and presents her husband with another man's child.

Not that slipups are unknown. One woman recounts her experience of unexpectedly finding herself on the delivery table with an olive-skinned baby when she was expecting a fair-skinned child—like her and her husband.

And then there is the possibility that the A.I.D. child will end up marrying his sister, another A.I.D.

offspring of the same donor. Donors are used more than once in even one sperm bank, and a popular donor could be the father of hundreds, unknown to each of them.

The old-fashioned way of accomplishing the same result was for the wife to step out on her husband. Handling this process with latex gloves does not make it any less adulterous.

Artificial Insemination by Husband. Your husband gets his copy of *Playboy* and is stimulated to eject his sperm. That sperm is handled by graceless hands, concentrated, and shot into you in the same manner that cows are inseminated. Now we have three parties to the conception: husband, wife, and scientist. It is your husband's sperm, true, but he didn't produce it in the confines of the marriage bed. The Bible calls sperm ejaculation outside the marriage bed "uncleanness"; only sex between husband and wife is "holy" and "undefiled."

Test-Tube Babies. Here we have the husband masturbating yet again, only this time he is joined by surgeons who harvest a number of eggs from his wife. To increase the chances of a viable offspring, several eggs are fertilized at once. The best egg is implanted in the mother's womb. (New wrinkle: some are considering "wombs for rent" where yet another woman is dragged in to carry the wife's baby. No such case has actually happened at the time of publication.) "Excess" fertilized eggs, little human babies waiting to grow, are flushed down the drain.

The little test-tube babies are cute and we wish them well, but this is not a technology that honors God. Again we see the scientist meddling with the marriage bed. Again we see babies conceived and destroyed.

Fertility Drugs. On its surface, fertility drug technology sounds pro-family. All you are doing is helping the couple conceive. But this attempt to force

How is taking a drug to *get* pregnant any different from taking a drug to *prevent* pregnancy? Both are an attempt to overrule God's authority and His perfect plan for our lives!

I struggled with this "infertility question" for a couple of months, then ended up on my knees, praising God for His wisdom, even if I didn't understand it. . . .

Praise God, I am now eight weeks pregnant, with no sign of problems! This "surprise" is my best pregnancy yet, because we know that it is truly a blessing and a *gift!*

—Lisa Gladden, CA

In our family the meaning of adoption is part of our whole understanding of life as rooted in the Christian faith. Thus, when we explain to our children what adoption means, we often add, "Mom and Dad are adopted too." As Christians we have been adopted into God's family; we have become God's children (Galatians 4:5). . . .

In looking to the Christian idea of being adopted into the family of God, we can see what adoption ideally should be. But more than this, many of these same principles are applicable to any family relationship; for to be adopted into God's family is to be a child of God in the fullest sense. As adopted children (whether as part of God's family or as part of a human family) there is no sense in which this is a "second-class" relationship. We are fully children of the family with all the privileges and responsibilities that any child enjoys, whether adopted or not (see Galatians 4:1-7). . . .

If a child is in genuine need of a home, and if God has called us to share in this particular need, His grace will be sufficient.

—Lane T. Dennis
Chosen Children

open wombs God has shut has led to some bizarre results. Often fertility drugs successfully dislodge more than one egg, producing an embarrassing wealth of conceived babies: four or five or even more. The doctors who caused this situation sometimes respond with a procedure called "pregnancy reduction," which means killing the "extra" babies in the womb. So once again the supposed desire for children, when coupled with an insistence on building one's own household by one's own efforts, actually leads to *killing* children.

Adoption: Not Just an Alternative to Infertility

Recognizing the moral problems with test-tube procreation, many couples who have not been able to have children have turned to adoption. We must be very careful, though, to have a proper understanding of what adoption means. Adoption can be wonderful and deeply Christian, or can be tragic if undertaken for the wrong reasons and under the wrong circumstances.

Adoption is a vocation, like natural parenthood. It requires the same lifelong commitment. Adoption is also a ministry, but it is not a disinterested service project. Ideally, the adoptive parents recognize their calling because God sheds His love abroad in their hearts through the Holy Spirit, causing them to desire to sacrificially love and serve one of "the least of these," a homeless child.

Creation and the Fall. "If the starting point for having children is rooted in Creation," says Lane Dennis, the president of Crossway Books and the father of eight children, including two who were adopted, "the starting point for adoption is the Fall and Redemption. Thus adoption is not 'an alternative way to have children,' but it is a way, by God's grace, to 're-deem' those little ones who have become tragic victims of the Fall. Thus adoption starts with a desperate need—of a little child who is lost, abandoned, homeless. In this sense it can be a clear picture of our own desperate need for salvation—to be adopted into God's family.

"Great care must be taken, then, to assure that children who are considered for adoption really are in this desperate situation. The primary responsibility for the love, nurture, and raising of any child belongs to the parents who gave him birth. Adoption is a morally acceptable alternative, therefore, only when the birth parents cannot assume this responsibility, either through death or some other tragic consequence of sin and the Fall. It goes without saying then that pressuring the birth parents to abandon their responsibility would be in violation of what God has ordained and tragically wrong. Likewise, we have a responsibility as Christians to minister in whatever way we can to birth parents who, out of tragedy or necessity, *do* give up a child for adoption."

Preserving the Natural Family. Before we go futher into the positive aspects of adoption, let's pause a minute and consider the positive aspects of preserving the child's original family, if he has one.

Whenever possible, we should be trying to build up whatever remains of the child's natural family structure, including his extended family, rather than removing him from it.

Guardianship in Cases of Temporary Need. As we look through the Scriptures on adoption and orphans, we see that "visiting" the orphans means to provide for their physical needs. Making an orphaned child your heir is not the only way to serve such a child. Job, the most righteous man of his time, rescued "the fatherless who had none to assist him," yet he did not legally adopt all the orphans in his vicinity (Job 29:12). The inference is that Job acted as these fatherless children's guardian, while they continued to live with their mothers or other family members.

Guardianship has traditionally been exercised on behalf of orphaned minor children who, on reaching their majority, will inherit substantial property of

The point I wanted to make is that adoption is not a means to fill our household (this is NOT how to be fruitful and multiply). Adoption is a ministry, it is not a "cute" and "new" way to have kids. Christians need to look at adoption as a calling to minister to children in need—as God leads—and they must be willing to follow through no matter what the cost, and there will be costs. It seems that today politicians have become increasingly concerned with placing once-abandoned children back into the very families that rejected them.

Thank you for also clarifying that Christians should be taking in the abandoned child and not trying to snatch a child from a home to fulfill a personal desire, thereby neglecting their duty to minister to families in need.

—A.K., WI (an adopted child)

their own. There are also a number of good reasons for considering guardianship for children with living parents who are *temporarily* unable to assume their parental responsibilities, as we will see later.

Teen and Unwed Mothers Are Mothers, Too. If the choice is simply between a girl aborting her baby or giving him up for adoption, the choice is obvious. But why should girls who want to keep their own children be made to feel selfish, and even pressured to give the children up?

Imagine what would happen today to the two single women who were arguing before King Solomon over who was the mother of the baby born in their house (1 Kings 3:16-28). A modern judge might well have decided that *neither* mother was "fit" to raise the child. After all, most Bible commentators have deduced that these women were prostitutes, based on their behavior and their domestic circumstances. But Solomon showed his wisdom, not by taking the child and giving him to some "more fit" infertile couple at the court, but by discerning the true mother. And this bit of Biblical history teaches us another fact as well: even the most down-and-out mother will usually love her child sacrificially. The true mother was known by her willingness to part with her child rather than see him sliced in half.

A Teen Mom Speaks Out. "I want to defend teenage mothers for a moment. Two of my pregnancies took place while I was teenaged, and they were conceived within marriage. While the situation was different from those who are not married and are not able to share the parental responsibilities with a loving husband, I don't believe your age automatically disqualifies you from being a fit parent.

"We were married right after my graduation from high school when I was sixteen and my husband was nineteen. Our first child was born when I was eighteen, and I was twenty when my second was born. Three more came along in my twenties and now I'm

I am an unwed mother of a 6½-year-old boy. I have always wondered whether I was being selfish in keeping him but always had this nagging feeling that no one could be more committed to raising him to be a godly man than I am.

I also believe that in giving up your child you are doing away with the consequences of sin. Raising my son has been really hard, but I also know I wouldn't have grown in maturity and in my relationship with Jesus if I had not lived with the consequences of my sin.

—D.M., IA

Recent studies of teen pregnancies show that if a young woman receives proper care, her pregnancy may be healthier than those in the 20-24 age bracket

—*Family Practice News*,
February 1978

thirty and awaiting my sixth. We have been married for fourteen years and our love for each other has grown and matured tremendously.

"I wish all teenage mothers could have their children under the same circumstances, but I know that is not so. At the very least, we should encourage them to keep and raise their babies as best they can and provide the emotional and financial support they need to remain with their babies (instead of finishing school and/or pursuing a career). That is the only way they can mature and bring something good out of the sin of fornication.

"I believe most teenage mothers want to keep their babies and want to be good mothers, but others are always trying to convince them that adoption is the best thing for their babies and for them. It is not right to force a loving mother and child apart, no matter what the mother's age or how the child was conceived. . . ."

Adoption Is More Than an Option. But having said this, it would be equally wrong not to reach out with the redemptive love of Christ to those children who really are in helpless need, lost and abandoned. As Lane Dennis says, "Adoption is a very specific kind of ministry and calling, which God lays on the heart of certain Christians who feel a specific call for this purpose. This call may be related in part to the normal God-given desire for children to love and care for. But in the case of adoption you need something in addition to this—namely, a genuine desire to reach out to a child in tragic need, to 'redeem' the child by God's grace from this need, and a willingness to minister to the special needs the child will have as a result of how his or her life has been affected by the Fall.

"This special sense of God's calling and God's grace will be invaluable to the adoptive parents as they raise their adoptive children. For example, it takes a special provision of God's grace to create a bond between adoptive parent and child comparable to the

The recognition that adoption involves a giving relationship needs to be complemented, however, by an appeciation for the *objective, legal* basis of adoption. It is interesting to note that the Apostle Paul actually used the *Roman legal* understanding of adoption into a human family to explain the *Christian* meaning of adoption into God's family (see Galatians 4:1-7).

It follows that we should not try to "de-institutionalize" adoption in our own society into a sentimental, subjective, individualized arrangement. Adoption must have an objective basis in law and must be carried out in compliance with all the legal formalities. Failure to do so can result in serious problems, if not tragedy.

—Lane T. Dennis
Chosen Children

natural bond that is there from the beginning between the natural parent and child. But where this happens it is just as real as the natural bond.

"For those who are called to this very special kind of ministry, adoption can be a beautiful picture of what it means for each of us who are Christians to be adopted as a child of God."

Foster Parents

Closely allied to adoption in people's minds, though very unlike it in reality, is foster parenting. Foster parents, in theory, take in needy children and act as their guardians until the children can be reunited with their natural families or put up for adoption. In practice, the system is a dreadful mess. Foster parents are neither fish nor fowl. They have no control over what happens to their foster children; children can be taken away at any time for any reason or none at all. They are supposed to meet all the needs of these children without bonding with them—an impossible task—and the children will be removed if it appears that bonding is taking place.

Reams have been written about the failure of foster care, but precious few solutions have been offered, other than the standard panacea of throwing more money at the people supervising the debacle. I am about to offer one: abandon foster parenting and institute guardianship. Instead of court-appointed guardians *ad litem*, foster children need *real* guardians. We in the church could really do something about this. We could put together a network of guardians who would be subsidized by the church (perhaps through a central parachurch organization) rather than by the state. This would provide the guardians with the supervision and assistance of a community body and prevent the present situation where too many unscrupulous incompetents go into foster parenting as their main source of income.

It would also make foster parenting (now guardianship) much safer. At present the state children and family service agencies expect their foster parents to

Long-term foster care can leave lasting psychological scars. It is an emotionally jarring experience which confuses young children and unsettles older ones. Over a long period, it can do irreparable damage to the bond of affection and commitment between parent and child. The period of separation may so completely tear the fragile family fabric that the parents have no chance of being able to cope with the child when he is returned. . . .

Increasingly, the graduates of the foster care system evidence such severe emotional and behavioral problems that some thoughtful observers believe that foster care is often more dangerous than the original home situation. Yet, according to data collected by the Federal Government, it appears that up to half of these children were in no immediate danger at home and could have been safely left there.

—Douglas J. Besharov
First head of the National
Center on Child Abuse and
Neglect

adhere to non-Christian standards of child training (e.g., no spanking). Well-meaning foster parents have found themselves accused of child abuse and their natural or adoptive children taken from them because they and the agency couldn't get along. I wrote a whole book on the subject of how the child abuse laws are used to attack Christian parents (*The Child Abuse Industry*). I strongly suggest you get a copy before considering volunteering as a foster parent.

Parents' Rights

We have no business judging who is or is not "fit" to raise their own children. Criminal behavior towards children should be punished: rape, murder, and attempted murder by execution, and torture by physical chastisement proportional to the damage inflicted. Aside from these rare instances, it's nobody's business, Biblically speaking, to come barging forcibly into another couple's family. Organizations or individuals can offer all the help they want, but threatening to take a family's children away unless the parents agree with them in every child-training jot and tittle is nothing short of tyranny.

We make another terrible mistake if we believe that all "fit" couples have a *right* to children. Many of the couples currently moving heaven and earth to have children are simply seeking to escape the consequences of their previous choices. Many would-be mothers and fathers are willing to murder their own conceived offspring if the babies are physically imperfect or otherwise inconvenient. These people were just not meant by God to have children, for reasons that should be obvious.

There is no such thing as a "need" for babies to adopt or mothers to sell their wombs to bear children for rich men, any more than there is a "need" for fifty million more Mercedes just because most of us don't have one. Children are a gift, not a right. We must not, in our sympathy for the heart-rending plight of truly loving infertile couples, fall into the trap of endorsing designer conception or assigned parenthood.

In Kansas City, a study conducted by federal court judges found that 57 percent of foster children were at high risk of being abused or neglected in their foster homes.

—Richard Wexler
The Progressive, 1985

So where do adoption and guardianship come in? Caring for the truly orphaned. The handicapped. The unlovely. The abandoned. All the children whom the acquirers of pet children do not want. Taking in your own flesh and blood—your niece whose parents died in an auto accident, your grandson whose mother ran off and whose dad is in prison. Looking after the orphaned children of your spiritual brothers and sisters. Some are called to these ministries. And God bless you if this is you!

Special Ministries of Infertile Couples

Others have been planning for adoption simply because it is what infertile couples do. I would encourage you, if this is your situation, to pray seriously about whether God has some special ministry for you that you could only fulfill (or could better fulfill) without children. An infertile wife, for example, can become a midwife and be a blessing to hundreds of women and their babies. Even by just bearing the pain of infertility, you will be a sermon to the rest of us not to take our fertility for granted.

All good things come to those who wait! Infertility can be a spiritual blessing for couples who learn to wait for God's will in it—whether God leads you eventually to adopt or to another ministry.

Trust God. He can and will give each of us the family that is perfect for us. He can also help us learn to appreciate what He has given. So the next chapter will look at how to enjoy the blessing of babies, right from the start!

A friend recently shared about how little support she gets for staying home since she has no children. Yet she serves God in her church, in the Gideon Auxiliary, and in a pro-life counseling ministry. The Lord may not grant her children, but He is using her to save the lives of other people's children. We need more women like her in the church!

—Liz Ensley, LA

Let's Enjoy Pregnancy
(As Much As Possible)

4

The minute she walked into the room, things started popping. Her husband jumped up and offered her his seat. Children ran from all directions, bringing cushions and pillows. A footstool appeared out of nowhere for her disposal. There were flutterings and comfortings and people asking if she had any special cravings and could they possibly get her anything?

That was the pampered pregnant woman of fifty years ago. But today woman are tougher. We Are Strong! We Are Invincible! We don't need silly things like footstools and cushions and a chance to lie down while hubby runs to the store to get us some special goodies. No, sir! We can work right up until the baby comes, and drive ourselves home from the hospital. We can do all our work without the least bit of help from anyone else, whether husband, children, or friends. We Are Superwoman . . .

"Earth to N.O.W.! Earth to N.O.W.! Come in, N.O.W.! Do you read me? Over!"

Now that it's too late, some feminist leaders are starting to discover that pregnant women really do need special courtesies. In the meantime, though, social graces that took hundreds of years to develop have evaporated. Men, not knowing any better, now often expect pregnant women to be self-sufficient.

But actually pregnancy is a time when the whole family has an incredibly rich opportunity to develop team spirit. It provides myriad occasions for the father to demonstrate courtesy to the mother, and for the children to be instructed in these courtesies. For all but those fortunate few of us who sail through pregnancy feeling great the whole time, the initial queasy period and the final bulky stage also make us aware of how useful an extended family and close community are, perhaps for the first time in our headstrong, independent lives.

Even if you are a woman who has been taught since childhood of a loving heavenly Father, you may not be fully convinced that he really loves *you, individually* and *unconditionally.* During pregnancy, perhaps more than at any other time of your life, you need to be *fully convinced* of his love. You need to rest in that love, allowing it to be the *stabilizing factor for your life,* and for the life of your family.

—Mari Hanes
The Child Within

51

I can't give any other advice on living through a difficult pregnancy other than *eat well* (the "Brewer diet") and trust God. So many pregnancy problems are diet-related! Eat 2400-2600 calories of fresh whole foods each day, including 100 grams of protein.

I also see problems caused by stress (worry). So many Christian women have amniocentesis, ultrasound, induced labor, etc., etc., so they can be sure "everything is OK." Where is their faith?! and joy?!

—L.G., CA
(A certified childbirth educator, R.N., and midwife)

Bouncing (with Help) over the Jolts

Babies are like Christmas packages; once they are chosen and wrapped, they still need to travel a ways to be delivered. When God picks out a baby for you, having decided at the beginning of time which combination of sperm and egg shall trip the light fantastic in your womb, there is still a long waiting period until the package is delivered! And just as with Christmas packages sent U.S. Mail, there may be bumps and jolts along the way.

Typical advice about how to handle the jolt of pregnancy nausea (eat crackers before you get up, drink pregnancy tea) has never helped me a bit. Nor has it done anything wonderful for anyone I know. But here are a few ideas that really do help:

■ Smells. You have never before in your life been made ill by cooking onions, but if you are now, ditch the onions. Ditto for anything else odiferous around you that you have the power to remove. Your family can help by not demanding highly spiced foods during this time—or go a step farther and do some of the cooking. And a hubby who will buy you an occasional carryout meal (which avoids *all* cooking smells) is worth more than rubies!

■ Fresh air. Maybe it's the ions or just the pleasant aromas—it doesn't matter. It helps. Now is the time for all cigarette smokers to come to the aid of their wives by not turning that fresh air into stale, cancer-laden fumes. Pregnant smokers have much higher risks of miscarriage, low birth weight babies, and babies with birth defects. Protecting your wife from secondhand smoke counts.

■ Exercise. Try walks, even if you feel terrible. Lying around will make you feel worse. Your family can help by taking over your chores while you exercise. If you have small children, your husband or a responsible older child can watch them.

■ Lemon juice. A midwife I know posits that the cause of pregnancy nausea is your liver trying to clean out the toxins before the baby starts drinking them in. A lemon's acid seems to "flush" the liver. Whether this is true or not, some lemon juice in a cup of water (or a lemon with salt, if you like it that way) will, surprisingly, often help. Bring her home a lemon!

- Classical music, easy listening, or no music at all. Rock 'n roll can boom those tummy contents right up and out. Hear this, teenagers? (You might want to get them a copy of Al Menconi's video on rock music, too.)

- The Brewer diet. This is the real winner. Gail and Tom Brewer have written a book called *What Every Pregnant Woman Should Know: The Truth About Diet and Drugs in Pregnancy.* Dr. Tom and his wife Gail, an R.N., share the results of Tom's research into what works dietetically and what doesn't in producing healthy babies and moms. Bottom line: dieting and skipping the salt is dangerous. Eating a lot of protein and a wide variety of vitamin-rich foods (the Brewers have specific recommendations) is the way to go. The Brewer diet won't take away the yukky feeling right away, but over the long haul it can really help. And if you start eating this way *before* you get pregnant, it will go much easier. That horrible feeling of sickness seems to hit women hardest who have been starving themselves and eating junk food before they got pregnant. Getting on a sane, healthy diet *before* you get pregnant helps a lot. For the same reason, women who are inspired by pregnancy to finally start eating right can usually expect an easier time of it the next time around.

- For effective alternatives to over-the-counter drugs for most discomforts of pregnancy (nausea, fatigue, headache, stuffy nose and allergies, heartburn, leg cramps, constipation, varicose veins and hemorrhoids, backache, difficulty sleeping, and edema) get *Safe Natural Remedies for Discomforts of Pregnancy* from the Coalition for the Medical Rights of Women (see Resources).

The last month of my pregnancies, when I feel tired and enormous, I try to plan a special project to take my mind off myself, like knitting or writing or planning what I want to do after the baby is born.

—Beryl Singer, MA

As Murphy's Law would have it, I again experienced pre-term labor with my third child at seven months of pregnancy. This time I ended up in the hospital twice, enduring overnight stays and I.V. needles and *lots* of medication. This slowed down but did not stop my contractions. Bedrest was again prescribed, this time with *two* lively little complications. . . .

God provided help through our friends at church with meals and outings for my boys, and our third son was born sixteen days early, also healthy. He is such a joy and the easiest baby so far. Despite difficult pregnancies, we look forward to the next addition to our family if God should so choose to bless us. . . .

We intend to plan for our next pregnancy to be a difficult one, and to make as many preparations in advance as possible. I can prepare and freeze meals in advance while I am still in the early stages of my pregnancy. . . .

I have a teenage girl as a mother's helper who cleans and does odd jobs for me. My children will be a little older and I plan to prepare them to take on a little more responsibility. If necessary, we will set aside the funds to again hire some extra help. Whatever happens, we know God will not leave us out on a limb, and His will will be done in our lives.

—C.F., CA

A Time to Grow (in More Ways Than One)

For most of us, pregnancy only gets us in the tummy. Once the queasies disappear, all we have to do is haul our big bellies around until Baby comes. But some women do have it tougher. God is giving their families an *extra* opportunity to grow.

See how one such family, the Lienhards of Nevada, managed to not only cope with six months of Mom's enforced bedrest, but even to creatively turn it into a blessing!

Lauri writes: "I found out I was pregnant with our fourth child in October, 1987, began bleeding in November, and spent the next six months in bed. In order to handle the worry and emotional strain myself, I had to stay in the Word, and the Lord was faithful to give me truth, comfort, hope, and encouragement. We also had lots of prayer support and didn't hesitate to ask for prayer each time a new worry came up.

"As for practical coping with everyday living with three children through this situation (ages 8, 5, and 2½), here are some ideas.

"We called on our church body to help at first—i.e., meals, housecleaning, childcare—but that was soon impractical as time went on. So we developed an attitude of 'Do only what's necessary to function daily.' In other words, don't worry about cleaning the corners, messy closets, drawers, etc. . . . We developed a daily routine of breakfast, dishes, schoolwork, lunch, schoolwork, dinner, clean-up, family time, bed.

"My children learned to cook easy things (oatmeal, scrambled eggs, french toast, meatloaf, frozen vegetables, sandwiches), how to work together to wash dishes, keep their toys picked up, etc. I laid on the couch and read directions from the cookbook, did the book work, corrected school papers, and read stories with them.

"We saved laundry and general housecleaning for Saturday when Dad was home, and had help from Grandma and Grandpa. We had friends take the kids on occasional outings, and made plans together as family as to what we would do after the baby came (i.e., camping trip, zoo, lake, etc.). . . .

"My husband and I also learned a lot and grew in the Lord. We made time nearly every weekend to have an evening or day alone together. We had candlelight dinners at the couch and lots of time to discuss things and encourage each other. . . . We also tried to have our friends and brothers and sisters come over frequently for informal dinner, pizza, or just to visit. This was encouraging to me, as I had no regular fellowship, not going to church during that time. It also kept us in touch with everyone and kept our perspective on the world outside our situation.

"I personally tried to use my time productively by reading, doing Bible studies, listening to tapes, catching up on correspondence, making plans and menus, and organizing closets and rooms in my head. This really helped when I was on my feet again. I refer to those lists and schedules I made when I had time to really think things out, as now I don't have as much time. . . .

"My children learned a lot of practical things that I wouldn't have thought them capable of. Life is easier now with four because everyone helps, than it was with three or two children when I did all the work. . . .

"God used this difficult time to make *all* of us better people and also blessed and rewarded us with a beautiful baby boy (3 pounds 5 ounces at birth—now 7 pounds and doing great!)."

The Lienhards turned a problem pregnancy into a time for organizing, for hospitality, for study, for quiet times as a couple, and for training the children, who not only got to help Mama themselves, but to see friends and relatives helping. This lesson in how blessed it is to receive is wonderful training in how blessed it is to give.

Enjoying Pregnancy as a Family

A widely underreported fact is that children of all ages love babies.

In our home church, a mother of a one-year-old was expecting another under dire circumstances. Four of us took turns spending days at her house through the worst of it, but we realized there are categories of people better equipped for that than us with our own small children. I'm just saying that there is a glaring ministry opportunity here, one which exists partly because so many of the women in the category most available to help are *not* available because they are pursuing careers . . . and partly because churches are too busy with programs to do such practical things

—Nancy Krumreich, IN

Even teenagers!

I remember one time I was changing my baby (our fifth) in a restroom at the Missouri State Capitol. The doors opened and several classes of high-school girls swarmed in. The first thing I noticed was how heavily made-up these girls were—and to what ill effect, I might add. They all were simultaneously trying to look cool and be passionately attractive to boys. An impossible task, and one not usually associated with maternal feelings.

As these hundreds of gum-chewing adultettes thronged around me with their jaded expressions and dripping mascara, I wondered what anti-child remarks they might make.

"Gosh, what a cute baby!"

"Oh, look, he's smiling!"

"Can I hold him?"

"I have a little brother just his age."

"I can't blankety-blank wait until I have a baby of my own!"

Well, the dialog *was* spiced with words appropriate to the cool teen image, but the content warmed my heart. Poor little girls! In spite of everything Planned Parenthood and Hollywood could throw at them, they still liked babies.

Most children are thrilled at the thought of a new brother and sister. Just keep them away from those wretched "I hate the new baby" books. These do *not* reflect the real feelings of children who are raised to think of others. I'm not even sure they reflect the true feelings of *any* children, except a small percentage of those whose parents show ridiculous favoritism to the baby. And I'm the oldest of seven. I should know!

Sharing the Joy of Pregnancy With Your Children. You and your husband can prepare the children for their new brother and sister by

- Showing your own excitement.
- Reading books about how babies develop in the womb to them.

- Playing Pat Mommy's Tummy (otherwise known as Come Feel the Baby Move!).
- Emphasizing the older children's superior status as leaders of the others (provided they exercise their leadership wisely).
- Telling the children their birth stories. "We were wishing very much for a little baby boy [or girl] and then we prayed to the Lord about it. Well, Mommy got pregnant, but we were worried because we had to move and she was not feeling well. . . ." Go right up to and through the birth itself, with whatever details you consider appropriate to the listeners' ages. Tell them what they were like when they were little, and what special attention you gave them. Then if any of them should complain later about how much time you spend with the baby or all the presents he is getting, just remind them that you spent that much time with them when they were that age and that they got presents, too. (A very simple, effective, unanswerable point that the "I hate the new baby" books *never* mention!)
- Requesting that they help Mommy because she needs extra help just now, and thanking them for it on Mommy's and the baby's behalf. Nothing makes people more committed to a project than working on it. If the children get the idea that the baby needs them, it will be easy for them to feel loving towards the baby.
- Squirrelling away some presents for the older children, and bringing them out when the baby starts getting presents.
- Calling the baby "your new brother [or sister]" and "our new baby." Convey to the children that the baby belongs to them, too!

A Mother's Simple Joys. But don't spend all your time worrying about how to develop a team spirit in the children! Pregnancy has joys of its own for the parents. Here are some of the mother's simple joys:

I am convinced that the single most important story that each child hears is his or her birth story. The sense of being wanted or unwanted, of being an individual with interesting characteristics or just another statistic with no personality, of knowing who one is and one's place in the world or of feeling lost—all this is conveyed most deeply in the way in which parents tell a child [how] he or she arrived in the world (or the way in which they avoid the subject altogether).

—Anne Pellowski
The Family Story-Telling Handbook

■ Being able for the first time in your life to eat a square meal without worrying about your figure.

■ Getting to pick out a whole new wardrobe. This can be supercheap as well as fun, since all the yuppy mothers of one get sterilized and send their almost-new maternity dresses to the consignment shop.

■ Having your husband pamper you. Pregnant wives fall directly in the category of those "weaker vessels" whom husbands are supposed to treat with special respect (1 Peter 3:7). (Are any husbands reading this? Good!)

■ Knowing you are accomplishing something by just existing. Women with low self-confidence often bloom during pregnancy.

■ Not having to worry about wolf whistles. You can go for a walk and be treated respectfully.

■ Gentling your disposition. Many of us have had to fight our way in the world and have in consequence lost some feminine sweetness. Pregnancy hormones can calm you down and sweeten you up!

■ Falling in love with your baby. You are in love with your baby. Admit it! Encourage it! Sing songs to your unborn child. Talk to him. Squeeze his little foot when he sticks it out against your belly. Sit with your hand on your belly, waiting to feel him flutter about in your womb.

Falling in Love with the Baby. Misguided people often feel that getting married means the end of falling in love. Not for mothers, it doesn't! We get to fall in love with each new baby before we even meet him. It makes me wonder if the huge market for romance novels isn't really a symptom of women forsaking our normal love objects—our own babies—and consequently desperately seeking for substitute thrills elsewhere.

I can still remember the almost physical shock I felt when I first realized I could kiss my newborn baby without asking *anyone's* permission! He was *mine!* It wasn't much longer before I was making up little love songs and singing them to him all the time. I still sing love songs to our babies while I change their diapers and nurse them and carry them around. (It's easy. Just pick a tune you know and make up new words!)

You will know this country is getting in better shape when you hear love songs from mothers and fathers to their babies on the radio more often than you hear mating songs—in which, oddly enough, the lovers call each other Baby.

The Simple Joys of Fatherhood. Pregnancy has its thrills for men, too:

- Getting your wife pregnant makes a man feel more manly.
- Feeling needed. A little baby of your own is depending on you. It makes a difference!
- Everyone likes presents! For those men who believe what the Bible says about children being a gift, there's the thrill of being selected to receive it.
- Looking forward to passing on your name and trade. Contrary to current social dogma, there is nothing wrong with this. More on this subject in a future chapter.
- Feeling protective. In an age like ours when men are badgered into repressing their protective instincts, it feels wonderful to have a chance to let 'em go. (So says my husband Bill!)
- Falling in love with the baby. Men may not have mothering hormones, but they (you) are not callous brutes, either. Getting kicked by the baby in the middle of the night is a thrill, whether you are kicked from the inside (Mom) or the outside (Dad).

You have developed a wonderful team spirit among the children. Mama is eating well and Papa is buying a banner to float from the house windows when the baby is born. You are gunning down the home stretch!

One tennis partner said to me when I was pregnant with David, "I'm sure glad it's you and not me!" I replied, "I'm sure glad it is, too!"
—Arlene Dryden, CA

But a brick wall looms up ahead. *Where* are you going to have this baby? And *who* is going to help you? Shall you get an OB-GYN doctor, or a family practice physician, or a midwife, or go solo? Shall you go to a hospital or a birth clinic . . . or have the baby at home? Is the best road in birth the road not widely taken, or the Main Highway? Read all about it in the next chapter.

The Good
Birth

5

*O*ne tubful of very warm water seasoned with a cup of sea salt—just what the midwife ordered. I sank in with a sigh. The warm water was so comforting, taking all the strain off my hardworking body. In the tub I prayed fervently that the Lord would help me handle the hard part of labor . . . coming right up.

Bill was right there, helping me remember how to breathe with his best tubside manner. I felt myself starting to shake, which meant I was entering transition . . . but the contractions were so easy to handle (compared to what I had experienced in hospital births) that I couldn't believe it.

"RRRing!" It was the doorbell. "Hurry back, Bill, please!" Yup, he would. Off to the door, in came the midwife. "How are you doing?" I begged her to examine me. She obliged after I climbed out of the tub. The glad news: "The baby is coming *now!*"

Oh boy, this is hurting! Don't tell me about how the Bible verses about pain in labor don't mean what they say. I was crying and struggling. Delivery had always been the easiest part of labor for me, but this baby really hurt. Tears were streaming down my face. Ruth was encouraging: "You can do it!" And with another determined push, out he came.

It was a he: the most beautifully-formed baby boy I have ever seen. This is not just a mother's prejudice; Ruth said so too. Franky had rounded little limbs, not like the usual scrawny newborn legs, and already was looking around with interest.

Ruth weighed him: eleven pounds and ten ounces. Later that day he would tip our home baby scales at twelve pounds ten ounces, causing us to wonder how much Franky actually did weigh at birth. With all that, I delivered without an episiotomy. The only (minor) tear was in a place already weakened by previous episiotomies that doctors gave me

THE FIVE STANDARDS OF
SAFE CHILDBEARING

☐ Good nutrition
☐ Skillful midwifery
☐ Natural childbirth
☐ Home birth
☐ Breastfeeding

What a radical departure from nature the medical profession has made of pregnancy and birth. Routine use of oxytocic drugs tells us that a woman's body does not know when and how to labor. Routine episiotomy tells us that the opening of the birth canal is incapable of stretching enough for the baby to be born. Routine separation of mother and baby tells us that mothers are incapable of taking care of their own babies without medical intervention.

—Lee Stewart, CCE
*The Five Standards of
Safe Childbearing*

As an R.N., a Bradley childbirth instructor, a La Leche League leader, and one who has attended several births, as well as having experienced a hospital and a home birth, I feel that I can speak with authority that Satan's first blow to the family is at childbirth.

—Joanie Etter, OR

against my wishes when I delivered babies that weighed one, two, and five pounds less than Franky.

Now we were in bed: baby and me. He was warm and cozy in his new baby suit and little cap. I was relaxed and overjoyed, both at the same time. The brothers and sister had all oohed and ahhed, Bill had taken some pictures, and Ruth had fixed me a sitz bath brew, cleaned up, and gone home in time for a good night's sleep.

Over the next few weeks, I did not suffer with episiotomy soreness or painfully engorged breasts. A few sitz baths took away the tenderness, and since the baby started nursing right away instead of being kept from me for twenty-four hours, I had only a slight bit of engorgement that passes in a day. I did not have to beg the nurses for permission to see my baby, or worry about him contracting one of the super-powerful hospital infections. No roommate inflicted her favorite loathsome soap opera on me. No nurses kept me awake all night with hall lights, chatter, and 2 A.M. wakings for pain pills. I did not have to recover from an unnecessary cesarean or hospital infection. Nobody pressured me to have my tubes tied. The kids didn't develop Mom Rejection Syndrome from missing me, and I didn't develop post-natal depression from missing them, or from the misery caused by hospital birth.

Family Authority, or Who's Having This Baby, Anyway?

Am I trying to tell you that modern hospitalized childbirth is not the best way to deliver babies? Precisely. In fact, it's *weird*. That's why we need special classes to prepare us to accept the strange things that will happen to our bodies and our babies. As the Spring 1986 newsletter of the InterNational Association of Parents and Professionals for Safe Alternatives in Childbirth said:

> Most couples in the United States take some form of childbirth classes. Often these are taught by hospitals. Many

times these classes are nothing more than "Obedience Classes," where the mother is taught how to "be nice," to "obey" the doctor, and where she learns to "lie down and roll over." As a result, the vast majority of births are medicated and couples are conditioned to accept even cesarean surgery without question.

If your childbirth educator is not teaching you to question everything, even her, and is not urging you to take personal responsibility and check things out for yourself, then you may be being misled, perhaps even being "conned" into compliance with routines designed more for the convenience of the hospital than for the safety of mother and baby.

A good test of your childbirth teacher is to find out what percent of her students have a truly natural childbirth, without drugs or devices, and how many end up with cesareans.

You may be better off to pay the price of a good, independent teacher than to place sole trust in the "free" classes offered or promoted by the hospital. The price of the "free" classes may be higher than you think, and not in terms of mere money. With the outside private classes, you could be both money and health ahead.

From the moment you enter the hospital it is not *your* baby and *your* childbirth, but the hospital's. The fact that few of us elect to go through this ordeal more than once or twice no matter how well we are trained to accept everything that happens to us speaks eloquently for how the hospital establishment has managed to make birth one of the most distressing and humiliating life experiences.

Your doctor promised not to give you a needless episiotomy? He promised to let you deliver standing up? Even if he ends up delivering you himself (which is doubtful), you have no power to make him abide by any of his promises. You can be monitored, pricked, sliced and diced against your consent. If your doctor thinks you "need" a c-section (and some doctors think the majority of their patients "need" them), he can get a court order to force it upon you.[1] If the nurses don't like your attitude, they can declare you are an "at risk" mother and refuse to let your baby go home with you.[2] Medical orthodoxy and even just plain nastiness have precedent over the family's natural authority.

36% of obstetricians surveyed in 1985 admitted that they had increased their cesarean rates for legal considerations.

—*AMA News* report
Cited by Sue Baker,
president of International
Childbirth Education Association
in a speech at a July 22-23,
1985 Washington, D.C. forum
on malpractice issues in
childbirth.

No reasonable form of government can have authority over our most private affairs—how we are born and how we die. I do not grant this authority to the state— nor does the United States Constitution.

—Ina May Gaskin
*The Five Standards for
Safe Childbearing*

In a massive computer study by Lewis Mehl, M.D., 98 variables were statistically compared to neonatal outcomes. The four obstetric procedures correlating most closely with bad outcomes for babies were as follows:

1. Oxytocin (a uterine stimulant)
2. Analgesia (pain killers or tranquilizers)
3. Forceps
4. Amniotomy (artificially breaking the bag of waters). . . .

In a British study it was found that simple amniotomy more than doubled the chances of a baby ending up in the intensive care nursery (ICN). If amniotomy were combined with even low doses of oxytocin, 3.5 times as many of these babies ended up in the ICN. With amniotomy and high doses of oxytocin, the number of babies requiring intensive care was 6.0 times greater than for those born by a natural, spontaneous birth.

Some will say, "The cases with amniotomy and oxytocin were probably fetuses already in distress, which is why these procedures were done; therefore the higher rates of intensive care were for underlying medical problems, not due to the procedures." The author of the study did not find this to be so. The implication of the study was that amniotomy and oxytocin pose additional hazards of their own.

—David Stewart
The Five Standards for Safe Childbearing

Safety Begins at Home

All this, of course, would be bearable if the humiliating and uncomfortable methods employed by hospitals actually were better for mothers and their babies. But the plain fact is that they are not. From the pre-birth enema and shave to the fetal monitor, from the episiotomy to the uphill delivery in stirrups, each and every intervention has been shown in scientific studies to be *harmful* in the vast majority of cases. In fact, doctor-attended hospital birth itself has been shown to be harmful. Consider the evidence:

Every valid study ever published comparing doctors to midwives shows better pregnancy outcomes for midwives.

For example, in a California study of midwives in a hospital setting published in 1969 and 1971 issues of the *American Journal of Obstetrics and Gynecology*, the neonatal mortality rates for midwives were 10 per 1,000 compared to 24 for family physicians and 32 for board-certified obstetrician/gynecologists. Each of these three types of birth attendants were dealing with identical birthing populations in the same setting, and yet the midwives had less than half the mortalities of family doctors and less than one-third that of certified obstetricians.

In a North Carolina study in the December 19, 1980 *Journal of the American Medical Association (JAMA)*, there were no preventable mortalities over a three-year period for home births attended by lay midwives. The actual statistics were 3 perinatal deaths in 768 births, or a rate of only 4 per 1,000, less than one-third the rate for doctors and hospitals in the state during the same time.

In a Kentucky study of 575 planned home births in the March 16, 1985 issue of *JAMA*, the neonatal mortality rates were, again, less than 4 per 1,000. In this study half were attended by doctors, the other half mostly by lay midwives. The only two mortalities were with doctors. There were no mortalities with midwives.

A U.S. Government study on midwife and out-of-hospital deliveries published in 1984 by the National Center for Health Statistics (Series 21, No. 40) tabulated information for tens of thousands of such births for the entire country over a two-year span. It clearly demonstrated that midwives, whether in or out of the hospital, have significantly lower rates of low-birth-weight babies, which is the primary factor associated with newborn death and morbidity.

There are dozens of such studies, published in the most highly respected sources, from the United States and abroad. All show the superiority of midwifery and the safety of planned, attended home birth. The superior results of midwives, both in and out of the hospital, cannot be discounted in terms of differences in risk factors of the clientele, nor in the methods of data tabulation, nor by any other method.

The above quote is from the Fall-Winter 1985 *NAPSAC News.* For a bibliography of exact citations for studies comparing obstetrics and midwifery, send an SASE to NAPSAC asking for the Spring 1985 issue. Or check out some of the books on this subject in the Resources.

Expense

While we're on the subject of hospital birth versus home birth, let's not forget which side the bread is buttered on. The only groups opposing home birth are those who make megabucks from hospital birth.

As usual, the more dependent you become on outsiders, the more you pay for the privilege. Hospital birth costs two to three times the price of the finest midwifery service—and that is not taking into account that the U.S. cesarean rate is 24.4 percent,[3] of which all but 2 percent or so are unnecessary.

Now when you are looking at a cesarean birth, you are looking at money. Big money. Not only does the operation cost more than normal birth services, but since 25 percent of c-sectioned mothers develop infections, that adds several profitable (to the hospital) days on the hospital stay. And since c-sectioned infants need, on the average, more care than other babies (partly due to the drugs pumped into them through their mothers' systems just before birth), the nursery and neonatal units get their slice of the pie, too.

The big push in maternal health care now is "regionalization." Big expensive facilities to treat "high-risk" mothers. Guess who has lots of incentive to declare all women high-risk? Guess who is putting ab-

While an occasional home birth could result in a death, preventable in the hospital environment, there are countless instances of deaths in the hospital caused by being there that would not have happened at home.

—David Stewart, Ph.D.
The Five Standards for Safe Childbearing

Medical institutions, medical drug manufacturers, medical device industries, and medical professionals, in general, receive their benefits and their incomes in an amount proportional to the abundance of abnormality, sickness and complications. For example, one sick mother and her premature baby can generate $100,000 or more in intensive care, medical supplies, and professional services.

—David Stewart, Ph.D.
The Five Standards for Safe Childbearing

solutely zero bucks into *preventing* pregnancy complications (a simple matter of proper nutrition, in most cases)?

Given a choice, I prefer to be far away from any facility who makes more money the sicker I and my baby get.

Bonding

Surprisingly, the #1 reason for choosing to give birth at home is not concern about family authority, expense, or even safety (although safety is high on the list). Mothers and fathers simply don't want to be separated from their babies at birth. They want to bond with their baby—and to let the brothers and sisters bond, too!

Tell me no tales about the great bonding experience in hospitals. How well I remember having Joseph, my second son, whisked away from me by a grouchy nurse almost as soon as he arrived. There I lay on the delivery table for half an hour while she slowly got around to wiping me up. After I finally was wheeled into my room, I didn't get to see him for twenty-four hours.

The point is not that this happens to every woman every time she gives birth in a hospital. It does not. The point is that it *can* happen, and when it does, you can do nothing about it.

When you give birth at home, the baby is immediately part of your family. You don't have to do anything special to make this happen; it just does. At the hospital, the baby is hospital property, to be handled by you and your husband and children only if and when hospital staff approve. And given the hospital's built-in motive for finding reasons to put Baby into special care or "under observation," you may find your budding relationship interrupted in strange ways, above and beyond the routine removal of your baby at birth for "observation."

Comfort

When it comes to giving birth, women are amazingly heroic. A majority of us consider our comfort

"At risk" mothers could have their children removed at birth and placed in "crisis nurseries." The "at risk" category included cases where "no current problem may exist."

—Discussion of *A Child Health Plan for Raising a New Generation,* submitted to and endorsed by the Governor of North Carolina. Words in quotes are from the plan.

last, well after the importance of the baby's safety and our bonding with him. That is why staff anesthesiologists go into such involved song-and-dance routines about how the drugs they use on us won't hurt the baby at all, etc., etc. If a doctor stood up before a roomful of pregnant women and announced that a certain drug was the best painkiller ever but that it was associated with a measurable risk of unnecessary infant deaths, no woman in the room would sign up for it.

But we do sign up for the doctors' drugs, because we are convinced that they will save us the pain God assigned to labor. Few of us have had enough children to know better. Fewer yet have experienced both hospital and home births. We who have are exceedingly ready to draw comparisons not at all favorable to the hospital.

They tell you that the wonder drugs will swoosh you through labor. This is baloney. If you are administered drugs too early on in labor, the drug will slow down or even stop your contractions. So hospital staff try to time the drug to take effect just before delivery—when you don't really need it. Transition labor, the part just before delivery, is the hard part, but drugs can't consistently help you with that.

What the hospital routine *can* do is keep you out of a nice warm tub. I have had six children, three in the hospital with varying degrees of drugs, and three at home, and I can tell you right now that no hospital drug can compare for sheer comfort with laboring in a nice warm tub. First of all, the water is relaxing all by itself. Second, you don't get chilly or hot or icky. Third, you don't have to worry about your labor stopping, causing draconian measures like Pitocin (which can rupture your uterus) or c-sections to be employed on you. You just haul yourself out of the tub when you get the irresistible urge to push, and that is that.

The only way to improve on laboring in a tub is to add a whirlpool. Make sure the tub is clean, and don't forget the sea salt (it prevents infections).

I am a walking statistic. My first two children were born by cesarean section, eight and six years ago. The first was due to a doctor who thought all babies should be delivered within a week of their due date, and twelve hours from the onset of labor. It was a nightmare of drugs, surgery and more drugs. I was so "grateful" for the doctor's great "judgment" and "skill" because I didn't know any better.

My second baby never got any labor—and after a ten-month pregnancy and many tests it was determined she *was* being compromised. This very sensitive physician still gave us a wonderful family-centerd birth. I was not away from my baby more than one hour (eighteen hours with my first!).

Well, after much searching and struggling, we found a physician who believed I could (and should) be normal. My third and fourth children (now two years old and four months old) were born in totally unmedicated births. I would encourage any woman to pray very hard and seek the same opportunity. Unnecessary surgery is destructive to the body and should be avoided! If a doctor tells you differently, study, read, research, and find somebody else!

—M.B., WA

Prenatal care by most physicians is little more than cesarean insurance. You pay your monthly premiums in pregnancy, and then if you need a section when labor comes, he'll do it.

—Gail Sforza Brewer, R.N.
Author, *What Every Pregnant Woman Should Know*

The rates of mortality for doctor-based systems are at least double, while the rates of morbidity [subsequent disease or complications] are at least quadruple that of midwifery systems. . . .

The data for midwifery versus doctoring, as philosophical approaches to maternal/newborn care, clearly prove that doctoring is more dangerous to the life and health of both babies and mothers. Why is this so? There are three fundamental reasons:

1. Most doctors use too much intervention;

2. Most doctors do not attend a woman in labor;

3. Most doctors do not develop the supportive rapport with laboring women to facilitate her ability to give birth safely and naturally by her own efforts.

—David Stewart
The Five Standards for Safe Childbearing

In the hospital, not only are you not in a tub, you are more likely than not flat on your back, which is the absolutely worst position for labor. Laboring on your back prevents gravity from helping you. When you have a contraction lying down, it can cause an oxygen blockage for the baby, which the dutiful fetal monitors present as fetal distress, which leads to a c-section to "save" the baby who was only endangered by you lying on your back in the first place. Thus are 24.4 percent c-section rates maintained.

Tender Loving Care

Doctors prefer patients who let the doctor run the show. A woman who studies up on subjects like home birth and VBAC (vaginal birth after cesarean) is likely to be tagged by the doctor as having a "bad attitude."

Are patients the ones with the bad attitudes? Reflect on the difference between the way a doctor and a midwife attend a birth.

The doctor does not arrive until the delivery (if then), unless he happens to be making rounds in the hospital earlier.

The midwife stays with you through the entire labor.

The doctor lays you flat on your back on a table, with your legs up in stirrups, so he can attend you comfortably without bending over.

The midwife lets you kneel or stand or squat or whatever is comfortable for you, while she gets down on the floor.

The doctor gives you an episiotomy (usually).

The midwife lets you deliver without episiotomy (usually). She helps you avoid tearing by supporting your perineum, helping you "breathe out" the baby instead of pushing, and perhaps rubbing the perineum with warm olive oil to make it more supple. If you need more help, she will suggest that you squat, since squatting increases the available room for baby to emerge by up to 30 percent.

The doctor leaves once the baby is born and you have held the baby a minute or two. If he stays longer, it is only to stitch up your episiotomy.

The midwife stays until you are comfortably in bed and both you and the baby appear to be doing well. She might make you a cup of tea and start a batch of herbal sitz bath brewing before she leaves.

The proof of the pudding is that women who have given birth with both doctors and midwives prefer midwives 100 percent to nothing. Even those who have never really thought through the issue have an intuitive leaning toward midwives. It just seems more natural to have another woman serving you humbly during your most crucial time, instead of a man who is not your husband controlling things and ordering you around.

The Principle of the Thing

You might feel that your own birth experiences were satisfactory, and wonder why I am making such a big issue about home birth. I have two answers:

(1) Are you sure you know what you were missing? If you have never given birth without an episiotomy, for example, you don't know how wonderful it is to be able to sit down on a normal chair the day after having your baby. This is not a trivial point: infections from episiotomies are the leading cause of *death* in women who have just given birth vaginally. You have no idea how much safer and more comfortable home birth can be until you have tried it.

(2) Just because you personally have managed to find a pleasant doctor and hospital doesn't mean nobody else has troubles. An analogy might help. Imagine you are the son of black parents growing up in the fifties in a middle-class neighborhood. Your parents are among the few blacks who have "made it," and your neighbors consist of white liberals who are delighted to have you among them. Would you be justified in declaring that blacks down South had no problem with racial discrimination just because life was easy for you?

Principles are important. The bottom-line issue here is, who has power over your family? Did God ever take authority over the family away from the

With my second child I was hoping for a VBAC, and went to the hospital after about 22 hours or so of labor. My doctor was out of town. The nurses got me comfortable, and my labor was going well. Then the nurse came back in and said, "Dr. X wants you prepped for surgery—shaved, enemaed and catheterized—just in case." She then added, confidentially, "You have the right to refuse."

I did refuse, and then, a few minutes later, a man burst into my room, livid with rage, and hollered at me, "I don't know who the #%$#% you think you are, but we have RULES in this hospital, and if you aren't on that bed and prepped for surgery in ten minutes, I'm off this case!"

Naturally I as politely as humanly possible under the circumstances asked him to drop my case long before my ten minutes were up! Can you imagine anyone treating a laboring woman in this manner? Can you imagine such a person delivering your child?

—Liz Messick, DE

husband and give it to the doctor? No, He did not. Biblically, there is no case for doctors wielding this kind of authority. Doctors should be family servants, giving us the facts and letting us make up our minds, with us responsible for the results of our own decisions.

Actually, it would be in doctors' best interest to give back our authority. Look at the medical malpractice crisis. Why can't doctors get decent insurance rates? Because people expect doctors to be gods. When the "god" slips up, they are furious. If the law said, and "patients" (we need a better word for doctor's customers) felt, that the person on whom the treatment was being used had the final authority and responsibility in all medical situations, this would put a stop to the kind of malpractice suits that have doctors grinding their teeth in frustration. It would also free doctors to stop the flood of unnecessary tests and overzealous interventions that they perform in order to defend themselves against potential malpractice suits.

We can hasten this happy day by avoiding as much unnecessary medical technology as possible. Home birth is not radical; it's the way most of the world has always been born. (To this day, Jimmy Carter was the only President not born at home.) Midwives not only protect your maidenly modesty (a consideration of some importance, considering how the Bible condemns exposing yourself to men other than your husband), they also save lives and safeguard your family's authority.

Midwife Crisis

Now here is a ministry opportunity for you older or childless women who feel like your life has no particular direction or meaning. We talk about "midlife crisis"; well, here is a midwife crisis! There is a great, glaring need for midwives out there. Training resources are available, from home study correspondence courses to classic nurse-midwifery programs. Or you can just follow around a practicing midwife

---

There may be people who enjoy good health care services without consciously bearing their share of the responsibility. If so, they are lucky to this point. In general, good health care is only available to those who educate themselves, question everything, make their own decision, and assume the primary responsibility for their own health.

—David Stewart
The Five Standards for Safe Childbearing

My advice to a woman expecting her first child would be that we have got to start looking at doctors as helpful professionals rather than as demi-gods.

—Liz Messick, DE

The midwives, however, feared God and did not do what the king of Egypt had told them to do; they let the boys live. . . . So God was kind to the midwives and the people increased and became even more numerous.

—Exodus 1:17, 20

and learn as an apprentice. You'll find resources for all these options at the end of this book.

All of you reading this who have given birth to a child have my respect. You have done something marvelously unselfish and courageous—an act of heroism almost unparalleled in the modern world.

Those of you who have given birth more than once deserve even more praise.

And to those men who have acted like gentlemen through your wives' pregnancies, doing your best to take the load off her suddenly weaker shoulders, all praise and honor to you as well. You deserve it!

Now that God has blessed you with that gorgeous little red, wrinkled mite, you feel the heavy responsibility of parenthood descending on your inexperienced shoulders. But not to worry: raising kids is easier and more fun than you think. Provided you kick out the rascals who are making it hard. More on these no-good, low-bellied sidewinders in the next chapter.

That night while praying, Chuck recalled that there were midwives in the Bible. On each occasion, the midwives were shown to be compassionate, faithful, and blessed by God.

—Sue Argenna
The Clarion, Volume 6, No. 1

The Three Little Hassles and How They Grew

6

*L*et's talk about kids a minute. Babies, to be specific. That cute little seven-pound rascal lying flat on her tummy in the crib. You are bigger than her, stronger than her, and smarter than her. This will remain the case for a long, long time. Even though she was born with a strong desire to get her own way (we adults call this "getting self-actualized" and "reaching my full potential"), she was also born wanting to please you. She will laugh with delight when she sees you smile, and will be chastened by your frowns. Furthermore, if she is your own natural child she is bone of your bone and flesh of your flesh. Natural bonds of love and all that. In any case, she smells sweet after her tub, her skin is soft and kissable, and she likes getting hugged.

If you are like most people, you were probably expecting this chapter to elaborate how hassled mothers can survive the daily assaults of our little bundles of joy.

Nope.

Moms today are hassled, all right, but our kids (bless their little hearts!) are not the true source of our hassles.

Throughout the history of the world, mothers (and fathers) never have felt as confused, diffident, scared, frustrated, worried, and incompetent as the parents of our generation. Proof: There never has been a market for How to Raise Your Baby books anywhere near the proportional size of the current one. That being so, our children must not be the real problem.

So what is?

In this chapter we are going to look at the three *real* hassles facing parents today. Then, instead of throwing up our hands hopelessly like the few books I have seen that acknowledge these obstacles exist, we are going to tackle the obstacles head-on and bring 'em down.

I would like to hear and read more about the sheer earthly joy we can experience in a large Christian family. The pleasures of parenthood are unique and nothing else in this life can compare. There seems to be no lack of literature which focuses on the negative aspects of child-raising—how to solve behavior problems, how to cope, etc.—but what about the positives?

—Pamela Boswell, CA

My friend L. and I also are asked (daily, it seems), "How do you do it?" regarding staying home with our children, home schooling, and wanting more. The ironic thing is that WE are the ones who are relaxed, happy, and enjoy our kids, and *they* are the ones who are frazzled and hate parenting!

—L.G., CA

Hassle #1: The Yak-Yak Amateur Hour

Once upon a time mothers and fathers considered babies a joy. And those that didn't knew enough to keep their mouths shut. Not liking your children was a sign of incompetence, and little sympathy was wasted on the whiners.

Somehow this has all changed. It is *chic* to knock babies and unfashionable to have good children. Parents are expected to have no control over their offspring's values and behavior, and those who beat the projected odds are looked on as freaks. Motherhood is considered a thankless drag, and fathers are not even expected to try.

Consider the typical young woman's expectations. According to recent research, "Young women in college in the 1980s see little hardship associated with career responsibilities, but view motherhood as filled with difficulty and stress."[1] Believe it or not, the over 300 female psychology students surveyed for this study "attribute all the 'role problems' in the wife/mother/career lifestyle to maternal duties."[2] Since these girls have never had jobs or children, we may reasonably conclude they are just echoing what they were taught. It's a simple lesson, and doesn't take long to learn.

(1) Don't Blame the Boss.

(2) Blame the Baby!

The truth is that as soon as we are able to read and view TV, we are taught that raising children is frenzied, frustrating, and ultimately futile. The world of work, however, is portrayed as fun, fascinating, and fulfilling. Unless you happen to be working at home surrounded by (horrors!) your own children. Staying home may be frugal, but it is also frumpy, fuddy-duddy, and friendless!

I would like to suggest that the young ladies interviewed for that study have it backwards. The 9-5 rat race is what gives people ulcers and drives them to psychiatrists. Children are a blessing—a source of joy!

Unless, that is, you *don't know how to raise them.*

Nothing is more frustrating than having responsibility for a job you know nothing about. Yes, millions of kids nowadays are (let's be honest) snotty little brats who drive their mothers wild, just like the kids on TV. But this is not the way kids are *supposed* to be! These pathetic children are what results when mothers and fathers let *amateurs* teach us how to raise our kids.

Yes, I said *amateurs*. Not that some of these people don't have impressive lists of initials after their names. They are just missing out on two essential ingredients:

■ Any *absolute authority* on which to base their theories.

■ Any *personal experience* with successful family life.

Chilled: The Ultimate Guide for Parents With Cold Hearts. Take, for example, an article in *Child* magazine. Or, for that matter, take *all* of *Child* magazine. In one typical issue of this self-proclaimed "Ultimate Guide for Parents" (September-October 1988) we find:

(1) An editorial by a mother of one who has left her three-month-old with a sitter to return to work. The editorial shows her turning to (a) a pediatrician and (b) a book written by an "expert," in order to understand what her son is trying to say to her. (The message is, "Come home, Mommy!" but with help she manages to avoid giving in to it.)

(2) "The Good-Bye Dad: A Day-Care Drama in Three Acts." Written by a father of one. The article chronicles his son's pilgrimage from one rotten babysitting arrangement to another, winding up at last in a day-care center. Moral: "Possibly we could have gotten by financially if one of us took care of him, but we both liked our work and didn't want to give it up to be 24-hours-a-day parents."

(3) "Romantic Getaways (You *Can* Leave Home Without Them)." The "them" you can leave home turn out to be the kids. Article highlight: A quote from the mother of a nine-month-old who returned

The parenting workshop soudned great. Let's face it; the psychologist had the right look: dark suit, chart, and several stapled handouts. He began by assuring the audience (parents from my son's preschool) that he was not going to instruct us on how to raise our children, only on how to make sure they turned to their parents instead of their peers for advice on sex, drugs, and alcohol.

He then proceeded to illustrate such techniques as not insisting your three-year-old wear a jacket in winter. "He will learn the responsibility of wearing a jacket when he gets cold enough," the psychologist told the wise-eyed moms. . . .

Finally a brave mother asked our authority, "Do you have children?"

"Hum . . . oh . . . (stammer, stammer). Not yet," was the reply. Another expert had lost his audience.

—Julia Dempsey Noblitt
Welcome Home,
February 1989

from a trip to Hawaii to find their daughter "so sick with intestinal flu that she couldn't lift her head." Here are the mother's words of wisdom: "I was glad that my parents hadn't called me to say she was sick. My husband and I both have demanding careers, and we really needed the break."

(4) "These Videos are 'S'-Rated (They're Sexist)." The article condemns *Lady and the Tramp, Sleeping Beauty,* and *The Shaggy Dog* for "cast[ing] male and female characters in traditional roles . . . the values of 40 years ago." Apparently the article's author is trapped in New York City and is totally unaware that in the real world some people still live like that.

(5) "Why Children Lie." A psychiatrist at U.C.L.A. School of Medicine informs us that "A child's first lie represents an important developmental step."

I could go on. Article after article was by and about the part-time parents of one day-care infant. Sprinkled throughout to add more authority were nuggets from "experts" like the U.C.L.A. psychiatrist mentioned above.

One mother I know, offended by the relentlessly anti-family tone of this magazine, wrote a civil letter of protest pointing out, "There *is* still such a person as a stay-at-home Mom."

Now it gets interesting. The editor wrote back. Her response is reproduced in the sidebar, from a photocopy I have of this letter. In case you have difficulty reading the small print, this is what it says:

Dear Mrs. M——:

It must be nice to be so smug and self-righteous as you. As a college educated person I've learned that no one has all the answers.

It must also be nice to have a husband paying all the bills. Most women in America work out of financial necessity.

You'll be interested in knowing—if you can
keep an open mind for five seconds—that most
studies show that children whose mothers
work grow up with a greater degree of self-
esteem.

Thank you for canceling your subscription.

**Where Seldom is Heard an Encouraging Word,
and the Guys Are Rowdy All Day.** Are you surprised? If you think about it, the only surprising
thing about this response is the editor's honesty. Just
about *every* mass-market magazine for women and
parents relentlessly knocks the Christian family
lifestyle. From page 1 through the full-color ad on the
back page, we get the message: kids are bothersome
pets who belong in a "quality" kennel. Taking care of
your child yourself is just too, too dreary.

The less personal experience of family life magazine writers and editors have, the more negative their
view of children seems to be. It couldn't be otherwise.
Sinning against someone makes you feel guilty, and
the oldest way invented to unload your guilt is to
blame the person you are sinning against. Adam tried
it in the Garden of Eden, blaming his own choice to
eat the forbidden fruit on God ("The woman *you put
here with me*—she gave me some fruit from the tree"
Genesis 3:12). The more the writers and editors of
magazines flee their children, the more they will promote negative attitudes towards children.

The same applies to all those Ph.D.-anointed types
quoted in magazine articles. Where are *their* children?
Do they even *have* children?

Revealingly, a recent mailer from *Parents* magazine says that "most"—not all—of their "experts" are
parents. In other words, some of their "experts" don't
even have *one* child.

Learn to translate what these people say (if you
insist on continuing to read it!).

I grew more and more im-
pressed with the effect that
the mere possession of money has upon the kind of information that is dispensed
through the media.

I already knew that, in
America, all advertisers spent
more than $25 billion a year
to disseminate their information. . . . Virtually all of the
$25 billion was being spent
by . . . the only people who
could afford to pay $30,000
for one page of advertising in
Time ($54,000 by 1977) or
$50,000 for one minute of
prime television time
($135,000 by 1977). . . . Only
the very rich buy mass national advertising. And they
do this to become richer.
What other motive could
they possibly have?

A. J. Liebling once said,
"Freedom of the press is limited to those who own one." I
was learning that access to
the press was similarly dis-
torted by the possession of
wealth. People with money
had a 25-billion-to-nearly-
zero advantage over people
without money. . . .

Twenty-five billion dollars
is nearly as much as the
whole country spends on
higher education every year.
I began to realize that a dis-
tortion was taking place in
the quality and kind of information offered to the public.
To a larger and larger extent,
people's minds were being
occupied by information of a
purely commercial nature.

—former adman Jerry Mander
*Four Arguments for the
Elimination of Television*

You know how the magazines love to tell you how much it costs to raise a child? Well, consider *these* statistics. The average person . . . will represent a combined liability, or economic cost, of $192,600 during his first 18 years plus his lifetime after retirement at age 65. But the same average person will occasion the production, directly and indirectly, of goods and services worth, if a male, $55,277 per year, or, if a female, $26,680 per year, every year from age 18 to 65. This means the average male will occasion the production of $2,598,000 worth of goods and services during his lifetime and the average female will occasion the production of $1,253,960 worth of goods and services in her lifetime. This means the average male's net worth to society . . . will be $2,405,400, and the average female's will be $1,061,300 . . . figuring solely on the basis of measurable economic income, not including the tremendous value of the financially unpaid work people—especially women—perform at home.

—E. Calvin Beisner
World, January 9, 1989.
Based on figures estimated by economist Marvin DeVries and reported by Allan C. Carlson in his book *Family Questions: Reflections on the American Social Crisis.*

ORIGINAL REMARK:	"Nobody today can protect children from XYZ [drugs, TV porn, child molesters . . .]."
TRANSLATION:	"I and my friends don't want to make the effort to protect our children."
ORIGINAL REMARK:	"Bad Behavior X is a normal developmental stage [teen promiscuity, drug abuse, lying, beating up little kids]."
TRANSLATION:	"I couldn't care less what my kids do."
ORIGINAL REMARK:	"Children have a need to be accepted by the peer group."
TRANSLATION:	"I gave up being a parent when Mikey turned five."
ORIGINAL REMARK:	"Children have to get ready to live in the real world."
TRANSLATION:	"I accept no responsibility for improving the world in which my children will be living."
ORIGINAL REMARK:	"Experts say . . ."
TRANSLATION:	"My buddies all agree that . . ."
ORIGINAL REMARK:	"Children today are different."
TRANSLATION:	"Parents today are different."

Dependence Sells. If today we spend way too much time worrying about our children and not nearly enough enjoying them, the reason is that we are listening to the wrong people. "A gossip separates close friends," says Proverbs 16:28. People are gossiping to us about our children. They have a good reason for gossiping, too: money.

At the risk of being thought hopelessly cynical, I am going to explain to you why the media are so relentlessly negative about children. The reason is simply that *dependence sells.* If you feel like you know how to feed, clothe, educate, and raise your children, nobody can sell you information and products about how to feed, clothe, educate, and (that loathsome word) *parent*.

What you may not know is that all the mainstream media make their money through advertising. You may have realized this is true of television and radio, but it's also true of magazines.

Magazines do not live by subscriptions alone. They hustle for subscribers so they can turn around and sell those subscribers to advertisers. Advertising is where the big bucks are. So today magazines design their editorial content not just to please the advertisers, but to help the advertisers sell. The reason articles always are "continued" in another section of the magazine is so the maximum number of ads can be displayed next to editorial content, giving the ads a better chance to be read.

Magazine sales people make their living persuading advertisers that their particular subscribers will buy more of the advertisers' products. They have moved beyond demographics (how many people read this magazine and where do they live?) to psychographics (what type of people read this magazine?).

Advertisers, it turns out, all want a certain psychological style of reader, who could best be summarized as Open Mind and Open Wallet. They do not want frugal, thoughtful, hard-to-convince readers. They want readers to believe what they are told and defer their judgment to that of others. So editorial content ends up, by the advertisers' irresistible pressure, producing dependent readers with an ever-increasing wealth of problems that need products to solve them.

The more wasteful and unnecessary a product is, it also turns out, the bigger the advertising budget available for selling it.

Advertising is for selling people what they would not buy on their own. If information was all we were getting, the whole world would advertise in the Clas-

In 1987 five advertisers spent $730 million out of the total revenue of $5.4 billion for all magazines that year. Here is the ad dollar breakdown [in millions]:

1. Philip Morris	$243
2. General Motors	153
3. Ford Motor	125
4. RJR Nabisco	105
5. Chrysler	100

The two largest cigarette advertisers cannot advertise on TV, thus the major expenditures in magazines of Philip Morris and R.J. Reynolds. Automotive advertising has always been a major source of magazine ad revenues.

—Leonard Mogel
The Magazine

People who take more pleasure in talking with friends than in machines, commodities and spectacles are outrageous to the system.

—Jerry Mander
Four Arguments for the Elimination of Television

sifieds. Glitzy two-page full-color spreads are for promoting luxury cars, cosmetics, fashion attire, and other high-ticket and low-usefulness items. Check this out for yourself the next time you read a consumer magazine.

So magazine editorial content is strongly skewed to promoting the mentality of people who buy these things and disparaging those that don't. You don't need a more complicated explanation than that for why media writers are always campaigning *for* new fads that undermine parental authority and responsibility and *against* a simpler, more traditional way of life.

Children as Problems, Children as Pets. Problems make money. Look at what happens when a new problem like Mid-Life Crisis comes along. Now people can write books, give seminars, produce videos, consult for industry, devise self-tests, and on and on, all about Mid-Life Crisis. All these products can be advertised and written about in magazines.

Children-as-problems is Big Money. Children-as-pets is also Big Money. Children as people we love, enjoy, and feel competent to raise is hardly a market at all. So today *every* women's, parent's, and baby magazine is busily promoting children as problems and pets. And so, of course, are television and radio.

The Mother's Declaration of Independence. I will not subscribe to, endorse, or buy anything that treats children like problems or pets. If enough of us do the same, the media might start sending us a better message.

I don't want to come along and sell you another product. I want you independent. I want you to have confidence in your mothering or fathering. All you have to do is

(1) not buy the vision promoted by the media,

(2) study the Bible, and

(3) iron out what's left with the help of older couples whose children turned out OK.

If you want my own advice, here is a foretaste:

- Think in positives instead of negatives. Think about "How can we build team spirit in our children?" instead of "How can we deal with sibling rivalry?"
- Expect the best from your children. Kids today are no different. Parents are what's changed, not kids. If you follow the tried-and-true wisdom of the past, you can expect the results of the past (honest, disciplined, affectionate children).
- Fight off the outside culture. We're here to change it, not to adjust to it. Don't take it for granted or accept its vision. Keep yourself and your children out of it as much as possible. Just as watching TV ads for cosmetics will make you feel ugly (the ads are designed for this), so soaking up the business world's present attitude towards children will taint your feelings towards them.

Hassle #2: The Youth Cultcha

The media may be just reinventing reality, but they succeed in getting our children to swim in it. Children today have all sorts of abnormal problems directly traceable to years of soaking in what is politely called the Youth Culture. (Or, perhaps more accurately, the Youth Cult.) Ninety-nine percent of the odd stuff experts are frantically trying to assure us is part of the normal developmental process comes from outside our kids. I'm talking about drugs, death rock, punk attitudes, peer dependency, sexual debauchery, and all those other great American traditions.

The Pilgrims had no problem with this stuff. And we don't have to, either. All we have to do is follow the Bible's advice and

(1) keep out of it ourselves and

(2) keep our kids away from it.

This is easier than it used to be, thanks to the home schooling movement. Home schoolers actually can protect their children from evil. Unlike the middle school where my church meets, my home school

I get weary of "support" group meetings in which the parents sigh and roll their eyes and act like they're barely making it. I hear not-so-funny jokes about what are really discipline problems. . . . I often wonder if their quiet desperation began with bottlefeeding, babysitters and birth control. They fail to see that their attitude toward the blessing of children affects them every day. Although they're trying to do what's best for the children they have, their attitude of limiting their family and "just getting through this stage of diapers, teething, home schooling, etc." makes the children an unpleasant chore instead of God's purpose for marriage.

—C.S., OK

One of the biggest influences as children grow into adolescence is the youth culture, that all-pervasive atmosphere that most American teenagers inhabit during most of their waking hours: listening to the radio, on the bus, at school, at after-school jobs, watching television, in the movies, and reflected in their friends. This culture gives no respect to parents. (Rock videos show parents being thrown out of windows and the like, to give you some idea of what you're up against.) Indeed, one of the main messages of the culture is that the teen is isolated and unloved, and certainly misunderstood except by fellow inhabitants of the teen culture, and that parents are the worst offenders.

—Connie Marshner
Decent Exposure: How to Teach Your Children About Sex

does not have a jukebox in the cafeteria loaded with degenerate rock music records. Nor are there any weird characters and drug dealers hanging around my front door. Since we have no TV, the kids also manage to miss the essential six thousand sex acts per year featured on that wondrous device, not to mention the heavy-handed promotion of violence and perversion in both programs and ads. As far as our kids are concerned, it's still 1950: "Leave it to Beaver" time.

Now, before you are tempted to tell me how horrible a mother I am to keep our kids outside mainstream American culture, let me ask you one question: Why not? Why should Christians buy the argument that all this degeneracy is the "real world"? It seems pretty unreal to me. A society that continues like this is not going to last, and I for one don't want my kids to get caught in the backwash. How much better to train our children in Christian culture, so they will be ready to lead others in the right direction!

Just because there are lots of bars out there, do we send our kids to bars?

Just because lots of couples divorce, should Christians divorce so our kids can share this common childhood experience?

I see no reason why Satanic rock music, lewd behavior, and general rebelliousness should form the environment for God's children. As an adult, I don't tolerate this kind of atmosphere. You won't find a Prince poster in my bedroom. So why should there be one in my daughter's?

New Testament Christians were widely accused of being antisocial. Seems they refused to attend the gladiatorial games and sexy plays of their day. As far as toting their kids to these events so they wouldn't be social misfits, that wasn't even considered. Funny thing was, their descendants ended up taking over the Roman Empire.

I look upon our modern American culture as David looked upon Goliath, not as a swimmer looks at the sea. If enough of us start looking at it this way, and if God responds the way He usually does by sending revival, by the time our kids grow up they won't have to know how to navigate through all this pollution. It won't be there anymore.

Hassle #3: The Generation Gap

Hassle #1 is amateurs telling us to feel hopeless about raising our children. Hassle #2 is the culture created and sustained by these amateurs. Hassle #3 is the professionals who should have taught us to raise our children, but didn't.

I'm talking about the generations of our parents and grandparents.

Young parents today have been disinherited. Winnebagos sprout the message on neon red bumper stickers: "We're Spending Our Children's Inheritance." While Grandpa and Grandma party, young parents struggle.

The sequence goes like this:

GENERATION ONE: These parents did a pretty good job, but neglected to teach their children how to teach *their* children.

GENERATION TWO: These parents counted on institutions (public school, Sunday school) to train their children.

GENERATION THREE: These parents haven't the faintest idea how to train their children.

While Generations One and Two were at it, they voted themselves a passel of federal programs to be paid for by their posterity. I don't know why we complain about Congress raising its own pay; Congressional pay raises are peanuts compared to the whopping sums our recent ancestors are still ladling out of our pockets and into theirs. These have so eroded the earning power of their descendants that today only 20 percent of young families can afford to buy a

We must never sacrifice personal time with our children for anyone or anything. . . . In every instance that I have heard about personally of children abandoning the faith and their parents' standards—this was one of the parents' key failings.

Another biggie is when parents allow peers and the Vanity Fair of this world system to entice our children from the simple, deep, abiding spiritual joys. We are foolish indeed to think that these babies can withstand a regular diet of exciting TV, movies, and star-studded shopping malls and continue to desire the simple pleasures of a life of self-denial.

—Laurie Sleeper, WA

Our project in "Family Living" was twaddle. What did those kids know about running a family? Or Miss Finchley?—unmarried and no kids. The class decided unanimously that every child should have a room of his own, and be given an allowance "to teach him to handle money." Great stuff . . . but how about the Quinlan family, nine kids in a five-room house? Let's not be foolish.

—Robert A. Heinlein
(in his early days)
Have Space Suit, Will Travel

THE OTHER SIDE

I chuckled when I read *HELP* readers requesting that older women should help the younger. This is true—but those of us who put in our time without working outside the home, took our children wherever we went, and had a well-behaved family—it is difficult to try to help those who want what we had but don't want to sacrifice and do what we did.

Don't get me wrong: we thoroughly enjoyed it. We never dreamed of babysitters. Walt played ball the first year and we went to the baseball banquet. I naturally took my nine-month-old with me. We had her in a high chair between us. They looked at us as though something was wrong with us. By the end of the evening we heard comments like, "If our children acted like yours, we'd take them along!". . .

Most young couples we see even have babysitters come in their home when they are entertaining in their home!

In the past week I met three babies in stores with their nannies. Such sweet babies and giving them to another to care for. One nanny told me that when the mother comes home from work (both parents have good jobs) the baby hangs on to the nanny for dear life and doesn't want her to go home. Sad, how many give away their heritage!

—Martha Pugacz, OH
Mother of seven adult children

house, while back in 1950 85 percent could afford one. And that's with *both* Mom and Dad working, as often as not!

So today young couples are hit with a double whammy: zero training for their job as parents and not enough money to provide a roof of their own over their heads.

To be fair, young couples today have higher expectations than their parents did. We were brought up to expect a life of wealth and success. Some young families will not consider a fifties-style starter home—they want a mansion!

All the same, I think few of us would say we were well-prepared for our responsibilities as parents and providers. Although there have been some noble exceptions, Dad and Granddad usually subscribed to the theory that each child (male *and* female) should earn his or her own way in the world. This translated into a dump-'em-out-the-door-at-eighteen policy that either sent us off to college or into our own apartment. While our parents would often stand at least part of the bill for our college education, few and far between were the parents who felt any responsibility for setting their children up in the world. Fewer and farther between were those who planned to offer their services as tutors and helpers after the children started coming. In fact, the idea that each generation should be totally independent of those preceding or following is so strongly ingrained in American society that even mentioning grandparents as helpers to young families sounds faintly pushy.

I sometimes wonder if the elderly's dogged insistence that they "don't want to be a burden" on their children by, say, living with them reflects an underlying fear that these same children who were left to sink or swim on their own will reciprocate when given the chance. These same independent-minded elderly vocally defend their Social Security and Medicare dollars, leading me to believe that independence is not so much the issue as is not wanting to admit that the generations in a family need each other.

The Bible, of course, clearly says that the generations *must* help each other. Grandparents are not supposed to hop into the Winnebago and vanish over the horizon. They are supposed to teach their children how to teach, and then help teach the grandchildren to make sure the parents follow through (Psalm 78:5-7). Adult women are supposed to have a home in their father's house until married (Genesis 38:11, Acts 21:9). Grown children, in turn, are supposed to take in the dependent oldsters in their families (1 Timothy 5:4).

The fact that our parents and grandparents never played by these rules (again, there are worthy exceptions) means that they are not trustworthy sources of information on family management. Today your grandma or mom is as likely to tell you to get sterilized after the second baby comes as she is to come and help after the birth. In fact, *more* likely. Judge the attitude of this generation by the adults-only rules in their Florida retirement communities. If they don't want to be around children, how are they going to be able to help you with yours?

Every new Christian woman reads Titus 2:3-5 and goes on a search for an older woman who will train her to love her husband and children, to be self-controlled and pure, to be busy at home, to be kind, and to be subject to her husband. I know, because a large number of them write to me complaining that such a female is not to be found. The older women are all busy with new careers or retirement plans. They have no time for their daughters' babies, or to give housecleaning lessons, or to hold a new couple's hands while they adjust to married life.

For the third time, I will mention the noble exceptions. I have the blessing of being related to a few. But realistically, most of us in this generation have to face the fact that we have to do two, or even three, generations' work at once unless we want our children stuck in a similar pickle.

I do heartily hope that some of the older people in the church will realize they *are* needed and start sharing the Biblical parts of their experience and exper-

When I first became a Christian in the '40s, young mothers were running to Bible studies, meetings, etc. I told them that it would be better to golf or play cards so that when the children grow up they could hate this instead.

—Martha Pugacz, OH

A serious problem among the midwives of today is that they are young—in their twenties or thirties—and are in the busiest years of raising their own children. This is the cause of a great deal of stress on the midwives, their husbands and their children. The granny midwife model did not have these problems.

In the granny model, the midwives were older women, often past fifty, who had no young children. . . .

—David Stewart
The Five Standards for Safe Childbearing

It might interest you to know also that the word "babysitter" was not in the *Webster Dictionary* until 1950.

—Tammy Alger, IL

tise. How wonderful it will be when the faithful older people finally realize that we need them, not to retire and make way for us, but to teach us!

But in the meantime, we have to help each other.

We have to rediscover how to beget and raise our children according to the Bible; how to build up our family's spiritual, moral, intellectual, and economic capital; and how to pass it on.

That is what the rest of this book is about.

The Hassled Mother's Quick & Dirty Guide to Child Training

7

*R*aising kids is like catching fish. You don't go for help to the guy with the best theories about how to tie flies. You go to the fellow with fish on his line. The people trying to tell us how to raise our kids today have lots of theories, but no fish on their lines. The questions they agonize over in print (e.g., sexist videos) show they are foolishly missing the point of what having kids is all about. And, I might point out, the more foolish we are if we waste even a nickel on advice from such sources.

Keep It Simple, Savvy?

Now here come some real experts: God and your fellow moms. Forget about all the important-sounding propaganda for "today's parenting lifestyle" promulgated by people who haven't even been living it long enough to know what it is.

The message from Real Moms is: Enjoy your kids! It's not as hard as you think!

Let's start with the newborn baby. Beryl Singer from Massachusetts, a mother of four, has some great advice.

"We just had our fourth baby seven weeks ago, and I came home from the hospital with several bags of those freebie samples they give you and lots of literature put out by the formula companies and baby magazines. I started reading through the literature and magazines while nursing the baby, and they were so funny I started reading them to Wayne and giggling. Some of them were inaccurate, and all of them were written for first-time mommies.

"In one article I actually read that babies don't recognize their parents until they are two months old. I read that one over several times, sure it was a misprint, but it wasn't! I also discovered I had four deprived little babies, because I never had half of the 'essential' baby equipment their article described.

To be a parent is more than a joy; it is to be related to the world in a radically different way from the way of youth, to see another who is not "wholly other," but a strangely free part of yourself.

—Joseph Sobran
National Review
December 31, 1985

It began with baby magazines and their lists of necessities. I still, to this day, do not know what to do with a dozen crib sheets. A newborn requires a washer load every day, and three or four would have been ample.

—Julia Dempsey Noblitt
Welcome Home
February 1989

Their layette list would clothe four babies easily! The pamphlet about breastfeeding was at least half-filled with instructions on bottle-feeding. There was a full typed page of instructions on how to put a diaper (disposable!) on a baby.

"The descriptions of life with your husband after baby were truly depressing. I couldn't believe it! It's nothing like they described. Our children have added to our happiness together—not made us angry and resentful of each other and the children!

"One article said something about not having any freedom and privacy since your baby was born. I wondered what privacy they were talking about, with the three children I had before the baby I was born interrupting me with 'emergencies' every time I go in the bathroom and shut the door. (You know, life-threatening things like, 'He gave this book to me last week and now he says it's still his!')

"Then there was that article on sex after baby. They said to choose a time when the baby usually sleeps for four hours (which is never with any newborn I ever had!). Then turn down the lights and put on soft music and a special nightgown (to hide the post-baby bulges) and have an unhurried time of enjoying each other. Well, it sounds nice, and it might even happen some day when the baby is three years old and all four of the children are visiting the grandparents at one time—if we don't have another baby by then! So anyway, I finally decided to write a more realistic postpartum guide of my own.

Beryl's Postpartum Guide for Fourth-Time Mommies

"ESSENTIAL
EQUIPMENT: One crib—for baby not to sleep in because he'd rather sleep with you, he doesn't want to take a nap right now, etc.

One car seat—For all those places you wanted to go after the baby was born, only now you'd rather stay home and take a nap.

Two arms and a lap—for cuddling baby.

TOYS: One father and several siblings will keep a baby entertained practically forever.

CLOTHES: For a summer baby: five dozen diapers and six undershirts.

HOUSEWORK: Delegate and ignore.

PRIVACY: Stand in the baby's room and say, "It's a poopie diaper—who wants to help me change it?" You'll have instant privacy as every family member disappears.

SEX: Set your alarm for 2 A.M. and make it a quickie.

DIAPERING: Put one half of the baby's diaper in front, and the other half in back. Fasten it at the waist with something. If it falls off, you did it wrong.

FEEDING: Put the breast and the baby in close proximity to each other. They'll make contact.

MEAL
PREPARATION: Serve only meals that can be prepared with one hand.

MARRIAGE
COUNSELING: With the ratio of children to parents at four-to-two, you have to get along, or the kids will win!"

I love being a mother. I love being pregnant, giving birth, breastfeeding, cuddling babies, toddlers, and even eleven-year-olds! I even love changing diapers and giving them baths. I love to look at their sleeping faces and marvel at their similarities and differences. I love their zest in the morning when I can barely wake up. I love to watch their first tentative steps turn into bold cartwheels in a few short years. I love to watch them love each other. I love it when they want another baby as much as I do. Children are wonderful!

—Pamela Boswell, CA

One reason I think God designed breastfeeding was for this very reason—so that a baby's very life would depend on the mother's physical presence.

　　　　　—Joanie Etter, OR

I fully expected this breastfeeding business, to which I was so committed because I knew it was the best thing for my baby, to be one of those things a mother just has to grit her teeth and bear!

I was pleasantly surprised to find that the feeling of nursing a baby is not at all akin to the feeling of being caressed by one's husband, and I was also pleased to realize that this was an extremely enjoyable experience.

Now I can say with joy that nursing my children has been one of the sweetest experiences of my life! It goes beyond the fact that breast milk is nutritionally superior, although that is important.

Nusing isn't just feeding; sometimes it is comforting, too. What a help it is to a brand-new mother with no baby-tending experience to be able to pick up your fussy baby and satisfy him or her at your breast! And from a nourishment standpoint, it is not necessary to monitor or measure your little one's intake of breast milk—if he is hungry, he'll nurse.

　　　　　—Liz Messick, DE

Playing It Close to the Chest

Now we come to one of motherhood's first pleasures—and first battlegrounds. The little tyke (or tykette) is hungry. *What* do you feed him or her? Bottle or breast milk? And for *how long?*

The decision to breastfeed rather than bottle-feed is relatively simple. Even formula manufacturers' brochures admit that breast milk is best for a young baby. That's not too surprising. After all, God designed it for that purpose!

The question of when to wean your breastfed baby is not all that complicated, either. Your three choices are:

(1) Forcibly wean the baby before he wants to stop nursing.

(2) Forcibly keep the baby at the breast long after he would have normally weaned himself.

(3) Begin to let the baby try solid food when he (a) shows signs of excessive hunger, e.g., waking up at night again after having slept through for months before or (b) begins to lose interest in breast milk, e.g., arching away, looking around at everything in the room instead of nursing, etc.

Most of us nowadays see that option #1 is not good mothering practice. No baby needs to be on solid food before he even cuts his first tooth! But option #2 is just as unnatural. Diane Moos of California addresses it:

"I wonder if you'd care to address what I call New Age Breast Feeding. . . . The idea is to nurse a baby on demand as long as she demands it—until she's two, or even older. This philosophy also requires the baby to sleep with you whenever she wants, even after she's no longer much of a baby anymore. Moreover, a baby *intuitively* knows what foods she should eat, and cows' milk equals *poison!* This doctrine fills the pages of *Mothering* magazine, as well as many 'expert' baby care manuals.

"Here's what happened to me: I raised my three oldest children (now ages thirteen, eleven, and ten) with a certain measure of common sense. My idea back then was that the sooner the little tykes adapted to our way of living, the happier we'd all be. It seemed reasonable to me that six-month-olds should sleep through the night, and with gentle nudging, they did. I felt vegetables and regularly scheduled naps were reasonable and good, so that's what we had, with no fuss. We were always complimented on the agreeableness of those children—we had no sleeping or eating problems. Everyone knew what to expect, I wasn't exhausted, and that period was one of the happiest of my life.

"After Timmy, our third child was born . . . during those seven years I read a lot of 'mothering' stuff, partly to prepare myself to be a childbirth educator at our Crisis Pregnancy Center, and partly because I just love the subject. The gist of a lot of this material was that babies must be clasped to their mothers' bosoms until they're old enough for preschool, practically. As a result, when God sent Rachel Grace, all my common sense had been replaced with these new ideas, and I nursed her every time she cried, which settled into a two-hour pattern, *day and night for sixteen months!* I was exhausted! I could barely remember how I raised the other three, so cloudy had my thinking become. My excuse was that Rachel was a special case and required extra attention. Actually, she had become the kind of baby I used to, in my saner days, criticize other mothers for producing.

"In desperation I called upon the Lord for help. He sent it. One night I was listening to a tape by Mrs. Dorothy Moore, nursing Rachel, and feeling grumpy. Mrs. Moore described what I was doing and labeled it 'humanistic.' Argh, the dreaded 'H' word! She suggested that there was nothing wrong with training up even a *tiny* child in the way she should go. Moreover, she stated that my method assumed that Rachel knew what was best instinctively, overlooking the fact that she was a little sinner. The next day I read in *Survivor's Guide to Home Schooling* [by Luanne Shackelford: see Resources] pretty much the same thing. So that night we moved a bewildered Rachel into her

---

In the *McGuffey Readers*, Book 2, are two poems on mothers and lullabies (Lessons LIX and LXXI). They both refer to breastfeeding your child to teach him to sleep and rest and for comfort, not just nutrition. It is of course because these books were written before bottlefeeding was invented.

In the Psalms it talks about a mother comforting her child at her breast.

—Tammy Alger, IL

Total breastfeeding means the following:

1. No bottles of water or juice. Bottles weren't available until this century and are unneeded.
2. No pacifiers. They again were not available until this century. A child was also comforted at his mother's breast.
3. No training cups. They again were not available until recently. Wait till your child is ready for a regular cup.
4. No baby food, either store-bought or home-made. This again is a modern convenience which encourages early return of fertility.
5. No baby swings to prolong periods between nursing.

I realize this sounds radical, but when you get rid of man's so-called "conveniences," then you can totally breastfeed and expect longer periods of time between the return of your periods.

—Tammy Alger, IL

My older son nursed for about 2½ years. My younger son nursed for almost four years. Now if there had been another sibling born, that probably would have been shortened some. However, I believe that God gave babies a very strong sucking urge, and this continues in young children for several years. Otherwise, why do we see three-, four-, and five-year-olds with thumbs in their mouths, or a pacifier or a bottle? . . .

Please don't get me wrong—both of my sons began eating some solids at around six months of age. They both continued to nurse for many months and years after that.

In Old Testament times children must have been nursed for years and not for months. In order for Moses to know of his history and culture he had to have stayed in his mother's house for years and not just for months. The same is true of Samuel. He must have been *several* years old when he was weaned and turned over to the priests to raise.

—Judy Pickens, CA

sister's room. (She'd been sleeping with us.) She cried for three nights, but has slept all night ever since, not counting a few bad dreams, when she gets cuddled but *not* nursed! Furthermore, I put her meals on a regular schedule. Since she wasn't full from nursing all night, she suddenly had an appetite. So, with the Lord's and Mrs. Moore's help, I came to my senses and we have a happy little girl.

"I think it is good to nurse a very young baby on demand, and to let them sleep with you for night feedings. That's one of the special things about having a new baby. But I do believe that there comes a time to exert gentle pressure to encourage a baby to conform to the habits of the household. No wonder those *Mothering* types were so eager to send their toddlers off to preschool! After three years of that kind of mothering, who *wouldn't* need a break!"

That about sums it up. As you can see, all three options have a germ of truth to them. Young babies need to nurse on demand and older babies need to learn to fit into the family's schedule. As to when to allow the baby to sample solid food: it seems to me that God gave us teeth to chew things with, and before a baby has teeth he is not likely to be meant to chew. With these parameters, you may end up nursing for six months or two years—it's all OK. Just enjoy your breastfeeding baby and don't worry about other people's timetables!

The Cheer of the Young Child

Now we move to the Young Child—you know, the kid they named a year after. Starting with the Terrible Twos and moving on to the Thrashing Threes and Fearsome Fours, you can expect a heap of trouble from kids this age. All you have to do is raise them according to the books instead of The Book.

The books make life complicated. Instead of playing Little Piggies with your children's toes, you are supposed to "stimulate the digital extremities." Instead of cuddling the baby, you are supposed to practice infant massage. Instead of keeping the children with you, you are supposed to find ways of keeping them penned up (playpens and kiddie gates) or looked after (babysitters and day care). Instead of teaching them anything, you are supposed to help them watch TV "creatively." Instead of breastfeeding and then graduating to blended table food, you are supposed to purchase expensive baby dinners. You are also supposed to keep up with all the latest baby exercises, infant designer wear, toddler videos, and kiddie camps. The list goes on, but I can't; it makes me tired just to think about it.

Then, after you've done all this hard work, the books tell you not to expect anything back in return. Not only is your youngster going to cost you hundreds of thousands of dollars (raised their way, of course, which is expensive), he is going to snort and snap at you as well. It will be up to you to change your behavior and learn to accept rudeness and ungratefulness as normal.

I don't buy this. I don't buy any of it. God didn't design children to be hopeless brats! Neither did He design them to need all this yuppy frippery.

Let's see what a list of essentials might look like for a young child:

ESSENTIAL
EQUIPMENT: One floor—where he'd rather sleep than his bed.

One yard—for running around in. If not available, take walks together.

Two arms and a lap—little kids still need hugs!

TOYS: Pots and pans for banging. Books for looking at and pretending to read. Socks for sorting. Sock balls for playing "basketball" with the laundry basket. One set of blocks (49¢ at a yard sale). Pencils, crayons, paper, and supervision. A broken TV set for not watching.

I recall going to a garage sale with our youngest when he was a toddler and overhearing someone say, "You can't be sick when you're a mother or the children will tear the house apart." To this I mentioned that ours would stay by the bed and hold my hand and rub my head. They asked if this was my only child and said I must be lucky. My reply was, "With one it may be luck—with seven it must be something else!"

—Martha Pugacz, OH

I do sometimes wonder whether all these books that are out now to read to children telling them that it's OK to feel jealous when the new baby arrives are causing the very problem they are intended to cure. Maybe the kids wouldn't feel jealous if we didn't tell them they should.
—Beryl Singer, MA

CLOTHES: Summertime: T-shirts, shorts, socks, and sneakers. Wintertime in the North: A coat, T-shirts, jeans, socks, and boots. All are available at yard sales and secondhand shops. Little girls may substitute skirts for shorts.

HOUSEWORK: Let him help. Even a one-year-old can start picking up after himself, and enjoy it too.

TOILET-TRAINING: When he's able to walk, talk, and follow commands. Any method will work sooner or later. Did you ever see an untrained eighteen-year-old?

SIBLING RIVALRY: Don't read him wretched books about kids who hate their new baby brother. Do encourage him to feel possessive about his little brothers and sisters. Do encourage the younger ones to look up to their older siblings. Do give them projects that require teamwork.

MEALS: Serve food.

Young children are super-easy to enjoy. They are also not all that much work, once you learn how to go with the flow and cancel your subscription to *House Beautiful*. Your young child can feed herself, go potty by herself, and do all sorts of creative things all by herself. Yes, there will be messes. Tell yourself, "That's what we bought her blocks for" . . . and then teach her to pick them up.

Muddling Along in the Middle

Middlers are even more fun. You can have grown-up conversations with these sprightly young minds. This is also the age where your values become consciously their own, if they have picked up the family team spirit. You can ask their opinion and get a logical answer. You will also be bombarded with ancient puns and riddles that they think are the freshest, most humorous things going. Middlers energize you!

Now is your chance to really cook along in your home teaching program. Middlers want to know the whys and wherefores, and will respect you for answering their questions. They love family jokes and stories; this is a great time to pass those along!

ESSENTIAL EQUIPMENT
FOR THE MIDDLE YEARS:

One floor—for lying on with a book, or practicing somersaults.

One world—for exploring (with supervision).

Two arms and a lap—middlers still need hugs!

TOYS:

Books from the library. Art supplies. Broken things to practice fixing. Rocks, beetles, flower heads, string, and any other kind of oddments for collecting. A weird assortment of shoeboxes and other hidey holes for "treasures."

CLOTHES:

Summertime: T-shirts, shorts or skirt, socks, and sneakers. Wintertime in the North: A coat, T-shirts, jeans or skirt, socks, and boots. Start now training your child to ignore fashion trends.

HOUSEWORK:

Dishes, vacuuming, dusting, laundry, folding, setting the table, mopping, and an occasional bit of cooking are well within this child's scope (not all

AGE CATEGORIES
FOR CHRISTIAN KIDS:

Wonderful Ones
Terrific Twos
Thrilling Threes
Fabulous Fours
Fantastic Fives
Super Sixes
Superior Sevens
Able-Bodied Eights
Nifty Nines
Tremendous Tens!

1. Welcome your children in Jesus' name.
2. Include them in family activities (no segregation).
3. Model by example.
4. Tell them how to live—use stories and precepts.
5 Practice good habits—walk them through it.
6. Give alternatives when they are tempted.
7. Give reasons for your rules.
8. Provide a nourishing environment.
9. Don't test them beyond their ability to bear.
10. Discipline for folly and rebellion.

One of the finest sermons I ever heard was preached by David Wilkerson . . . some two dozen years ago. He called it "The Number One Teenage Sin." He said this sin is not drug addiction, or drinking, or smoking. It is not a sex sin. It is not cursing or blaspheming or telling dirty stories. It is not engaging in crime, violence, backbiting, or slander. It is not cruelty to animals or breaking the law.

The number one teen-age sin in our part of the world today, he said, is wasting time.

—Sherwood E. Wirt
World
September 26, 1988

at once, of course!). See discussion of Chores in Chapter 11.

ACADEMICS: If he hasn't learned to read, teach him. (See *The New Big Book of Home Learning* for dozens of excellent phonics programs.) If he has, take him to the library.

MEALS: Serve lots of home-baked cookies. You're building memories!

The Teening Masses

Now we move on to the not-so-young child. Here you have someone with the body of a man or woman who is given absolutely no responsibility. This bothered me when I was a teen, and it bothers me today.

No other culture enforces childhood as long as ours. And it's not even all that great a childhood. Where is the freckle-faced barefoot lad of the 1890s with his fishing rod? Today he is sweating over teeny-weeny "skills" he should have learned in the fifth grade. He is bombarded with unheard-of social pressure to use drugs and fornicate. He is depressed with the family disasters of his friends and the media's prophecies of nuclear holocaust. If this is childhood, Peter Pan had it all wrong. I will grow up—and pronto!

Aside from families that hang together and train their children, all today's teens really need can be summed up in two words: meaningful work. I don't mean that neophytes deserve a seat at the executive board meeting. There's nothing wrong with stuffing envelopes or digging ditches. I've done both myself. But teens need to feel they are contributing something important. They need a chance to practice adult virtues (after all, they are already tempted with adult vices).

This doesn't mean your offspring will spring off and do his work without grumbling. Be honest—you grumble about your work sometimes! Just keep reminding him how important his efforts are to the family.

ESSENTIAL EQUIPMENT
FOR THE TEEN YEARS:

One listening ear.

Two arms—don't forget the hugs now!

Many encouraging words.

TOYS:

No, not the family car. This should also be the age to start mastering and owning real tools. "When I became a man I put away childish things"— 1 Corinthians 13:11.

CLOTHES:

Every sensible culture provides different clothes for children and young adults (e.g., knickers v. long pants). We can take a step in that direction, too. Wouldn't it be nice to see teens looking like young ladies and gentlemen again?

HOUSEWORK:

Any mother of big, strong teens who takes out the trash herself has only herself to blame.

DATING:

You gotta be kidding! Teach him to blow skyscrapers down with dynamite instead. It's safer.

MATING:

This is a different story. Once a young man or woman is well-trained, and the young man is capable of supporting a family (which can be sooner than we expect if he has incentive and some help) it's time to start matchmaking. Help the poor kids out by locating likely marriage prospects

WHAT YOU CAN EXPECT FROM YOUR TEENS

THE WISE CHILD	THE WILD CHILD
Wise	Foolish
Godly	Self-centered
Confident	Insecure/proud
Independent	Peer-dependent
Productive	Unreliable
Humble	Vain
Works to prepare for marriage	Wants to play before marriage
Respects authority	Defies authority
Affectionate	Cold

James Dobson in his second big film series, "Turn Your Heart Toward Home," has a depressing episode entitled "Power in Parenting: The Adolescent." What's depressing is that he doesn't believe parents *have* any power over teenagers. He teaches parents to *expect* (!) rebellion as an inevitable hormonal manifestation. Then he advises that all the parents can do during this stage of childraising is, "Hang in there, it'll be over soon enough."

Above all, Dobson warns parents, *don't feel guilty* over children who abandon the faith. You did your best. It's not your fault.

I wish this man who has the ear of evangelicals would tell parents the truth: the reason your kids rebel is because you've let them drink in the spirit of rebellion from their peers, their public school teachers, their music, their TV shows, etc. Rebellion is *not* normal or inevitable. It is the very logical result of letting our children conform to the pattern of this world. The flip side of the promise in Proverbs 22:6 is a curse.

—Pastor Phil Lancaster, MO

and providing supervised social situations where they can meet each other.

GETTING READY: Now is the time to start training your fledgling in motherhood and fatherhood. How to discipline children. How to teach the Bible. How to lead family devotions. How to run a household (girls) and lead the family (boys). Focus their eyes on the bright future to keep them out of dark pits in the present.

MEALS: Serve *lots* of food!

How to Enjoy Your Children

Now we're going to talk about motivating you.

What do you get out of all this?

How can you get more out of being a parent?

For starters, children are a gift from the Lord. They are cute. Cuddly. Enthusiastic. Energetic.

Children Give You Energy. I remember when our first son, Teddy, was just a baby. His crib was in our bedroom, and every morning he would wake us up by yelling, "Hi, there!" His cute little face smiling at us over the edge of the crib was just like a sunbeam. Melancholy as I am by nature, Teddy's happiness helped me start a lot of days on the right foot. And his brothers and sisters have kept it up since! It's hard to get up a really deep gloom with all that bounce and bobance dashing around the house.

Another time we were coming home from a long car trip. We had decided on impulse to drive to Amish Country in Arthur, Illinois, and the trip turned out to be a lot longer and more draining than expected. I was feeling physically rotten, since some undiagnosed health problems had been plaguing me, and the trip didn't help at all. After what seemed like hours of staring into glaring sunlight, we stopped at a gas station. Sarah, our oldest girl, got out of the car and walked to where I was sitting on the front seat with my feet on the gravel of the parking lot. "I love you, Mommy," she whispered and hugged me. Honestly, peace just flowed into me from her dear little hug.

Hugging and Kissing. Cleaning expert Don Aslett says, "Don't love anything that can't love you back." Well, kids can love you back. And loving them first isn't hard at all, since God designed little folks to be lovable. Even their physical features—big eyes, soft skin, different body proportions—have been shown to arouse protective emotions. Baby humans are cute.

Children's rights types try to make us feel bad about doing what comes naturally: hugging and kissing our little ones. In the same spirit as those who want us to keep our kids away from church until they are "old enough" to decide if they want to go (eighty years old, perhaps?), the self-styled child advocates try to make parent-child bonding sound perverse by warning us not to "use" kids as "love objects." But to be the object of someone's love isn't bad—in fact, it's the goal of just about every person on this earth. Cuddling and hugging your kids is good for you and them. And cuddling does not lead to sexual abuse, in spite of all the revolting speculations written on this subject, any more than breathing leads to hyperventilation, whereas lack of cuddling greatly increases the statistical risks that a child will grow up to be sexually perverse.

Children should learn early on to associate physical touching with innocent pleasure. Kissing the top of the baby's downy head; letting the two-year-old snuggle in your lap with a storybook; hugging the five-year-old; Dad wrestling with the sixteen-year-old boy or letting the toddlers climb on his back for a horsey ride—all this is great fun for you and your children, besides teaching them to enjoy physical contact in a wholesome manner.

When our first baby was born I remember working hard to have and express the attitude that I was glad to see my child and glad that he was here. As time went by, with this continual practice, this attitude became easier and easier. To this day when I see any of my children across the room, at school, or playing outside, my eyes light up and my heart swells with love. To me they are like a light in the room wherever they are. And I have noticed that they feel the same way. No matter what age they have been, from baby to toddler, to teenager to young adult, when they see me across the room their eyes light up, and they are glad to see me.

So it all comes back full circle. What you give, you receive in return. . . .

—Lee Stewart
NAPSAC News,
Fall 1987

I wanted to share the example of my grandparents, who had eight children, thirty grandchildren, and (so far) forty-three great-grandchildren. These two people have made a great impact on the lives of so many—not only their direct descendants, but on the husbands and wives of two generations as well. In fact, my husband credits my grandfather as being the most influential person in his decision to become a Christian. All of their children and grandchildren are Christians, and all of my cousins are building Christian homes for the next generation.

Only in recent years, as I've seen more and more of the world around me, have I become aware of what a blessing it was to be born into this family. Last summer we had a family reunion in Portland, Oregon, and the memories are still sweet today. . . .

The point I want to make is that your idea of "evangelism through reproduction" is a realistic goal. My grandparents began as poor farmers in Missouri. Their first child was born in 1916, and now, seventy years later, their influence has spread to eleven states and dozens of their descendants working for the Lord. All of us could duplicate this and in a relatively short period of time make a marked change in the course of our nation. . . .

—Pamela Boswell, CA

A Chip off the Old Block. We parents also enjoy our children taking after us. We get great delight from seeing our mannerisms and values expressed by our own two-year-old or ten-year-old. I, for example, love to see my daughter Magdalene cooing over the baby the same way I do, and Bill beams with pride to see Ted and Joe repeating his trademarked puns.

Again, the killjoys have invaded this territory, claiming that it is somehow exploitative and un-American to train our children to follow in our footsteps. Ignore them. The Bible calls this process "discipling," and as long as you aren't teaching them anything bad, it's more than OK, it's great!

Dads should encourage their sons to follow in their footsteps. Why should every boy be supposed to start from scratch and make his own way in the world—well, every boy except the Kennedys and the Rockefellers?

American dads faded out of the picture because they became convinced they were not needed for anything. Well, Dad, it's time to fade back in and throw the kids a pass. You *are* needed. You *do* have a right to the kids' respect. It's OK to want Johnny to grow up to be like you (it's also great motivation for you to get better in a hurry!).

Does taking an active hand in your children's life mean hassles, miseries, boredom? No way! God wants you to enjoy your children—and He wants them to enjoy you!

The family that plays together stays together. Find out some great ways to spend time having fun as a family in the next chapter.

Is There Life
After TV?

8

"*M*ommy, I'm bored! There's nothing to *do!*"
Ah, the gracious tune of a child on a rainy
day! But we parents know how to quell rebellion in
the ranks.

"Go watch TV, dear."

Away thud the little feet (who ever said they *pat-tered?*). And here they come back again with the en-core:

"There's nothing *on!*"

All this is tremendously helpful for building up
our families, of course. Those happy hours we spend
"together," a row of zombies in front of the sacred
screen, not daring to speak for fear of being shouted
down in favor of the voice from the tube, not daring
to look each other in the eyes lest we miss one twitch
of the action, not even thinking our own thoughts be-cause the scriptwriter and admen so thoughtfully
have provided others for us. Even better, if we get
really rich the family head can generously provide
personal sets for all of us, so we can sit in separate
dark rooms staring at separate flickering images.
There's togetherness for you!

I know you agree with me that television is not a
positive social force. Almost everyone does. Almost
everyone you talk to deplores TV, thinks it should not
be used as a babysitter, admits that the vast majority
of programming is stupid or obscene, claims to hate
the manipulative and boorish advertising, and (this is
the real killer) maintains he, personally, hardly
watches any TV.

This is odd, because the statistics say the average
household has the set going more than six hours a
day. If there is a child in the family, the parents show
their concern for the child's mental hygiene by
adding another two hours to their daily TV hours to-tal. Children watch more than adults, but adults still
watch plenty: four hours a day in the 1970s and more

Creative recreation, in my
personal definition, can be
thought of in two ways.
Firstly, it is recreation which
produces creative results,
stimulates creativity, refresh-es one's ideas and stirs one to
"produce." Secondly, it is
recreation which is the *result*
of original ideas, creative be-cause someone has creatively
planned an evening, a day, an
occupation which in itself is
fresh and different.

—Edith Schaeffer
The Hidden Art of Homemaking

today. Lumped all together, the average American of any age spends more than half of his free time plunked in front of a turned-on TV screen.

Turn On, Tune In, Drop Out

People have written whole books about what TV has done to modern family life. I have read some of them, and do not intend to write another. To paraphrase Karl Marx (a guy who had a way with words, even if his ideas were screwy), who cares what TV does to families? The point is to get rid of it.

I can hear the ouches from that last sentence. "Get rid of our TV? How can we live? Whatever will we do?" This reaction actually is the best argument for getting rid of the TV. As the Apostle Paul says in 1 Corinthians 6:12, "'Everything is permissible for me'—but not everything is beneficial. 'Everything is permissible for me'—but I will not be mastered by anything."

If you absolutely can't live without your TV, you have become its slave. Your best possible move is to get rid of it (Matthew 5:29, 30). If you *can* live without your TV, surely you will agree that if I can find you something better to do than TV you are willing to do it. After all, if it *really* doesn't mean that much to you, you would just as soon be doing something else.

Let's get this straight before we go any further: God will not send you to hell for watching TV. (He might, however, have something to say on Judgment Day about a good number of popular shows watched by self-proclaimed Christians.) But, on the other hand, you won't help anyone else to heaven by watching it either. That time in front of the TV, with exceptions so rare I can't think of any at the moment, is a dead loss.

Remember the parable of the servants and the talents in Matthew 25? Jesus said that the master gave the first servant five talents (a talent was a sum of money), the second two, and the third only one. The first two servants got busy investing their talents, but the third hid his in the ground. When the master came back, he praised the servants who had doubled their talents by investing them. Then he turned on the third servant, who was standing there offering the master his talent back. "You wicked, lazy servant!" the master exclaimed. "You should have put my money on deposit with the bankers, so that when I returned I would have received it back with interest." Then the master commanded that the lazy servant's talent be taken from him and given to the servant who now had ten.

Jesus' listeners all got the point, which is why today we use the word "talent" to mean a special ability the Lord has given us. He wanted His hearers to maximize their talents, not vegetate on top of them.

Hmm. Let's try to think of our favorite modern way of vegetating . . . or should I say Couch Potatoing? Just exactly what are we accomplishing all those long hours in front of the set?

Wait a minute—don't bother to answer that last question. I will help you answer it myself.

"I just watch the news and sports." As Gregg Harris says, I have news for you, sports! The "news" on television has been shown by numerous studies to be deliberately slanted *against* Christianity. The myth of objective journalism today is looking mighty tattered. Look at the Quayle hunt last election, for example.

As for sports, TV people are so anxious to help you "only" watch sports shows that they are on all evening long all year long, not to mention the better part of what used to be our family holidays.

I used to be a Boston Bruins hockey fanatic myself, back when Bruin fans lived for the moment the team was shorthanded so the Bobby Orr-Phil Esposito-Derek Sanderson-Dallas Smith line could come out and score. I now have the opportunity to be a St. Louis Blues and St. Louis Cardinals fan, not including all the sundry local teams for sports like soccer. If I wanted to, I could fill every spare hour with watch-

As Ben Stein pointed out in *The View from Sunset Boulevard*, dramatic television shows are increasingly didactic. No longer content to entertain, which they do poorly, they set out to advance an agenda. This agenda bears a remarkable resemblance to that of the Democratic Party's left wing. . . .

And while dramatic shows are increasingly didactic, so-called "public affairs" programs have become highly dramatic and sensational. . . .

Enter now the schlock brigade, the talk-show troops. . . . Aside from their usual preoccupation with such subjects as transvestites, liposuction, and breast enlargement, these shows now intrude on the public debate.

Topics covered include Supreme Court decisions, presidential elections, covert operations, and even the Kennedy assassination. These too are show-trials, and the one with the microphone controls the debate. . . .

In a review of [Professor Neil Postman's book *Amusing Ourselves to Death*] , critic Terry Teachout discussed the idea that television is the force that made America stupid. . . . Teachout offered a related but more penetrating thesis: Television was also the force that made America's stupid people powerful.

—K. L. Billingsley
World, February 18, 1989

A few years back two re-searchers (Robert Lichter and Stanley Rothman) inter-viewed 104 key TV people—-writers, producers, directors and creators. Here's what they found.

☐ Fully 93% said they never attend religious services or seldom do.
☐ Only 5% strongly agree that homosexuality is morally wrong.
☐ Only 16% strongly agree that adultery is wrong.
☐ These people feel that reli-gion (meaning Christiani-ty) should have little in-fluence on society.

But most revealing of all was the authors' conclusion:

"But perhaps the most surprising finding of our study is that TV's creators seek to move their audience toward their own vision of the good society."

And as you can see, their society is anti-family and anti-Christian.

— American Family Association fundraising letter, mailed February 1989

The news elicits from you a variety of opinions about which you can do nothing except offer them as more news, about which you can do nothing. . . . There is no murder so brutal, no earth-quake so devastating, no po-litical blunder so costly . . . that it cannot be erased from our minds by a newscaster saying, 'Now . . . this.'"

— Neil Postman
Amusing Ourselves to Death

ing or reading about or talking about the local sports heroes. The reason I don't is not just because I am fe-male and don't have the male hormonal reaction to sweaty fellows running around a playing field and voice-overs from old players explaining why Number Seven "is having a hard day, Pat, it's been a tough season for him." My husband Bill does have the hor-monal reaction, but he fights it for the same reason I can't see starting to follow the playing season myself: when would we spend time with the kids and get our work done?

If we were here on earth only to play, I can tell you right now that I'd be a sports fan. But we're not. There are better things to do. I'll tell you about some of them in a minute.

"I only watch the TV evangelists." I won't say anything about how some of these mighty have fallen lately, and good riddance to the fallen, too. Let me just draw your attention to that word "evangelist." What is an evangelist supposed to do? Answer: Win the lost. Are you lost? Answer: No. Then why do you need to watch these shows? Answer: It's more than evangelism . . . they have all kinds of guests . . . it keeps me informed. Do we have any Christian maga-zines that cover the same topics as the TV shows? An-swer: Yes (see the Resources section for my favorite). Then why do you *really* watch these shows? Answer: For entertainment. OK, I'll buy that. All I want to know is, Do you and your family keep the entertain-ment in its proper place? Or do you run your lives by the TV schedule?

Believe it or not, the *good* TV evangelists would re-ally rather you were doing what they asked you to do than watching their program. Really. I can't see Jerry Falwell getting all bent out of shape because you were too involved in local Christian activism and evangelism to watch his show.

Besides, there are more positive ways to be enter-tained. I'll tell you about them in a minute.

"I watch any old thing that catches my fancy."
Now we're getting honest! According to the polls, that is exactly what the vast majority of people who call themselves Christians do. They watch the same sexy, violent, stupid, anti-Christian junk that everyone else does. Why? Because it's there. It's tempting. It's easier to turn on and tune in than to get up and go. And besides they have this terrible feeling that they would be missing something if they didn't stay on top of all the current shows.

Let me tell you (I'm assuming you are not a Super Saint but one of the millions who watches junk he knows he shouldn't) what you are missing. Then we'll get to the good part: how to have so much fun you won't even want to watch TV.

Stay tuned!

The Family That Plays Together Stays Together

Baking and eating homemade fudge. Star-gazing on the back porch. Toasting S'Mores in the campfire. Rocking on the porch swing. Helping the kids catch fireflies. Taking on the neighbors at volleyball. Building something wild and wooly with a toy construction set. Having several families in the church over for dinner. Designing a Treasure Hunt for your son's birthday party. Planting a tree. Stringing popcorn for the Christmas tree. These are a few of your favorite things . . . that you *could* find time to do again.

I was about to say you could find time to do all this, and much more, if you gave up at least most of your passive entertainment (the stuff you tune into by twiddling a dial or by paying for a seat). But the phrase "gave up" is misleading. It sounds self-righteous—"We had this terrible struggle and although it is like cutting off our right arms, we still are denying ourselves all the wonderful pleasures of television." Fact is, we haven't had a TV set for twelve years now, and I don't feel like I gave up anything. Really, I *rediscovered real life*.

Everything those sleek, glamorous folks on TV do you can do. You can sing, play a musical instrument,

Not seeing the news certainly does not cut us off from current events—we still have the radio and the newspaper, just as they did about sixty years ago!

—Tamra Orr
Priority Parenting
June 1988

We've never had a TV in our home. Kevin reads in the evening to us, we play "memory game" with the children, listen to "Unshackled," a half-hour radio program (real-life dramas of how people have come to know Jesus). In the warmer months we often go to a nearby park to swing or cook out, or go for a walk around the block. We most often just sit in the living room and talk as the little ones play or romp nearby.

We all look forward to our camping trips. Especially Joshua. He was picking up little sticks all over the yard. When I asked what he was doing, he answered matter of factly, "MAKING A FIRE!" The state park we go to has a wonderful hiking trail and you can see so many stars on a clear night. We honestly don't miss the TV at all. Once a week we let them "camp" on our bedroom floor. Kevin tells an extra-long story on that night. They love to do this.

Many people never discover how much fun and good times you can have just staying at home with the children. Know what I mean?

—Mary Jane Kestner, MN

What *don't* we miss because we don't have a TV? Reading (usually at least three hours a day), making up our own stories, thinking our own thoughts, drawing, wood-working, sewing, fixing our own cars and house, listening, dancing and singing to music, playing in the sun, eating and sleeping when we need to (rather than as dictated by the television schedule), making plans and models of the house we will soon build and most importantly, talking and playing together.

Our children are active all day and can find things to do on their own, so their muscles are well-developed and their minds are creative. They stick to one activity until they are done with it, so they have very long attention spans and confidence in their ability to accomplish what they set out to do. Their TV-addicted cousins are relatively uncoordinated and underdeveloped, they have short, scattered attention spans and exhibit little creativity. They expect to have everything done for them and yet they are starved for affection.

—Denise Cherrington and
Bill Patterson
Priority Parenting
June 1988

crack jokes, cook fancy meals, entertain friends, and play a sport. You've just forgotten you can do these things because you are so used to watching other people do them for you.

We Americans buy canned music, canned humor, canned cooking, canned sports, and canned life. "Just add one cupful of water and stir lightly for that homemade flavor." But the real thing is a lot tastier *and* better for you than the canned variety!

We can make our own goodies and our own good times. I'll go farther than that. We should make some of our goodies and most of our good times. Why? Lots of reasons. Because God is creative, and His children should follow in His footsteps instead of just swallowing down whatever the world chooses to offer us. Because you get more joy out of real-life shared times than canned experiences. Because children who are included in family good times are spared many of the temptations of children whose good times are artificial. Because the family that plays together stays together.

Homegrown Entertainment

Now let's look at how we can build family ties through homegrown entertainment. We're going to include the children and have those wonderful family times we love to read about but never find time to do.

Where do we start?

Homemade Goodies. Among my happiest childhood memories is licking out the bowl when my mother made goodies. She didn't let me measure and mix, or even fetch her ingredients, but baking-time was still a shared family experience as all we children hovered around waiting for the mixing spoon, beaters, and bowl to be divvied up for licking.

My sister Theresa and I also used to hang out in the hall, long after we were supposed to be in bed, waiting for the fragrant loaves of fresh bread to emerge from the oven. Invariably, my mother's delight in our appreciation of her baking would overcome her disciplinary urges, and we would end up in the kitchen sharing yummy slices of piping-hot bread.

Home schooling books all urge parents to let kids participate in the baking. This is OK, but not necessary. To build fond memories, all they really need is to participate in the batter-tasting and eating!

Homemade Music. For some reason, our culture considers tools to be useful, important purchases whereas musical instruments are luxuries. That is why it took me so many years to get up the courage to put aside some money to buy what I had always wanted: a classical guitar.

Our home musical apparatus now includes the aforementioned guitar, a tenor banjo, a trumpet (for Bill), a shofar (rams' horn trumpet, for fun), a very nice harmonica, several different sizes of recorders, a marching-band drum with drumsticks, a kiddie-styled tambourine, and a piano.

Now the million-dollar question: Do we have tremendous musical talent? As far as I can figure it, the answer is no. We don't have all these instruments because we are a Christian version of the Osmond Family. Rather, we picked them up one at a time because we enjoyed the thought of making a joyful noise together unto the Lord.

I can barely play a few chords on the guitar (no time for lessons!), but I enjoy singing hymns while the kids sing along. Bill and I can do recorder duets, and soon the older ones will be playing the recorder too. Teddy likes trying his lungs out on Daddy's trumpet or bashing his drum while Sarah, Joey, and I sing "I'm In the Lord's Army." Mercy Grace, the baby, is old enough to jiggle and chew on the tambourine.

As music therapist Mary Ann Froehlich says, music education is not an option. God commands all His children to sing, play instruments, and make a joyful noise. And let me tell you—jamming with your family is *fun!*

THESE ARE A FEW OF OUR FAVORITE THINGS

- ☐ Singing rounds
- ☐ Watching Daddy try to juggle (fun!)
- ☐ Watching Mommy try to juggle (a laugh riot!)
- ☐ Making and eating chocolate chip cooky batter
- ☐ Baking and eating what remains into chocolate chip cookies
- ☐ Watching the baby take her bath
- ☐ Catalog-shopping together for clothes, toys, seeds, science kits, presents . . .
- ☐ Playing chess (and kibbitzing)
- ☐ Making silly faces
- ☐ Playing "Please Don't Smile" while making silly faces
- ☐ Reading the best bits of our books and magazines to each other
- ☐ Asking riddles
- ☐ Solving a crossword puzzle all together
- ☐ Telling stories
- ☐ Making up funny songs and poems

First thing, you'll have to pick an instrument. Now that choice needn't be a hard one to make. For one thing, you were born with several choices built in. I mean you can clap your hands! You can snap your fingers! You can whistle and sing! . . .

So next time you hear some folks playing music— join in somehow.
    —Marc Bristol
    Homegrown Music

You don't have to have money to accumulate a lot of music-makers, either. Several years ago I picked up a book called *Homegrown Music* by Marc Bristol (Seattle: Madrona Publishers). This one book tells how to make all kinds of instruments from odds and ends and how to acquire or recycle used instruments. I have never actually gone out to the garage and tried swatting out tunes on Bill's saw, but I intend to someday soon. Naturally, all the kids will want to try playing the saw if they see me do it, and naturally (with a few safety precautions) I will let them try it.

As a matter of fact, there is no better recipe for instant family togetherness than for one family member to sit down and start quietly playing an instrument, assuming that family member is known to be friendly and willing to let others try their hands at his songmaker. Almost magically, little children will start popping out of the woodwork and clustering around the musician. Remember the Pied Piper!

Singing, of course, is a great togetherness event. Rounds and harmony are more fun than straight unison singing; our kids will keep these up for hours without tiring. If you want to learn some good rounds and harmonies, I suggest you pick up the *Wee Sing* cassette tapes and songbooks. These are available at any bookstore, or send for the publisher's brochure (address listed in the Resources section).

Homemade Projects. Sometimes mistakenly listed under the category of "work," family projects can actually be a tremendous amount of fun. I'm talking about getting together and building things: a birdhouse, a set of shelves for the kitchen, a new garden. When you all pitch in and work together to make something you can look at with pride, you feel like a team.

Normally children enjoy learning to do grownup things, especially grownup things that don't smack of school desks and chalkboards. Little kids just adore to follow Daddy around and help him with his tools. Older kids beg for a chance to sand a piece of wood or drive in some nails. I get the same treatment when I'm braiding bread loaves ("Let me help, Mommy! See? I washed my hands special!").

We're assuming that the project is something children might want to do, not something horrendous like lugging ten tons of rocks from the quarry to build a retaining wall for the bottom of the yard. I got to help my parents do just that when I was five years old. I had absolutely no interest in building that wall, and all I can remember of those days lugging rocks was being hot, exhausted, bored, and miserable.

Projects are also not the same as chores, which arrive whether you want them or not. Projects are special extras that yield semi-permanent results; chores need redoing again and again. Chores, since they are more work for less visible reward, need extra motivation power.

We'll discuss motivating for chores in a future chapter. For now, consider this: if you want to see the children helping with chores, try getting them involved in some projects first.

Homeplayed Games. It takes two to tango. It also takes two to play badminton, or catch, or One-Two-Three Red Light. Someone has to turn the rope while the jumpers jump. Someone has to throw the ball so you can practice catching.

Unless you are blessed with a listing on the mailing list of a Yuppie Catalog. Opening the catalog, you find that today's entrepreneurs have invented hosts of devices that substitute for other people, so your children can play games all by their little lonesomes. Machines pitch the balls or make the chess moves. Software takes the place of a Ping-Pong opponent or a whole sandlot baseball team.

As Curley of the Three Stooges used to say, "Yuk, yuk, yuk!" He was laughing; I am revolted. How close we have come to Bonzo, the Robot Friend of Children! "Go play with Bonzo, dear. Mommy and Daddy are busy."

If, indeed, T.V. stifles creativity, then it should be of great benefit and joy for a family to eliminate it. But we have found that creativity is another word for WORK! Tonight my fifteen-year-old boy was replacing a bathroom lavatory sink for almost two hours. Not quite finished, but tomorrow he will be. Would this have happened if the TV had been blaring? Home maintenance has become one of our major indoor pastimes.

Another activity that has borne fruit for us is various handcrafts. Library sources are legion for finding out how to do old-timey things like making fabric dye out of vegetables, making pioneer-type toys, potato stamp printing, etc.

—Garland Brock, TX

"Work-play" is what I call it when there is an expected outcome from the play. The child has to hit the ball, earn a badge, learn to play an instrument, turn a cartwheel. This kind of "play" has a hidden edge to it—failure.

Can I, as a parent, accept as legitimate the kind of play my children revel in—the kind with no object, direction, or result? Running the hose in the sandbox, dreaming through an old catalog, looking at baseball cards, and digging up "treasure" in the dirt are a few favorites at our house. I shouldn't lose sight of the fact that my children consider it fun to run an errand just with mom, or to help wash dishes, or water plants, or look through old photo albums, work a jigsaw puzzle, or get out a few of the old toys I played with as a child.

—Nanette Ford
Parenting for Peace and Justice
Network Newsletter
Cited in *Family Reader*
March-April 1989

You and I didn't have Bonzo around to amuse us while we grew up. Somehow we managed to play Scrabble and Monopoly even so. I was particularly blessed with two parents and six siblings, so I could rattle off the names of dozens of board games I played on rainy afternoons. Someone always was available to play kickball or knock a badminton birdie around.

If you actually follow my advice and tune out the TV, you will discover your kids have a lot of energy that delights to be channeled into physical exercise. Starting with romps on the floor with the baby and graduating to mock wrestling matches with the two-year-old, the father who allows himself to do what comes naturally will find himself exercising with the kids. This leads to pitch-and-bat sessions as they get older, and even impromptu family softball games if you are blessed with enough children in your neighborhood.

Board games, on the other hand, are just the ticket for rainy days. Board games slow down the pace of life, provided you steer away from the hard-hitting competitive kill-your-opponent games.

Where a little bit of athletic competition is good for children, building team spirit and discipline, vicious board games hurt more than they help. For one thing, unlike athletics, board games all have a strong random element. "Winning" can't mean as much when it is based on the luck of the draw. For another thing, the meanness of doing your opponent out of his Boardwalk property is completely different from beating the others fair and square in a footrace. You don't take anything away from others when you win at athletics; most competitive board games are based on the concept of killing or economically demolishing your opposition. To win you must do these things.

(I suspect that *Pictionary*'s huge success is because it provides a true competition: who can draw and understand a picture the fastest. This has nothing to do with twiddling dice or drawing the best cards.)

Reading Aloud. Bill was complaining that he seemed to have no dramatic ability. "I just can't loosen up. Everything comes out in a monotone."

"Why don't you try reading to us, with expression?" I asked. Sneaky me! I had read Edith Schaeffer's *Hidden Art of Homemaking*. One chapter had suggested reading aloud as a way to develop dramatic ability.

That was years ago. Today Bill's reading is so interesting that I can't concentrate on writing when he is reading in the next room. His bad guys have gravely voices, or Peter Lorre voices, or sinister husky voices. His good guys sound noble. When Bill is saying lines for Little Red Riding Hood, his voice is high and childlike. When the wolf speaks, he snaps and snarls. My personal favorite is his Dudley Do-right of the Canadian Mounties imitation. It cracks me up no matter how many times I hear it.

The kids eat this all up, of course. Which is why even shy people can blossom from reading to their children. Where else can you find an audience that applauds every time?

Bill reads to us at mealtimes and at family devotions. We have journeyed through the entire *Lord of the Rings* trilogy, Anne deVries' *Journey Through the Night* opus about the Nazi occupation of Holland, various tales of Sherlock Holmes, Frank and Ernestine Gilbreth's *Cheaper by the Dozen* and *Belles on Their Toes*, the *Complete Yes Minister* book based on the popular British TV series by the same name, and many more, all at the supper table.

I also read to the children. Not that I have any choice! Every time I sit down, in about five seconds some little one is sitting in my lap and waving a book before my face. "Read book, Mumma!"

Reading aloud to your children is the Number One guarantee that they will be successful readers *and* thinkers later on. Especially interactive reading, where you encourage them to point to picture elements or share their thoughts about what has just

---

We are seeing more and more children who are behind in reading ability. They are coming from both public and private schools. The interesting thing is that many of these kids have *good* phonics backgrounds. They can sound out almost any word you put before them. Their problem is comprehension. . . .

The question then is, *"What is it that people who read well do with groups of words that these kids are not able to do?"* The answer is that they convert these groups of words into mental pictures and thus "see" and "hear" what is happening in the story. . . .

What keeps some people from developing this "word processing" ability? It is my opinion that it is usually the result of too much TV and/or not being read to enough.

Listening comprehension is essential to reading comprehension. . . .

—Luanne Shackelford
*A Survivor's Guide to
Home Schooling*

Reading aloud to teenagers seems to have gone the way of the husking bee and the taffy pull. . . . Yet reading aloud to teenagers has many rewards. . . .

Seesawing emotions often swamp the teenager with feelings of self-criticism and emotional isolation. Sharing stories helps bridge this loneliness and strengthens family bonds.

—DeeAnne Lamb
Mothering, volume 45

Our ancestors, whether they were Christian or not, believed four things about teaching morality:

1. There was a right way to behave and a wrong way.
2. You learned the right way by being trained in it.
3. You also needed models of virtue to imitate.
4. These models could be found in stories of wisdom and courage.

—William Kirk Kilpatrick
Psychological Seduction: The Failure of Modern Psychology

SOME OF OUR FAVORITE FAMIILY VIDEOS

☐ *It's a Wonderful Life*
☐ *Robin Hood* (with Errol Flynn)
☐ *The Mark of Zorro*
☐ *The Sound of Music*
☐ *Cinderella* (Disney)
☐ *Sleeping Beauty* (Disney)
☐ *Lady and the Tramp*
☐ *Papa Was a Preacher*
☐ *The Gospel Blimp*
☐ *The Fighting Prince of Donegal*
☐ *Old Yeller*
☐ *Pilgrim's Progress* (cartoon version)
☐ Dolores Demers how-to-paint videos
☐ Don Aslett's *Is There Life After Housework?* video

happened or will happen next. It just also happens to be a marvelous source of shared pleasure for both parents and children. The only reason more of us don't do it more often is that we are too busy passively absorbing television. Honestly. Try it, you'll like it!

Home Box Office. OK. So you've played games, read aloud, made music, baked cookies, and built projects. Now you're starting to suffer from that dread disease: TV withdrawal! You salivate every time you see *TV Guide* at the supermarket. You find yourself humming the *Miami Vice* theme song. You dream technicolor dreams starring Bill Cosby.

What to do?

Well, you still don't want to go back to four hours or more a day of TV-vegetating. You don't miss the commercials, and you are a little concerned about the nudity showing up as you flip channels at 10 P.M. You are just freaking out for lack of moving pictures in color.

The answer can be just to keep on keeping on. You can break TV addiction if you just keep busy with more edifying things. Or you can satisfy your craving with a much more edifying version of TV: the video player.

Videos put you in control. I don't mean the kind you tape off the air, since those have all the problems of real-time TV itself. I mean the videos from the corner store or offered in an educational catalog. If you pick up *It's a Wonderful Life* starring James Stewart, that's what you get. No party-animal Budweiser mutts, no scantily-clad dancing girls. You can pause it, rewind it, fast-forward it, stop it, and still come back to it later.

TV pushes you to conform to *its* schedule. "If you don't pay close attention, you'll miss something!" Video lets you take it easier. You can always replay it. I am convinced that this is why the well-known effect of TV hypnosis is not so strong in video-watchers.

Video, in short, frees you from TV slavery.

The only problem is that if you are watching videos on your TV, the little kiddies can still turn on the set and catch some hot sex action when you aren't watching. You are not protected from whatever the media moguls choose to broadcast. You also have to constantly fight the TV addict's temptation to watch whatever is on, no matter how boring. ("Great Moments in Tiddlywinks.")

Happily, stand-alone video players are now available. We have one in our home and enjoy using it a few hours a week. For educational video, such as how-to-paint lessons, it's enormously helpful. We also enjoy watching an occasional old movie together, if only for the taste it gives of a more Christian society. Since it has no TV tuner, we have no TV worries. We now offer these video players through our home business, Home Life. See the Resources section for details.

For Confirmed Addicts: How to Kick the TV Habit

You may remember how in the Introduction I promised you a story of how God intervened miraculously in one couple's life to free them from TV addiction. Here it is—the true story as told by Judy Goshorn of Indiana.

"While growing up in my parents' home, I watched my share of TV and, as an only child, became quite absorbed in some of it. However, during six years of college and graduate school I had little time nor interest in the screen. What spare time I had was devoted to reading.

"When my husband and I were married, some kind relatives donated a used TV which we promptly sold to buy a freezer. We then bought a small, used, black and white set, but didn't watch it much.

"I had become increasingly appalled at the changes wrought in six years, and very little programming (or commercials) appealed to me. My husband, however, enjoyed losing himself occasionally in a ball game or a movie. This was not a problem until his thirteen-year-old son came to live with us. This teen spent hours watching anything, and my hus-

Jerry Mander, author of *Four Arguments for the Elimination of Television*, challenges his readers to take the "Technical Events Test." Flick on the TV and "simply count the number of times there is a cut, a zoom, a superimposition, a voice-over, the appearance of words on the screeen—a technical event of some kind."

Mander wants us to become aware of "the degree to which technique, rather than anything intrinsivally interesting, keeps [us] fixed to the screen." He says that once we realize how much of TV's excitement is a direct function of the number of technical events per minute, it's the first step to curing TV addiction. "I have seen this happen with my own children," Mander says. "Once I had put them to the task of counting and timing these technical events, their absorption was never the same."

Mander also recommends "meditation," which for Christians would mean prayer, as an antidote to TV fixation. Interesting thought, that the more you pray the less you will want to watch! Part of the reason for this phenomenon, according to Mander is, that "television addiction might itself be symptomatic of an inability to produce one's own mental imagery," while prayer helps you develop inner spiritual resources (i.e., something important to think about and Someone real to talk to).

band often joined him, becoming completely oblivious to the rest of life. In his words, it was 'something they could do together.' Yes, I thought inwardly, you can vegetate and degenerate together.

"I began to lobby (not nag, of course!) for some limits to viewing. We could curtail the number of hours that Mike watched or, even better, put the tube in a closet and take it out only for special programs. My husband, a Christian, could not see what I was so upset about. His argument was that to take away TV would further widen the gulf between us and his son, a non-Christian. To his credit, however, he did somewhat monitor the shows that Mike watched.

"When my first child was born, I became desperate. I could not let my baby grow up ingesting all the trash watched by a teenager, even the evening news. Still, there was little or no understanding from my husband. So (and why is this often the *last* resort?) I prayed. I believed that God was saying, 'No TV.' But, if so, He would have to get the message across to my husband. I couldn't.

"Shortly after I had prayed this particular prayer, we experienced an ordinary thunderstorm. Afterwards, the TV did not work. When my husband investigated, he found the inside parts of the TV completely fried, *fused together!* We had had no indication that lightning had struck. The TV was in the middle of an inside wall; the antenna was in the attic. I was thrilled and reported my prayer to my husband. He was speechless (highly unusual) and, thankfully, convinced. God had spoken!

"And so we lived for five years with no TV. After the teenager moved out, we bought a small set and video cassette player for using videotapes. The children watch no network TV. Occasionally my husband will decide to watch a special show of some sort. Then the real miracle occurs. Now he can see and recognize the degradation. It affects him and he wants to protect his remaining children from it. Before the zero-TV years, he would not have been aware of the filth that he was taking in.

"Incidentally, the children have terrific imaginations and are wonderful at entertaining themselves. . . ."

Pagan Parties *v.* Christian Celebrations

Speaking of entertaining ourselves, a lot has been written lately on the subject of family rituals and celebrations. Some of it makes me downright uneasy. I think, for example, of *Festivals* magazine. *Festivals* is "focused on personal and communal transformation through ritual, celebration and festivity . . . about people who celebrate and how they have found more health, enjoyment and power by discovering the festive spirit . . . honors what is best in all traditions and fosters the creativity needed to adapt old traditions and build new ones."[1] This could be quite good. Then again, it could be sheer, utter paganism.

New Agers are drawn to festivals as moths are to the flame. They hope to find some kind of salvation in rituals. They share this misbegotten hope with pagans throughout the ages, who have always put great emphasis on colorful, involved ceremonies.

What difference, if any, is there between a Christian celebration and a pagan ceremony?

Christian celebration is geared towards thanking God and enjoying His good gifts. It is limited by God's rules for proper conduct (no drunkenness, flirting, showing off, and so on). It is designed to refresh the participants and hearten them to continue in their work for the Lord. Everyone is welcomed and included. A special effort is made to include the poor, helpless, weak, and unlovely.

Pagan ceremonies give all glory to the idol: Money, Sex, Power, Beauty, Strength, or whatever. They are typified by frenzy and gluttonous self-indulgence. You are urged to let go of your self-control ("shed your hangups" or "erase your old tapes") and join in uncritically. Typically, the strong are honored and the weak are sacrificed (sometimes literally).

When a celebration excludes kids, watch out! If children seem really out of place, it's probably because the entertainment is pagan. Kids don't really fit

TYPES OF ENTERTAINMENT	
CHRISTIAN	PAGAN
God-centered	Self-centered
Break from work	Instead of work
Refreshing	Depleting
Joyous	Frenetic (druglike, carnal excitement)

in at cocktail parties, or séances, or stag parties. Casino Nights and Las Vegas parties aren't designed for infants, either. Where there is gambling, dancing by couples (as opposed to the more Biblical dancing in groups), wine, women, and song, kids are a nuisance. Bless their little hearts! All you have to do is stick with the kids and you'll be preserved from much so-called "adult"—but really pagan—rituals.

Family Holidays

So we're going to avoid all celebrations out of fear they might be pagan, right?

Wrong! The Bible says, "Every man should eat and drink, and enjoy the good of all his labour, it is the gift of God" (Ecclesiastes 3:13).

Family celebrations are a time to stop and honor God for what He has done for us. They also provide a break from the day-to-day routine—very important for personal sanity!

Most of us celebrate at least a few times a year, on the children's birthdays. Most of us also celebrate the major holidays: Christmas, Easter, and Thanksgiving. Some celebrate the entire Christian Year, following the feast days of various important Christians of ages past. Others celebrate on Valentine's Day, Labor Day, and the military holidays.

The Bible says that whether we do or do not consider a particular day sacred is not worth arguing over. Rather, we should look into these matters, be firmly convinced in our own minds, and then celebrate (or abstain) heartily as unto the Lord (Romans 14:5-8).

Nobody needs special instructions on how not to celebrate a holiday. You just go about your normal work, that's all. But some of us, especially those who grew up in less-than-ideal families, could use some inspiration about how to celebrate as a family.

I have read several books on this topic. Frankly, they were not too helpful. The authors suggested all sorts of creative, time-consuming, difficult ideas that I'm sure took a long time to develop in their own families. You can grow into a fancy celebration little by little, year after year, but it's daunting to be faced with the full-blown article and told this is how to do it!

So here is my own list of tips for family celebrations, straight from a mom who'd rather lie on the couch than make adorable heart-shaped placemats for Valentine's Day.

The Lazy Mother's Guide to Birthday Parties

(1) Make sure *everyone* gets a present, if presents are given. We always buy one little gift apiece for the other children when one is celebrating his birthday. This prevents jealousy.

(2) Keep it simple. The more excess effort you exert when designing the celebration, the bigger the success it has to be to keep you from feeling like a failure. Children are just as happy with a Betty Crocker cake with supermarket frosting as with a three-story wonder covered with chocolate clowns and licorice lions.

(3) That is, unless you like and are good at doing decorations. Just don't let Gertie Goodwife's bravura performances bamboozle you into feeling you have to match her artistry. (Hint: M&M's and other candies stuck on a cake look fancy and take almost no time. The kids can even do it!)

(4) Balloons are always a hit with little kids.

(5) If you buy presents, choose items that allow children to be creative. Art supplies are great!

(6) Out of a dozen miserable childhood memories I beg you not to organize competitive games, and especially not to award prizes to the winners. Someone always has to be the loser, and to be the only loser with no prize in the midst of a crowd of excited, romping children is almost unbearable.

(7) A birthday party is an opportunity for the birthday child and his brothers and sisters to practice hospitality. Remind them that their job is to make sure the guests have a good time. This turns the birthday child away from a selfish concern about "What am I gonna get?"

In a survey conducted several years ago, 1,500 schoolchildren were asked, "What do you think makes a happy family?" Children often surprise us with their wisdom. They didn't list money, cars, fine homes, or televisions. The answer they gave most frequently was *doing things together.*

—Nick Stinnett and
John DeFrain
Secrets of Strong Families

I believe another reason families don't always have fun even while they are recreating can be traced to the push in our society to make the most of our time. We view free time as time that needs to be filled up, to be scheduled. We do, do, do and go, go, go. . . . How easily our sense of wanting to accomplish, to attain, to produce can make work out of activities that we choose because they might be fun.

—Jim Vogt
*Parenting for Peace and Justice
Network Newsletter*
Cited in *Family Reader*
March-April 1989

(8) Presents are twice as much fun if you put together a Treasure Hunt with clues leading to the presents. This need not be elaborate. I myself write the clues on Post-Its and let the other children put them in their hiding places ahead of time.

(9) I personally feel it is worth it to buy special birthday paper plates and tablecloths, etc. Set-up and clean-up are much easier, and they add a lot to the party atmosphere.

(10) Our family's rule is to not give a party to a one-year-old. He or she is too little to enjoy it. Two-year-olds get their first party with just brothers and sisters. Three-year-olds can invite one or two guests. Four-year-olds and up can invite more. This way each child is able to enjoy the event without becoming overwhelmed.

We purchase presents up to a month in advance, and party gear the week of the party. I always make the cake the day before, and usually frost and decorate it the night before. Then all I have to do for the party is set the party plates, make a Treasure Hunt, and watch the children have fun!

Other mothers give much more elaborate parties. I have avoided this, not just out of laziness, but because I don't want our children to become jaded connoisseurs. Too much fanciness distracts from the food and the guests.

Since a birthday is our chance to thank God for giving us this child and preserving him for us, we make a point of thanking God for this during our evening prayers, and also at the party itself. We also slow down the present-opening time enough to make sure the birthday child thanks the giver and the Lord for every present.

The Lazy Mother's Guide to Other Holidays

(1) The ingredients remain the same as at birthday parties: good food, guests, and possibly presents and games. Thank the Lord for all of these, and make sure you don't include anything you can't thank Him for!

(2) Children love crafts, so let them make the decorations. Some suggestions: popcorn strings for Christmas trees, dyeing Easter eggs, and even those Valentines Day placemats.

(3) Halloween seems to be heading back to its Satanic roots, judging from the costumes offered in stores and the witchy emphasis at this time of year. You can stay home and let the children hand out tracts and candy to the doorbell-ringers (making sure to reserve enough candy for them so they don't feel left out!). Or you can go out with them and Tract 'n Treat, like my friend Alida Gookin from Mississippi suggests. Dress up in Bible costumes, take along some tracts, and give them to the people whose doorbells you ring. These both seem better options to me than the usual church Halloween party, which neither reaches non-Christians nor edifies our children.

(4) Christmas and Easter present special problems. Our materialistic culture has managed to turn these into Santa Claus Day and Spring Fashion Day respectively. If you want to celebrate Christmas and Easter as Christian holidays, you would be wise to start weeks ahead by sharing the Bible stories of Christ's birth, sufferings, and resurrection, to counteract the secular hoopla.

(5) Teach the children to use these holidays to bless other people, not to seek things for themselves. The reason so many people commit suicide during holidays is that our culture has taught us that the holidays are a time to indulge ourselves and receive homage from friends and family. So let the older children share in preparing the festivities. This will help them develop servant hearts. They will learn to enjoy making other people happy instead of demanding more and more for themselves. Let the ten-year-old hide the chocolate Easter eggs for his brothers and sisters to find (we do this the Saturday after Easter, so as not to confuse the Resurrection with Easter eggs!). Let the five-year-old come up with Treasure Hunt clues. Let the two-year-old set out the party paper plates.

SOME IDEAS FOR MAKING HOLIDAYS CHRISTIAN

We have separated the seasonal/cultural parts of Easter from the celebration of Christ's Resurrection. The first day of spring is our time for baskets, eggs, candies, and bunnies. During Passion Week we have a progression of devotionals and special activities leading up to Resurrection Day. . . .

How about celebrating Reformation Day instead of Halloween? . . .

Visit nursing homes during the holidays (and all year) and leave little seasonal gifts. The older people love the attention and the chance to see some children. The kids learn it *is* more blessed to give than to receive.

—Pastor Phil Lancaster, MO

(6) Hospitality: If you are new to the entertaining biz, don't start by inviting the most scruffy types you can find to your family celebrations. Start with your own family, branch out to friends, then include easy-to-get-along-with strangers, and only when you are comfortable and practiced invite the hard cases. This advice was given to me by a dear and trusted older friend years ago. He pointed out to Bill and me that we had to learn to practice hospitality and get to the point of enjoying it before we could expect to do a good job in difficult circumstances. We also are responsible for our children's safety, and must consider their emotional readiness before bringing disturbed or strange people into our homes. Reaching out to the hard cases is a ministry for single people and older couples. The "poor" Jesus expects us to reach out to as families seem to be the virtuous poor, especially our fellow Christians.

So you see, there *is* life after TV. Your family can have fun that builds it up in the Lord, creating precious memories and lifelong bonds. But you can do even more than that with the time you would otherwise lose in front of a blinking screen. Discover the ultimate investment strategy for your time, energy, and money in the next section.

The Omega
Strategy

9

*W*ould you like to Get Rich Quick? Then you ought to read our mail. Lately every time we open the mailbox, we find at least one envelope adorned with blurbs promising The Investment Strategy of a Lifetime! "Why recession is inevitable . . . and how you can make big bucks when it hits!" "The Ten Biggest Little Investments of the Year—paying up to 54% profit!" "The surprise stash of the future (Nope, It's Not Gold)." And so on. And on. And on.

Each of these investment guys proudly lists his credentials. He'd better, when he's trying to talk us into blowing somewhere in the neighborhood of $100 per year on his investment newsletter! Some boast about how they predicted the 1988 Black Monday stock market crash. Others point to proven track records over five, ten, or fifteen years, during which time their clients' investments outperformed the stock market.

So what's wrong with all this hype? Is there any good reason why Christians shouldn't try to make a few bucks by playing the market, or line our pillows with Treasury bonds? Is there a better way to invest whatever extra funds might come our way after the mortgage, food, and fuel bills have been paid? Is there any way people who don't have even middling-sized sums of money to invest can increase their family's net worth?

Yes, there is! I have discovered an amazingly simple principle I call the Omega Strategy. Using this strategy, and with the blessing of the Lord, we have vastly increased our family's productivity over the past few years. Our financial picture has also improved considerably. Not that we are wallowing in the lap of outrageous luxury. We don't even *want* outrageous luxury, for reasons I'll explain in a minute. But it would be fair to say that *in the things that really matter* our situation has improved almost immeasurably.

Wealth is made up of real things. It is hammers, lathes, shovels, typewriters, windows, doors, walls, pencils, shirts, shoes, rugs, apples, automobiles, and bread. . . . It should be obvious by now that real wealth is your objective. Paper, once it is printed into money, cannot be consumed; it can only be traded for real wealth. Stocks, bonds, and savings accounts, then, are only ways in which to store purchasing power until you are ready to use it. . . .

As long as you have your wealth in the form of paper claims, you are prey to swindlers and con men, both those who work through government and those who work outside the law. . . .

—John A. Pugsley
The Alpha Strategy: The Ultimate Plan of Financial Self-Defense

Why Other Investment Strategies Fail . . . and This One Doesn't

The Omega Strategy got its start from some principles in a wonderful book called *The Alpha Strategy*, by investor John Pugsley. Simply stated, Pugsley pointed out that the traditional methods of saving money don't work over the long run. Bank interest runs less than inflation, so you actually lose money on your savings account. Playing the stock market for short-term gains more resembles casino gambling than a sensible investment strategy. Bonds, T-bills, mutual funds—Pugsley goes down the list and debunks them all as investment vehicles. None consistently makes your invested return more valuable than the original purchasing power of the dollars you used to buy the investment.

So what is left? Here is where Pugsley shines. He points out that *investing in yourself*—your skills and knowledge—and *investing in tools and real goods* are really the wisest investments. Both are inflation-proof and deflation-proof. It doesn't matter if inflation is at 70%, as it has been in some South American countries lately. It doesn't matter if money is so scarce that you can't afford to buy gas to even get to the supermarket. If you own it, you own it. Those cans of beans in the basement are still food even if war destroys the nation's entire infrastructure. And what's in your head nobody can take from you, even if your home is wiped out by a tornado or you have to flee a hostile government.

Let's take Pugsley a little farther now, and mix in some Scriptural teaching about how a wise woman, in particular, maximizes returns on her investments. I am referring to the famous wife in Proverbs 31. The sequence, as you recall, goes like this:

> She selects wool and flax
>   and works with eager hands.
> She is like the merchant ships,
>   bringing her food from afar.
> She gets up while it is still dark;
>   she provides food for her family
>   and portions for her servant girls.

She considers a field and buys it;
    out of her earnings she plants a vineyard.
She sets about her work vigorously;
    her arms are strong for her tasks.
She sees that her trading is profitable,
    and her lamp does not go out at night. . . .
She opens her arms to the poor
    and extends her hands to the needy.
When it snows, she has no fear for her household;
    for all of them are clothed in scarlet.
She makes coverings for her bed;
    she is clothed in fine linen and purple. . . .
She makes linen garments and sells them
    and supplies the merchants with sashes.
She is clothed with strength and dignity;
    she can laugh at the days to come.
She speaks with wisdom,
    and faithful instruction is on her tongue.
She watches over the affairs of her household,
    and does not eat the bread of idleness. . . .
Charm is deceptive, and beauty is fleeting,
    but a woman who fears the Lord is to be praised.
Give her the reward she has earned,
    and let her works bring her praise at the city gate.

> Tangible wealth consists of all the real products produced by man from the raw materials of nature, and by the use of which man derives survival, comfort, and pleasure. . . . There is also intangible wealth. It consists of knowledge and ideas, the things we must have in order to produce tangible wealth.
>
> —John A. Pugsley
> *The Alpha Strategy*

I left out the parts about her relationship to her husband and children, since we are looking at those in other chapters. For now, we will be looking at the portion of this passage quoted above, since it is *the most concentrated description of a successful family investing policy* you are ever likely to find.

First Things First

You notice that Proverbs 31 is talking about "a woman who fears the Lord." This woman "speaks with wisdom" and is also a fountain of "faithful instruction." These are the underpinnings of everything she is able to accomplish. She has *spiritual capital*—spiritual understanding and knowledge.

In a minute I'll explain how and why we should get spiritual capital *first*. Let me now share with you a bit of our pilgrimage that led us to realize this truth.

Bill and I had quite different backgrounds where money was concerned. My father was a Depression

baby and my mother a Hungarian refugee. They both
raised me to count the pennies. Bill's father, on the
other hand, had become quite successful financially,
and his family had enjoyed a lot of luxuries mine had
missed. However, he was in the same financial condition as I was when we met—loaded down with college loans. Bill also brought to our marriage a car
loan.

As new Christians, we were convinced that we
needed to get out of debt, so this became a top priority. Every penny, and I mean *every* penny, that we did
not give away to Christian groups or spend on pinch-
ingly frugal meals went to kill off our debts. We sold
our jewelry, including my engagement ring and a
ring I had given Bill. We sold almost all our other
possessions as well. On top of this, Bill was going to
seminary, so the family income was what could chari-
tably be called slender.

In this state of almost total capital destitution—
owning almost nothing, buying almost nothing, but
heading toward freedom from debt—I had become so
stingy that I wouldn't buy myself *anything,* not even a
new dress, no matter how ragged and ancient the
hand-me-downs I was wearing had become.

Bill helped me to see I was being a bit extreme one
day, as I was agonizing over whether it would be a
waste of money to buy some new clothes. "After all,"
I moaned, "I am not naked. Clothes are just for function. When children are starving overseas, how can I
justify spending money just on appearance?"

"Good thinking," Bill chimed in. "Why don't we
just get you some burlap sacks?"

"Burlap sacks?" I echoed foolishly.

"Yes!" Bill smiled. "We can chop a hole in the top
for your head and two holes at the sides for your
arms. Maybe we can even get a sack that used to hold
flower seeds so you can have a picture of a flower on
the front!"

I couldn't help smiling back. Bill was referring to
the story my mother used to tell about how, as
refugees in wartime Germany, she and her friends

had been reduced to wearing burlap sacks for clothing. Mom had felt herself especially fortunate, because her sack had a picture of a flower on it!

I realized I was being silly, and managed to buy a few clothes for myself, even though it still felt painful to spend money on "unnecessary" items.

Not too long after this, I was mooning over a list of books I wanted to buy from Puritan-Reformed Discount Books (now Great Christian Books). The Christian bookstore in our town did not carry anything of much more depth than testimony tales like *I Was a Mafia Hit Man*. "If only we could afford to get some of these books!" I sighed.

Bill once again came to my rescue. "Why can't we?" he asked.

"You know we can't afford to spend $50 on books!" I retorted, shocked.

"Why not?" he repeated. "Haven't we got that much in our checking account?"

Bill knew perfectly well that we had money to buy the books. My problem was that I had it all mentally earmarked as prepayment on loans.

Bill pressed on. "Why not get the books, if you want them?" he demanded. "Doesn't the Bible say, 'Seek ye first the kingdom of God and his righteousness, and all these things'—meaning all our earthly needs—'will be added unto ye'? Where does it say, 'First prepay all your debts, and then you can buy some Christian books?'"

He had a point there, so with a great act of willpower I wrote out a check and ordered the books. Over the next year or two we kept this practice up. Sometimes we had to wait two or three months before we could afford to buy our next "wish list" of Christian books, but pretty soon we had accumulated quite a little library of Christian classics.

That reading, pursued when I still had a good amount of free time, provided the spiritual knowledge that enabled me to write *The Way Home*, my first book. It also helped change us in many ways for the better, as our emotional problems, bad habits, and

---

Is there any biblical evidence to indicate that possessions can really "tempt" us? Are they truly "dangerous"? Such pharisaical, environmentalist notions are completely condemned by Scripture. It is an implication that God is really to blame, since He created possessions in the first place. . . .

The problem is *sin*, not possessions. God owns everything, yet He is not tempted by evil (James 1:13). . . . The fact that a rich man forsakes God is not due to his riches "seducing" him, but to his own evil heart. You could as easily say that the poor man's *lack* of possessions "seduces" him to steal (Proverbs 30:9b). . . .

The point of the biblical passage [Luke 12:22-31] is to underscore the fact that all economic success comes from God, and that our concern about the future must not conflict with the demands of His kingdom. Jesus is saying, "Where is your heart? What is your motivation?" . . . The goal of success is a necessary aspect of all human action. But we must never try to be autonomous. In all that we do we must work in the fear of God, desiring to glorify Him by our labors. . . .

There are valid needs in the present. But God's law is structured so that, usually, a good portion of income can go toward production.

—David Chilton
Productive Christians in an Age of Guilt-Manipulators

We now have a home with four bedrooms and two baths, and many say, "That's why you had a big family." We proceed to tell them—we first had the family, then God gave us this home.

—Martha Pugacz, OH

other hindrances were challenged and corrected by men who lived and died years before we were born.

As the Bible says, "Wisdom is supreme; therefore get wisdom. Though it cost all you have, get understanding" (Proverbs 4:7). Elsewhere the Bible says that wisdom is a better investment than rubies, and that it yields better returns than gold (Proverbs 3:14, 15). In other words, *wisdom is your very best investment* and *whatever helps you get wiser is the best investment of your time and money.*

How to Invest in Spiritual Capital

Most people today have the same attitude towards Christian books and other teaching aids such as cassettes, videos, and seminars that I used to have. When budgeting or buying, books come last. This is a serious mistake. Anything that you have reason to believe will improve your spiritual life, your wisdom, or your knowledge should be top priority. I'm not saying this just because I now write books, either!

We still live by this rule today. If we see a book, or a tape series, or a video that looks like it can answer questions we have been pondering, if we can afford it, we get it.

We want to know more about prophecy, about holy living, about how to raise children, about how civil government should be structured. We want to learn how to educate our children better, how to evangelize more powerfully, how to help people without making them dependent, how to overcome our spiritual weaknesses. We want to know church history and Biblical languages, and be acquainted with the great Christian writers, thinkers, and martyrs.

None of this is going to fall on us for free. We have to go out and *search* for it. We have to pay for it, and find the time to study it. So do you. We also have to make use of whatever wisdom we have already gained to separate the wheat from the chaff, the tomes by "experts" from the books solidly based on the Bible. This is hard work. But it is *worthwhile.*

During the California Gold Rush, men would live for years on beans and hardtack, camping in the open, hardly ever washing or going to town for any social life. They were totally dedicated to finding that gold and getting it out of the ground or the creek bed. "If I ever get my lucky strike," a 49-er would muse, "I'll have it made for the rest of my life." Well, there are veins of spiritual gold waiting to be mined, too! And the really neat thing is that *this* gold is there for everyone who persistently searches for it. "He who seeks, finds" (Matthew 7:8).

Some of us will have joyful homes, cheerful children, contentment in good times and bad, and spiritual power to burn. Others will live from crisis to crisis, never getting or doing much good on this earth. The difference is just the amount of spiritual capital each of us has. Search for more. Make it grow. You won't be sorry.

How to Invest in Your Children

After the Israelites left Egypt they were in sad shape. They had been slaves for four hundred years and were not used to doing things for themselves. Nonetheless, the Lord commanded the Israelites, "Impress them [His commandments] on your children. Talk about them when you sit at home and when you walk along the road, when you lie down and when you get up" (Deuteronomy 6:7). God told the parents, who themselves were short of spiritual capital, to provide their children with spiritual capital.

Why did He do this?

Why didn't He just have Moses set up a school and teach all the Israelite children?

I think the answer is tied up with two things:

(1) God wants children to honor their parents. (See the Fifth Commandment in Deuteronomy 5:16.) This is almost impossible when the parents don't disciple the children, and absurdly easy when we do.

(2) God knows that we parents increase our own spiritual capital by training our youngsters.

It occurred to me that even though we didn't own a home, were not able to afford a big entertainment budget and didn't have the money for all the consumer items we dreamed about—on the other hand, our life experiences were a pretty valuable thing in and of themselves. The experience of having time to leisurely read, take long walks, and have fascinating conversations with friends and loved ones is worth something and needs to be considered when figuring out just what your standard of living amounts to.

—Sally Roskin
New Families, Spring 1987

Public education once could teach children things. So history says. But centralized public ed run by bureaucrats with strange ideological passions flagrantly falls short. Part of the reason is not just the bureaucrats, but the effect bureaucrats have on those who used to teach children: their parents.

Teach Your Own. You see, once people get the idea that a job they used to do is about to be done by someone else with enormous resources, they lose interest in that job. So many parents today actually expect the public schools to teach their children *everything,* from sexual morals to the right way to blow their noses.

I'm not afraid to blame the bureaucrats for most of what has happened to American education. Heaven knows they have deliberately inflicted enough educational calamities on us. But we needn't sit around waiting for them to come up with yet another "solution." For one thing, we already know that their solution is to throw more money at the people who caused the mess. For another thing, *we* are the real solution.

"It's too hard! I couldn't teach my children anything!" Oh yes you can! Even impatient, stressed-out parents can teach their children. During the process, if you are willing to let God teach you, you become *less* impatient and stressed-out. I'm speaking from experience!

Of course, to teach a child the moral law it helps to not have other people constantly undermining you. Thus, the home schooling and Christian school movements.

Today you can get resources to help you teach every subject under the sun, from art to zoology. I myself have written several rather large resource books reviewing thousands of educational items perfect for home instruction (*The New Big Book of Home Learning* and *The Next Book of Home Learning*). I have also written a how-to book for parents and others who want to teach children (*Schoolproof*). These are listed in the

Resources, along with the best home-school teacher training workshop I have found. So getting started teaching your children is no problem.

A Sound Investment Strategy. Once again, I must stress that we have to change our perceptions of what is worth spending money on. Many people wince at the thought of spending, say, $210 for a first-rate reusable phonics program for their child. These same people will pay $300 for *one* college credit and think nothing of it. But learning to read is far more important than a college credit!

Which is worth more:

- A fine restaurant meal for two . . . or a year's art supplies for your children?
- Tickets for the family to a first-run movie . . . or a full-color laminated history timeline?
- A new set of chairs for the kitchen . . . or a Bible memory curriculum?

A savvy home schooler will pick the second option every time. And he or she will be right, too. Long after you have digested the restaurant meal, gone home from the movie theater, and scratched up the new chairs, an investment in learning will still be bearing fruit in your family's life.

And that fruit is more than brighter children, too. Let me tell you what happens when you start teaching your children.

(1) You discover gaps in your own education and start filling them. This increases your confidence in the long run, if you can make it through the short-term feeling of panic ("Help! I don't know how to spell!").

(2) You find what you lack in management skills. These are the exact skills you need for leadership in every other area of life. The main problem with trying to increase your management skills in other arenas (work, the church) is that nobody tells you honestly what you are doing right or wrong. Not to worry. Your kids will now tell you.

> Wisdom is supreme; therefore get wisdom.
> Though it cost all you have, get understanding.
>
> —Proverbs 4:7

The only safe, rational investment program for the average person in today's turbulent economy is to *eliminate the intermediate step.* Instead of converting labor into money, money into investments, investments back into money, and money into real goods once again, convert your surplus earnings directly into real goods. . . .

Goods to be saved will include (1) the knowledge and skills of [your] trade, (2) the tools, supplies, and inventory for [your] business, (3) the regular consumer products [you] use in [your] everyday life, and (4) raw materials and finished products that [you] can later store for trade with others.

—John A. Pugsley
The Alpha Strategy

(3) As you hang in there showing real love for your children and improving daily in skill and knowledge, your children gain respect for you! This is the beginning of a real team spirit that gives your family the power to be its best.

How to Invest in Yourself

So the first step in the Omega Strategy is to invest in your own and your family's spiritual capital, including both knowledge of God's Word and academic knowledge. Now that we're solid on this first step, we're ready to tackle the rest of the Omega Strategy. It goes like this:

"She selects wool and flax and works with eager hands." First, develop your home skills. Edith Schaeffer calls this "Hidden Art." Do your normal household tasks: writing letters, cleaning the kitchen, cooking, sewing and mending, gardening, designing, and so on. As you become excellent at these tasks, you will be investing in the first part of your portfolio: personal skills.

The next chapter will explain in detail how and why to increase these skills.

"She is like the merchant ships, bringing her food from afar." Step One in money management is saving what you can of what comes in. The noble wife of Proverbs 31 searched far afield for the best bargains, like the merchant ships.

"She gets up while it is still dark; she provides food for her family and portions for her servant girls." Of the family income, the first portion after returning the Lord His tithe goes to provide for the family and its helpers. In our modern age, this includes providing the gas and electricity to run the household machinery. It also includes purchasing tools to help you with your work: a very important point.

"**She opens her arms to the poor and extends her hands to the needy.**" Next, she looks after the poor, investing part of the household funds in personally-supervised charity.

"**When it snows, she has no fear for her household; for all of them are clothed in scarlet.**" Some portion of money is used, as available, for nice things and comforts.

"**She makes linen garments and sells them and supplies the merchants with sashes.**" Her household skills eventually blossom into a home business, as she is producing more goods than the family can consume.

"**She considers a field and buys it; out of her earnings she plants a vineyard.**" Reinvestment. Instead of cashing out, as is the rage among modern companies, the wise family businesswoman reinvests in capital goods under her personal control that can be counted on to yield even more income in the future.

"**She sets about her work vigorously; her arms are strong for her tasks. She sees that her trading is profitable, and her lamp does not go out at night. . . . She watches over the affairs of her household, and does not eat the bread of idleness.**" She does not leave the management of her family's investments to others, hoping it will all turn out all right somehow. Instead, she personally supervises the household. "Her lamp does not go out at night" does not mean she stays up all night, but that she keeps the home fires burning.

"**She is clothed with strength and dignity; she can laugh at the days to come.**" This woman's investments are secure. She is as well set up as she can be. No matter what happens, her family is in the best possible state.

Comment from Mary: BUY THAT BOOK! Mr. Pugsley not only explains everything you need to know about money and investing in the clearest language I have ever seen, but he provides the information you need to choose *which* raw materials or finished goods, etc., make most sense for you to invest in—plus much more! See Resources.

Every man will sit under his
  own vine
and under his own fig tree,
and no one will make them
  afraid,
for the Lord Almighty has
  spoken.
—Micah 4:4

To summarize the Omega Strategy:

(1) Invest first in your family's wisdom—spiritual capital.
(2) Invest next in your skills—mental capital.
(3) Save all the money you can, while providing for:
    (a) The Lord's tithe;
    (b) Your family's needs;
    (c) The poor;
    (d) Your family's comforts.
(4) Invest what is left over in tools and nonperishable goods—physical capital.
(5) Once your skills have reached the level where people are willing to pay for your creations, start a business.
(6) Reinvest money made by the business (monetary capital) in income-producing property.

Cashing Out v. Spreading the Wealth

The Omega Strategy might seem obvious on its face. But it is completely different from the way worldly authorities tell you to start. They say, "Make a business plan and take out a huge loan," if you are thinking of starting a business. If you want to invest your earnings, they tell you to buy stocks and bonds, or T-bills, or futures, or put it all in gold and bury it in the ground. (Remember the parable of the servant with the one talent who did just that?)

Our economy today is a mess because the worldly way never works in the long run. In the short run a few win the lottery. They sell their businesses at a huge profit to new buyers, who typically finance the takeover with even more debt. That is why every book on business and every business magazine devotes so much space to the engrossing subject of how to get in debt and how to keep the bank happy. Meanwhile, the business world becomes increasingly unstable and the small- and middle-sized businesses are increasingly gobbled up by bigger players with better financing.

Then take a look at Wall Street. Or should I say, Las Vegas East. "Investors" today treat the stock market like the lottery. Few and far between are investors who put their money into a company and leave it there. Even fewer are those who invest in a business because they believe in that business. The name of the game is quick profits: get in, get out, and take the loot. These stockholders put enormous pressure on business management to go for quick profits instead of reinvesting for long-term growth and development. This is no way to run a business!

Socialism is not the answer. What is gained by taking control of the country from the increasingly small number of major business owners and giving it to the bureaucrats? Nothing, except greater inefficiency and corruption.

The Omega Strategy supplies a middle road between greedy debt-based hoggism and repressive tax-based statism. (And don't any of you Free Marketeers write to tell me that a perfectly free market solves all its problems. Once it gets in the hands of too few players, it stops being a free market and becomes a closed shop.) What we really want is what G. K. Chesterton in a fit of brilliance once named "Distributism"—every family having as much of a piece of the action as they deserve. Every man under his own vine and fig tree. Nobody muscling in and taking away the fruit of your labor. Millions and millions of little businesses—the Fortune Fifty Million instead of the Fortune 500.

So, should your little business bloom and prosper, go on to the final step of the Omega Strategy:

(7) Invest in someone else's dream that you, too, believe in. Help another family get its business going. I call this IBM stock: I'm Being Merciful. (IBM can also stand for I'm Being Mercenary, and that's just what it is when you invest in a company without even knowing or caring about what they produce.) What God has given us, above and beyond our needs, should be passed on to others who have shown themselves faithful in the little things, so they too can have a blessing.

Thru the stock market, short-term next-quarter mentality is evident. Inside traders & corporate raiders have become the new buccaneers, pursuing profit with little thought to consequences. A SEC survey of large Wall Street firms that speculate on takeovers showed 80% of those firms also help underwrite the deals. . . . Even union/worker pension fund managers push for immediate gain at expense of longer-term stability, thus hurting the very employees they're supposed to help.

Focus today is on investments, money-making potential (e.g., *USA Today* business section is titled "Money") while long-term productivity issues are back-burnered. In making decisions that can affect hundreds of employees or whole communities, many busines owners act like they have absolute, not limited rights. . . . *Where are the corporate spokespersons out there saying,* "We must compete in the long-run as well as the short-term!"

—*PR Reporter*
October 12, 1987

The next three chapters will now detail how you can put the Omega Strategy to work in your family, and perhaps even end up with your own piece of the pie.

The Cinderella
Principle

10

"I too was in a career in Computer Systems before becoming a homeworker. I felt I knew nothing of cooking or sewing, only of writing computer programs. I do so hope you will write a second book explaining how to accomplish the goals and objectives put forth in *The Way Home!"*

Thank you, Mary Ellen from Ohio! You have captured what is missing in the education of girls today. In a nutshell, real-life skills. Our unisex, office-job-oriented educational system is great at providing courses in typing, but not so hot at teaching us how to clean up after ourselves or do the laundry.

Today any woman who tries taking care of her own home is likely to feel like Cinderella. You remember Cinderella—the poor girl whose wicked stepmother and stepsisters had her slaving morning, noon, and night.

For one thing, the feminist lobby has spent the last twenty years downgrading the value of this work.

For another thing, few of us have ever learned how to do it right.

This chapter will deal with both subjects: why the work is worth doing and how to do it professionally.

Cinderella's Apprenticeship

You remember in the last chapter that Step Two of the Omega Strategy was developing your own skills. After Step One, developing your spiritual capital, you invest in your future productivity by increasing your abilities.

Normally today we try to learn new skills by signing up for a course somewhere. The Bible says this is not the proper way to start. We are supposed to begin where we are, learning to be "faithful in the little things."

To help you understand what little things I am talking about, I'll name some of them: dirty dishes,

It's hard to get excited about current obligations. The term itself has no glamor: current obligations. We would rather begin a new adventure off somewhere in the distance than follow through with the ordinary details of our present circumstances. But current obligations are a part of every godly adventure. They comprise a springboard that will launch you into the plan and purpose of God for your life. . . .

But what are our current obligations? If you have a family to take care of, you have many obligations to fulfill. Your adventure starts in the daily routine of managing your household. But it is not simply a grin-and-bear-it proposition. There is room for excitement in the management of your household, if you are willing to get away from the herd and take a path that is less traveled. . . .

Don't try to be faithful only when you think it really counts. . . . God's adventures come most quickly to those who buckle down and fulfill their current obligations.

—Gregg Harris
Family Restoration Quarterly
February 1987

When we had only two or three children I used to feel frustrated and inadequate almost all the time. The sense of failure as a Christian wife and mother was especially acute when I would read the books about *being* one.

My husband and I have been blessed with three out of five fussy babies. . . . . During those tense months when it took every ounce of my strength just to get through the day with the children cared for, laundry done, and meals made, being told that I also needed to tithe my time to the Lord, greet my husband at the door dressed in Saran Wrap with a rose between my teeth, and do my bit for the church by teaching Sunday school and singing in the choir, made me feel that I had to be the world's most unspiritual and faithless mother! . . .

Two things helped me a great deal: the realization that Jesus spent ten times more of his life ministering in the hidden years, as a carpenter quietly living at home, than he spent in his public ministry, and the Scripture in Titus 2:4, 5 which seemed to say to me as a young mother that there were different priorities for my life than for that of an older woman. I felt very freed by that to listen to the Holy Spirit's prompting in my life rather than the guilt-producing expectations of other people.

—Kim Jeffery, PA

meals, clothes that need mending or washing, seeds to plant and water, and children to teach. These God-given natural opportunities are God's training workshop.

Now the plain fact is that hardly any of us were taught how to teach and cook and clean and sew and garden and launder at our mother's knee. The generation of our parents (and, to a lesser extent, *their* parents) firmly believed that outside institutions could and should teach us all these things. We would learn cooking in home ec class and how to use tools in woodworking shop. Teachers would teach our children, so we would never have to. Dirty laundry could go to the laundromat, and if we were successful a housekeeper would clean up our messes, just like Mom used to.

The ancient fairy tale of Cinderella teaches us otherwise. This tale, which is found all over the world in many different cultures, features a dear young thing who is put to work for an unsparing female taskmaster. Though she is overworked, Cinderella always is sweet and willing. She dreams of her Prince who will someday take her away from this life of labor, and against all odds, with a special magical assist, she gets him.

The Walt Disney version of this story has a scene where Cinderella is down on her hands and knees scrubbing the floor. This scene captures the feeling of the Cinderella story perfectly. Cinderella is not only exquisitely beautiful, reflected with Disney art in the pool of scrubwater, but she is cleaning the floor with style. She swishes the floor so beautifully that if the Prince had first seen her there instead of at the ball, she would have won his heart just the same. Cinderella's two ugly stepsisters, in contrast, pin their hopes on fancy clothes and social status. All their efforts, of course, come to naught as the Prince is heartily bored by them when introduced.

The underlying moral of the Cinderella tale is perfectly plain. Hard work and faithfulness in the unpleasing tasks of life fit a young girl for the company of the Prince. Vanity and self-indulgence do not. Following the Biblical teaching that says, "Do you see a man who is skilled in his work? He will serve before kings; he will not serve before obscure men" (Proverbs 22:29), Cinderella is supernaturally assisted to triumph over her favored stepsisters.

Putting this into Christian terms: *Becoming skilled in your most mundane tasks is is God's appointed means of training Christians for future leadership.*

Is There Life After Housework?

So here we go, future leaders! We're going to tackle your dirty floors, grungy dishes, ripped clothes, weedy yard, and more besides!

First on the docket is that dreaded word CLEANING. If there is one skill more than others that American women have totally forgotten (and would like to forget even more) it is CLEANING. We struggle, we suffer, we fume, we howl when it's CLEANING time. We try to talk our husbands and kids into doing it for us. We bribe, we wheedle, we threaten, we whimper. Finally we give up, take off our glasses, and pretend the mess isn't there.

And it's all so unnecessary! Consider: Some people make their whole livelihood cleaning—janitors, housemaids, the ladies from Tidy Team. It doesn't take *them* all day to clean one house. If it did, they wouldn't make any money. So they must know something you don't. If they know it, you can learn it. If you learn how to clean like a professional, you will come to enjoy it.

Cleaning has been a special study of mine, since I am specially bad at it. I even drove a college roommate away by my excessive untidiness! You can just imagine my rapture when I found a set of books that told a slob like me how to clean up my act.

Don Aslett, the author of the books in question, is America's cleaning expert. He started a cleaning service in college, called Varsity Cleaners, and it's now one of the biggest cleaning companies in the world. Starting out like most of us, with very little knowl-

---

A CLEAN HOUSE

How does everyone else do it?
- [ ] Some lie . . .
- [ ] Some have mighty lumpy rugs . . .
- [ ] Some have no children . . .
- [ ] Some browbeat their husbands to do the work . . .
- [ ] Some use only one room in the house . . .
- [ ] Some never let anyone in . . .

It's amazing that no real training is provided for the most complicated, life-affecting job on earth—homemaking.

Yet I assure you there are proven ways to have a clean house, and they don't hinge on magic, good luck, or genies in a cleaner jug. By learning how to *prevent* housework, and by using *professional* cleaning methods, you can reduce your household chore time by as much as 75 percent.

—Don Aslett
Is There Life After Housework?

One great testimony from reading your book is I am faithful to do my dishes. Trivial? No way! I got pretty good at stacking and hiding. I would do anything rather than my dishes. I kept thinking, "There has to be a way out of this!" You know how simple and concrete God is—well, He gave me this great revelation for my dirty dishes—wash them! Can you believe that? I never would have come up with an answer like that all by myself. After seeing the kitchen clean for the third day in a row, my husband got suspicious. He looked around, grabbed my hand, and gently led me to the oven. Well, I gladly obliged. After all, I knew he would find it empty [of dirty dishes]. Praise God!

—D.T., NY

edge of how to clean, Don interviewed the housewives he worked for, collecting their tips. What makes Don unusual is that even now, as head of this massive company, he still gets in there and cleans with his crews. So his knowledge of cleaning is really hands-on.

Somewhere along the line, Don's wife Barbara persuaded him to give a talk to her women's group. It was a smashing success, and led to more talks, which led to several books, a video, and a mail-order catalog for professional cleaning products (all in the Resources).

We have used Don's system for years, and it Really Works! It's based on a few simple principles:

■ De-junk. "Don't love it if it can't love you back." Get rid of the clutter that you spend hours sorting through, climbing over, and shuffling from place to place.

■ Eliminate work. Keep out the dirt with mats. Design your living space to eliminate dirt-causers and dirt-catchers.

■ Save your energy. Do cleaning tasks in the most efficient order. Dust first, then vacuum. Wash walls from top to bottom.

■ Use professional tools and equipment: squeegees for windows, Scrubby-Doos for floors, beater-bar vacuums for rugs, Masslin cloths for dusting, and so on.

■ Use professional techniques. Don's video, on which he demonstrates his stuff before a studio audience, shows how you really can clean with style.

I am not going to try to spell out all of Don's tips and tricks here. For one thing, it wouldn't be honest even to try. For another, I don't want to deprive you of the joy of reading his books. They are so well-written and so artistically laid-out that I hope they sell *another* million copies! All I can say is that if you get them, study them, and faithfully follow their instructions you too can actually enjoy cleaning house for the first time in your life.

The Joy of Cooking

My parents did teach me how to cook. At the age of eight I could make bacon, toast, eggs, and coffee. I have since forgotten how to make coffee, given up bacon except for special treats, hardly ever cook eggs, and eat my bread untoasted, but even so it was a fine start.

In my teens I learned to bake. Baking is where it's at if you want to gain a lot of weight in a short time or (alternatively) entice some fine young man into marrying you. It just depends on who eats what you bake. No matter what anyone says about chemistry and physical attractiveness, the way to a man's heart still seems to pass through his stomach!

Although I did suffer through a couple of semesters of Home Ec (when I really wanted to take woodworking instead), I actually learned to cook from reading the instructions in recipe books.

So I offer this suggestion to those of you who are eating out of cans and would like to move up to real food: get a good basic cookbook, like *The Fanny Farmer Cookbook*, and study it. Read the section explaining what all the terms mean, and note its location. Then start with a few simple dishes, looking up anything you don't understand as you go. Ask a friend if you need help. Just take it easy; don't begin with a dinner for twenty, including your husband's boss! Start baking with cookies, frying with eggs, roasting with chicken, microwaving with veggies in a microwave-proof steamer. Honestly, simple is better anyway. The more elaborate a dish, the higher the likelihood it will contain all kinds of expensive and fattening ingredients.

To preserve our family's health, I do play with recipes a little. For example, I always substitute whole wheat flour for white flour and only put in half as much sugar in cookie recipes. Health food purists out there would excoriate me for the sugar, but I stick by it. Have you ever seen a crispy cookie made with honey or fruit juice? But crispy is just the way *we* like cookies. You may like them better some other way.

The way to a man's heart is through his stomach.

—Wise old proverb

Around our house, it is a proven fact that you *can* reach a man's heart through his stomach. My heart-to-stomach connection is pretty firmly set, especially just before mealtimes!

This must be pretty common among men. A reader of *Focus on the Family* magazine pointed out that, after all the talk about PMS for women, her own husband exhibited all the symptoms: crankiness, inability to cope, pangs in the lower torso—only in his case it was Pre-Meal Syndrome!

—Bill Pride
Flirting with the Devil

The romance of cooking is playing around with recipes, substituting this and that as you become more experienced, and eventually inventing your own recipes. Cooking is a skill that you can always improve, so it never will become dull if you take the time to study it. And I'm not even getting into the art of garnishing or other ways of making the food you prepare look more attractive. Or the art of table-setting (which I myself totally neglect).

The world recognizes a Food Artist when it sees one. Even the most adamant careerist male will admit he is envious of a colleague whose wife stays home and bakes bread and other goodies. And mmmm, does it make the house smell good!

Shop Around

Time is money, and it does no good to spend so much time shopping that you could have made the item yourself. Shopping can also be another way to escape home duties. "Let's get the girls together and go hang out at the mall."

Some places are also better to shop than others. Did you know malls are designed to promote impulse buying? Older buildings and shopping centers tend to be more architecturally respectful of their customers. Yard sales have no particular architecture at all, but some of the worst (if cheapest) impulse buying goes on there.

Since every dollar saved is worth three earned, a really good shopper can actually be worth more economically to her family than a not-so-good shopper with an outside job—and that's not even counting the possibility of a home business income, which we will discuss in a future chapter.

I personally do as much of my shopping as I possibly can by mail. When you are buying new items, mail-order shopping saves both time and money. Time, because the shopper doesn't have to drive to the store, park, walk inside, search up and down aisles for the desired item, and maybe repeat that process several times before coming home. Money, because mail-order buying does not lend itself nearly as well to wild impulse spending, especially if you pay by check instead of calling the handy toll-free number.

A good rule of thumb for preventing accidental indebtedness caused by overzealous buying is to wait a week after deciding to purchase an item. This is easy when you shop by mail. Just make up a list of what you want on a Post-It, listing the page numbers and prices of all items, and stick it in the catalog. A week later, cross out the items you have discovered you can live without and order the rest. Simple.

For those who have trouble spending less than they make, the envelope system of budgeting works well. Just write the name of each category on a separate envelope: rent, food, clothes, books, insurance, etc. On each envelope write the monthly (or weekly, or whatever) amount you have budgeted for that category. Every time you purchase an item, add its price onto a slip kept for that purpose in the envelope. When the amount on the slip is about as much as you have budgeted, stop spending. You can try some variations, such as taking money saved from one category to use on another, but the basic principle is easy enough to follow.

Other Ideas for Saving Money

■ **Clothes.** Marcia Hoehne, in an article in *Priority Parenting* of March 1989, suggests you try a "double rummage" sale. Sell the clothes you no longer wear and use that money to shop for "new" secondhands. Marcia also suggests you tap friends for outgrown children's clothes. This works beautifully if you have friends with similar tastes whose children are the same sex but a little older than yours. And for babies, try living without disposable diapers. Cloth diapers can save you a ton of money, besides avoiding exposing your baby's bottom to potentially dangerous chemicals. Many companies now sell natural or semi-natural fabric diaper covers that close with velcro, and these make diapering as easy as with disposables.

I'd like to comment on home business for home schooling mothers. My husband has a paid job that he enjoys, and I have found that I can come out better financially if I practice thrift and careful shopping, and make or grow everything possible myself, rather than trying to earn money with a home business. The old adage of the penny saved being a penny earned is very true today when we are taxed on what we earn, *and* taxed again when we spend it! I enjoy being able to use as little money as I can, especially as I am *against* so many of the things our taxes fund. I guess I'd like to have you pass on the idea that *not spending* money can be as helpful as *earning* it! (That of course presupposes *some* income for the family—I can't make books, pens, dental work, etc., etc., etc.!!)

—Diane Stearns-Smith, FL

Use it up,
  Wear it out,
Make it over,
  Or do without.

—Folk proverb

■ **Bulk purchases.** *The Alpha Strategy* recommends buying large institutional sizes of products that store well and that your family uses a lot of. Calculate how much you use in three months or a year and buy that amount. Buy beauty supplies from a beauty supply shop, food staples from a restaurant supply shop, and laundry soaps from a laundry supply outlet. This also used to apply to janitorial supplies, but now Don Aslett's Cleaning Store offers professional supplies in condensed household sizes at a really good price (see the Resources). Check prices against co-ops, discount stores, catalog suppliers, and even retail stores first to make sure the institutional supplier's prices are really better.

■ **Living without.** Primping and entertainment can suffer first, but don't neglect them altogether! Get rid of subscriptions to magazines and newspapers you don't really enjoy. Wait longer after choosing an item to order it.

■ **Cleaning up.** Sell your junk! Recycle newspapers, aluminum, glass. Put those old lamps, outgrown tricycles, and stacks of old *National Geographic* on the market. Almost everything is collectible these days, so if you have a lot of old stuff it might be worth checking out a few books on the subject down at the library. Some people have turned their ongoing yard sale into a home business by offering to sell items for others on consignment. Others find they make more money pulling out their hot items to sell to an antiques dealer. Either way, you'll end up with more space in the house—especially important if it is small to begin with!

■ **Spending money to save money.** Some books and newsletters specialize in money-saving tips. If the money saved from tips exceeds the cost of the information source, it's worth it.

I'm Sew-Sew, You're Sew-Sew

Sewing and other fabric crafts have been the backbone of women's work almost since the foundation of

Sewing is making a comeback, and one in four adult women sewed or mended clothes in the last six months, according to Mediamark Research. Purchases of fabrics and patterns declined from 1974 to 1986 [and I could give them some hints why, having seen the patterns!], but have picked up since then.

—*Focus on the Family*
March 1989

the world. The Bible says both Adam and Eve made themselves garments of fig leaves, but ever since then Eve seems to have cornered the market. Women twisted the flax, cotton, or wool into thread, dyed the thread, wove it into fabric, and made the fabric into clothes and decorations. Quilts, needlepointed chair seats, tapestry, crocheted afghans, hooked or woven rugs, and fancy tatting are only a few of the ways women have turned the needle crafts into art. And in days past a country wife would make all her family's clothes, including coats and hats.

The Industrial Revolution hit this cozy home industry, and hit it hard. Huge machines now were able to churn out fabric inexpensively and put it together in fancy ways. Very few people could afford these machines, so the housewife could not buy her own and compete that way. Instead, many women found themselves forced into factory jobs making the fabrics and clothes they used to make in their own homes.

Mass marketing now provides us with very affordable clothing, and the secondhand market offers even greater savings. You can't realistically compete with either one economically most of the time. So my main reason for urging you and your daughters to learn needlework is not that you will save scads of money. If money is tight and you have free time, you *can* acquire a nice wardrobe inexpensively by learning to sew—especially if you are one of those odd sizes that garage-sale clothes never come in! But needlework is mainly important as a character-developing womanly art.

I say "character-developing" because my first successful experience with learning Christian patience came while undoing and redoing pieces of tatting, knitting, and crocheting. These arts operate at an unhurried pace—great for developing motherly serenity and unfreezing us from the rat-race pace!

God uses these arts to develop womanliness (note the example of the Proverbs 31 woman). If teenage girls today would spend more time knitting and less time primping, this would be a better world.

> She selects wool and flax
>   and works with eager
>   hands.
> In her hand she holds the
>   distaff
>   and grasps the spindle
>   with her fingers. . . .
> She makes coverings for her
>   bed;
>   she is clothed in fine linen
>   and purple. . . .
> She makes linen garments
>   and sells them
>   and supplies the mer-
>   chants with sashes.
>
> —Proverbs 31:13, 19, 22, 24

I feel it may be helpful to consider some of the possibilities all of us have of really *living* artistically, but which are often ignored. People so often look with longing into a daydream future, while ignoring the importance of the present. We are all in danger of thinking, "Someday I shall be fulfilled. Someday I shall have the courage to start another life which will develop my talent," without ever considering the very practical use of that talent *today* in a way which will enrich other people's lives, develop the talent, and express the fact of being a creative creature.

—Edith Schaeffer
The Hidden Art of Homemaking

If you want to learn how to sew, quilt, knit, crochet, tat, make lace, hook rugs, tie-dye, knot macramé, cross-stitch samplers, embroider, or any of the hundreds of fabric- and thread-based arts, the simplest and most pleasurable way to proceed is to ask an accomplished needle-wielder to teach you. Beyond that, you can take classes at your local community center or community college, buy instructional videos, subscribe to a crafts magazine or newsletter, or hop on down to your local bookstore or library and pick out the best-looking books on the craft of your choice.

If you get *really* good at needlework, you can parlay your art into a home business.

I have located a source or two for this kind of instruction. See the Resources.

Greener Pastures

Now we come to a subject in which I have considerable expertise. Of how not to do it, that is. I started out my gardening career with a black thumb that is only slowly becoming greener.

The ingredients of a successful garden, it turns out, are:

- Good soil. Yours probably isn't. To make it better, pick out the rocks and add lots of compost. Compost is what happens when all your garden leftovers, weeds, grass clippings, and veggie scraps are mixed in proper proportions and kept moist enough to heat up and decay into yummy brown superstuff.
- Good plant material: seeds, bulbs, trees, shrubs. It really doesn't pay to buy your stock from bargain-basement discounters, since you'll spend many times its price in labor and supplies on preparing beds for the plants, feeding the plants, and tending them.
- The right kind of plant food and the right amount of water, applied at the right time. Here is where your black thumb, if you have one, will show up.

You will forget to water the new zoysia plugs or burn the lilac seedlings with fertilizer stakes. Some people believe in organic fertilizers only—plant food as God designed it. Others go for the scientific-seeming chemical formulations. I used to be able to trust *Organic Gardening* magazine for advice on natural gardening, but now that they've simultaneously gone yuppie and New Age on me, I'm stuck with thumbing through back issues of the magazine or Rodale Press's old books.

■ Bug-killers. You don't want little beasties munching your prize plants. Here again we have an even sharper division between the do-it-God's-way bunch and the kill-everything-in-sight types. A related issue is the question of how much of this poison ends up on your food. Since natural pesticides tend to be less effective, many settle for a compromise position where they use natural pesticides on the food crops, for health's sake, and zap the ornamentals with an occasional chemical.

■ Gardening equipment. If you don't garden, you're probably thinking of hoes and spades. They work, but you'd never know it from all the tractor and shredder ads in gardening magazines. Today's gardener can end up with as much machinery as a steel mill, not to mention rolls of plastic mulch, special tomato cages, flower-propping stakes, overhead sprinkler systems, and on and on. We have resisted some of the more odd and lazy-making items, but the siren song of garden appliances can be hard to withstand. You should see our garage!

■ Information on how to garden. You might have thought you just drop seeds into the soil, water, weed, and wait. Not today! How can you *live* without the latest updates on mushroom soil as a fertilizer or fast-breaking news about the newest seedless watermelons? You need books and magazines and videos and gardening-club memberships! (Not really . . . but it's fun!)

One touch of nature makes the whole world kin.

—Shakespeare

157

There is something very exciting about holding tiny brown seeds in one's hand, in rubbing soil in one's fingers to make it fine in texture, in placing the seeds with one's own fingers in the rows, in covering them up and patting them. There is something exciting in watering the bare brown ground, wondering whether the hidden seeds are doing anything at all, wondering whether they will burst out of the little shell and become roots going down and stem and leaves coming up. The day the first tips of green are seen, if they are *your* seeds, planted by your own fingers, there is a thrill that is surely similar to producing an art work. . . .

Human beings were made to interact with growing things, not to be born, live, and die in the midst of concrete set in the middle of polluted air. . . . There is something tremendously fresh and healthy in having one's mind filled with thought of whether the lettuce is up yet.

—Edith Schaeffer
The Hidden Art of Homemaking

■ A nice garden design. This should have come first, but hardly any gardener starts with a design. You work your way into gardening by plopping a shrub here or a marigold bed there, and only later in the game do you start to think about how to make a lovely landscaped composition. (Two books from Rodale Press, *The Perennial Garden: Color Harmonies Through the Seasons* and *Flowers for All Seasons*, both by Jeff and Marilyn Cox, are really helpful here.)

All kidding aside, gardening really is about the most creatively relaxing activity going. In this world where we spend so much time in man-made environments, a garden is your chance to slow down to Creation's rhythm and admire the handiwork of your Creator. For this reason, people with emotional problems benefit tremendously from gardening. Like anyone who ever feels stressed. All of us, in other words.

Children adore gardens, especially when they have the chance for a little garden of their own. And nothing breaks the winter monotony better than an evening planting petunia seeds into flats.

This very minute in January a reluctant Christmas amaryllis is coquettishly considering whether to bloom on top of my lateral file. Tonight the children will be making out their seed orders (late again!) for the coming spring. Ted wants to plant ornamental popcorn, and is full of plans for marketing it. Joseph leans towards carrots. Sarah stoutly states her preference for peas and carrots. Magda is banging on my back wanting to know which seeds *she* will plant. I am looking forward to experimenting with a few beautiful perennial flowers. Bill will help me choose which ones, and undoubtedly do the bulk of the rototilling and planting.

We have gone through the seasonal plant-weed-harvest ritual for many years now, first with a garden planted by our former landlord (who crammed half the plants in the St. Louis Botanical Garden into a postage-stamp yard) and now on our home property.

We have tried many garden suppliers and weeded out the bad ones (pardon the pun). The very best we could find are listed in the Resources. Try 'em; you'll like 'em!

Cinderella finally did get her prince and put away her mop. You, too, can put away the mop (most of the time) once you learn to manage your household successfully. Find out how to take the step from apprentice to manager in the next chapter.

The Two-Minute Manager Comes Home

11

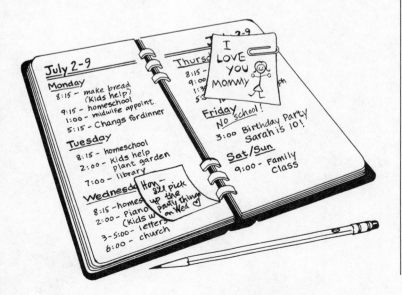

*B*usinessmen love efficiency. So when a book called *The One Minute Manager* came along, they snapped up hundreds of thousands of copies.

A copy of this book traveled home one day with my husband Bill. At the time Bill was working as a manager in a computer systems department. Upper management, in a fit of generosity, had decided to enhance lower management's skills by buying copies for all.

The heart of *The One Minute Manager* was that managers should not farble around with "open door" policies, letting underlings interrupt them at the underlings' pleasure, or waste time in endless conferences and meetings. Nor should they haphazardly slam or reward employees. Instead, the manager should:

(1) Require one-minute goal settings. Each goal should fit on one piece of paper and be readable in less than one minute. The employee had to know up front what was expected of him.

(2) Watch his people closely and either give them (a) one minute of positive feedback ("I really appreciate you tracking down that part for me so quickly") or (b) one minute of explaining what he did wrong ("This is not the part I asked for and it arrived too late anyway, which embarrassed me before the client"), followed by brief, warm encouragement of him as a person and his ability to solve this problem in the future.

Although the complete One Minute Managing system was more complicated than this, of course (which is why you should buy the book for yourself), its main idea was to solve the dilemma caused by pitting "people management" against "results management." An employee was supposed to go out the door of his boss's office feeling that his boss really cared about him and had specific plans for his future.

The young man's face showed surprise. He'd never heard of a One Minute Manager. "You're a what?"

The manager laughed and said, "I'm a One Minute Manager. I call myself that because it takes very little time for me to get very big results from people."

—Kenneth Blanchard and
Spencer Johnson
The One Minute Manager

One-minute managing not only frees the manager from annoying interruptions, but forces him to develop concrete goals for each employee, and if the employee falters, to offer specific suggestions for getting back on target. It also insures that each employee who successfully accomplishes a task can count on at least *one* minute of hearty praise for his work—until he reaches the point of being able to recognize and praise his own accomplishments, at which point he is usually ready to become a One Minute Manager himself.

Introducing the Two-Minute Manager

What does a book on company management have to do with the family? More than you think! You already are a people manager, if you are a married man or a mother.

Most women today have not been taught anything about home *management.* We have been trained to think of ourselves as presiding over the pots or chairing the kitchen chairs, but not to consider ourselves as managers in the corporation sense.

Most husbands and fathers also fail to recognize their home management opportunities. They are not entirely to blame for this. Even our vocabulary disguises the need for managing the family. Our roles as family members are looked at in terms of gooey emotional relationships with no goals other than those based on feelings. The very word *parenting* was invented to replace *child-training,* with its connotations of goals to be reached and the need for management skills.

Let me lay this down as a set of Biblical principles in management language:

(1) The husband is responsible to manage his household. He is his wife's manager, responsible for developing her to reach her godly potential.

(2) The wife is responsible to support and help to implement the husband's godly goals, while taking care of her own sphere of authority.

(3) The father is responsible to manage his children, including training them to become parents, with help from his wife (*not* the other way around!).

(4) The lessons learned at home enable both parents and children to manage greater responsibilities in the church and community. The home is simultaneously a "factory" of finished products—the creative output of its members— and a "training center" for people.

Not that the home is exactly like a corporation. Your household is *harder* to manage than a Wall Street business—at least at first. We can safely say your home management efforts will take twice as long, because of the special nature of home interruptions and the fact that your "employees" are children.

Hence the title of this chapter: "The Two-Minute Manager Comes Home."

In this chapter we will be applying management theory to your home. We will be talking about how to organize projects and how to manage people. In the next chapter we will take this one step farther, and apply your new management skills to the ever-fascinating question of how to start your own home business.

Am I going overboard to apply management theory to the home? No. The Bible quite firmly and clearly outlines the corporate structure of your home—what we now call "family roles." It also explains how those in charge are supposed to exercise their roles, and to what end. Over and over again the ideas of authority, stewardship, and productivity ("fruitfulness") appear on the Bible's pages.

We will now start to seriously examine how you can develop as a Christian leader while making your home productive for Jesus Christ.

The Bottom Line

First, let's ask the Great Business Question: What's the bottom line?

It is said that the bottom line of American business today is making money. This is not the place to discuss whether that bottom line is right or wrong. The fact remains that when a business fails to make more money than it spends, it's history. So company

> A manager can either *overmanage* or *undermanage*. When a manager overmanages, he or she watches each movement a subordinate makes and is almost literally "watching over their shoulder." This is obviously inefficient because *two* people are doing the job that only one should be doing.
>
> A manager can undermanage by not paying enough attention to what a subordinate is doing. The work is simply dumped on the employee and the manager disappears.
>
> —Lin Grensing
> *Office Systems '89*, February

He [John McCormack, "Hottest Entrepreneur in America," founder of the Visible Changes hairdressing chain] views business as a game of great and diverse possibilities, many of which may not be apparent when you start out. That's because you can never predict how much people are capable of doing. Since you can't know the possibilities, you run the risk of missing them if you don't begin with big enough goals.

—Bruce Posner and Bo Burlingham *Inc.*, January 1988

survival turns out to be the real bottom line. Businesses are judged, right or wrong, by whether they

(1) Last, and

(2) Make money.

Paralleling the business experience, many today take "family survival" as the bottom line for a family. Whatever keeps the family together is OK in their thinking. This could include allowing the teen daughter to have overnight dates if she threatens to run away otherwise, or the husband caving in to his wife's unreasonable whims out of fear she may leave.

I suggest that the Scriptural bottom line for a family is to glorify God and enjoy Him as much as possible.

Mission Possible

Now we can talk about the family's mission, as distinct from its bottom line. Every business needs to know its particular mission. Businessmen spend much time agonizing over definitions of their company's missions. The mission of Ben & Jerry's Ice Cream is "To make the best superpremium ice cream in the world." Henry Ford's mission was "To make a reliable car most American families can afford to own." Once the mission is defined, you can at least tell whether you are heading towards or away from that basic goal. You also have a much easier time defining the intermediate goals that will enable you to carry out your mission.

We know the church's mission: to evangelize and disciple the nations. We know the state's mission: to punish evildoers and encourage those who do well, so the church will have a hospitable environment in which to flourish. But what is the family's mission?

Maybe we can get a clue by looking at the family's "product." Every business has a product: clothing or cars or lipstick or typing services. What is the family's?

Children. The only thing the family produces that no other unit of society does is children. Meals, educational services, health services, and other family services can be obtained elsewhere. This is not automatically to say that they all should be obtained elsewhere! I have argued at some length that when the family hands these over to any significant extent it undermines social freedom. However, children remain the one "product" only available from the family. Further, God has specifically commanded parents to "process" this "product," training the children up in the nurture and admonition of the Lord.

Therefore, an important part of the family's mission is bearing children and training them into godly adults.

Roles and Relationships. Does this mean infertile couples or those whose children have grown have no mission? No: for another part of the family's mission is to serve as an example of proper roles and relationships. You and your spouse are meant to provide a living illustration of the relationship between Christ and the church. Older couples have the job of instructing younger couples in how to do this properly, as well as assisting them in their child-bearing-and-training mission.

So the family's mission is twofold: to *illustrate proper roles and loving relationships*, and to *bear children and train them into godly adults*.

The home, in other words, is a hotbed of leadership training! Children are trained to be adults. Adults are trained to be leaders. Those who are leaders become the next generation's trainers.

Special Missions. On top of this, individual families have special missions of their own, as we will see in detail in future chapters. My own family, for example, has a calling to "turn the hearts of the fathers to the children" by helping families find and fulfill their ministries. Both our home business and our Christian ministry reflect that calling. Another family might have a calling to help Christian refugees in South America, and yet another might be hard at work perfecting a family musical show. The Bachs, for example, were definitely called to musicianship!

The genius of his [John McCormack's] setup is that it forces people to decide for themselves whether they want to grow and develop. . . . Those who do, are offered opportunities beyond their wildest dreams.

—Bruce Posner and
Bo Burlingham
Inc., January 1988

All men should aspire to be the kind of men described in 1 Timothy 3, and the home is the place to train them. A man is *not qualified* for leadership in church (or elsewhere) if he is not a successful manager of his own family.

—Pastor Phil Lancaster, MO

THE BIBLICAL CHAIN OF COMMAND

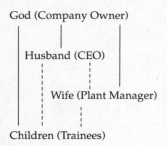

God (Company Owner)

Husband (CEO)

Wife (Plant Manager)

Children (Trainees)

LEGEND:
——— = Direct authority
------ = Delegated authority

Women and Children First. These added-on missions should *never* take the place of the basic mission: showing Christ in our roles and relationships and bearing and raising children. A pastor who neglects his family for the sake of his "calling" is really neglecting his *basic* calling. A missionary who ignores his wife so he can spend more time translating the gospel is failing his most important mission. If a man is called to such strenuous exertions that he has no time for a family, he is called to *celibacy*. Otherwise, the world will see our wretched family lives and apply *that* lesson instead of the one we think we are preaching. Failure to understand this simple truth is perhaps the biggest reason why the nations where Christian missionaries have labored so long almost universally end up humanist or communist.

So here comes management principle number one: First Things First. Make sure your "company" is fulfilling its basic mission before chasing after any others.

People Who Train People

Now let's talk for a minute (oops, I mean *two* minutes) about people management.

Who is in charge of this outfit, anyway?

According to the Bible, it works like this. God, Company Owner. Tarzan, Chief Executive Officer (CEO). Jane, Plant Manager. Boy, Trainee. Not hard to understand. We can also pretty easily see what is wrong when Tarzan and Jane start battling over who should be boss. Alligators hang out below and eat whoever falls out of the tree.

Tarzan has his own problems. Like for instance, what to do when Jane refuses to obey him, or when Boy becomes rebellious and unmotivated. Management literature is full of suggestions on what to do in these situations, some of it even in accord with Biblical principles.

But the literature, until recently, has been less replete with advice for lower managers with upper-management problems. Yet this is the most common issue for wives today.

What can Jane do when Tarzan is wrong-headed? Or, worse, when he refuses to act like a head at all?

TARZAN: Me want spend our life savings on new red Corvette.

JANE: (You fill in the blank)

or . . .

JANE: Boy's teacher says he is falling behind in math and reading . . . He needs new clothes, but there is no money for them in the budget . . . The car is developing problems . . . What should we do?

TARZAN: *You* decide, dear!

How to Keep Your Husband From Becoming a Leader

The modern solution is for Jane to try to become Tarzan. Heap big chiefess! Bang on chest. Oy-ai-ay-ee-ohhhh! We women are trained naturally for this leadership role by our female elementary school teachers and Sunday school teachers and social workers. Talk mean, show your anger, and intimidate the hairy-chested opposition, who still suffers from the lingering conviction that he shouldn't hit back. All he can do is leave . . . and often he does.

Some women like to wear down their men by relentless negotiations and round-table discussions. This is the liberal version of hitting the lord and master over the head with the rolling pin. He learns to flinch every time she opens her mouth.

Others take a lesson from the kids. Whatever their husband decides, they ask him "Why?" For a change of pace, sometimes they ask, "Why not?" No decision goes unchallenged.

And there's the winning-by-intimidation type. She never shows appreciation for any of his decisions or actions that do work out, and constantly reminds him of his failures. To produce a husband like cartoon character Dagwood Bumstead, let his wife Blondie be your model.

Several effective strategies . . . you can use to get *your* hard-to-budge boss moving:

☐ Fathom the fear.
☐ Offer reassurance.
☐ Cater to your boss's decision-making style.
☐ Move fast when you get a go-ahead.
☐ Rally round your goals.
☐ Anticipate second thoughts.

You don't have to change jobs to get free of an indecisive boss. With some careful planning and the right information to back you up, you can give your wishy-washy boss a nudge in the direction you both need to go.

—Melanie LeMay
"Working with a Wishy-Washy Boss"
Executive Female
January/February 1989

Wives, submit to your husbands as to the Lord. For the husband is the head of the wife as Christ is the head of the church, his body, of which he is the Savior. Now as the church submits to Christ, so also wives should submit to their husbands in everything.

Husbands, love your wives, just as Christ loved the church and gave himself up for her to make her holy. . . . In this same way, husbands ought to love their wives as their own bodies. He who loves his wife loves himself. After all, no one ever hated his own body, but he feeds and cares for it, just as Christ does the church—for we are members of his body. . . .

Each one of you also must love his wife as he loves himself, and the wife must respect her husband.

—Ephesians 5:22-32

How to Help Your Husband Be a Head Without Losing Yours

Your man is going to blow it now and then. This is a fact of life, along with the flu season and stockings that run. If you're not perfect, what makes you think he can be?

Now we're going to separate the women from the girls. The question to Jane is, "What do you do when Tarzan is wrong?"

Higher Laws. The answer is, "It depends." Is he asking you to involve yourself in a sin? You note that I said "Involve yourself in a sin," not "Commit a sin." Sometimes not opposing sin is a sin in itself. For example, if your husband decides to pull a Jim Jones routine and feed the family poison, you would be sinning to stand sweetly by and ignore his actions. Your highest responsibility is to Jesus Christ, not your husband. This is the logic behind Operation Rescue and other pro-life direct action missions. If your husband wants to rape and murder, it's your job to foil him, if you can.

We've taken care of $1/10$ of one percent of cases facing women in their families so far. Now let's go for another $1/10$ of a percent: the situation where your husband asks *you* to sin. He wants to practice "Open Marriage," say, which being translated means he wants you to commit adultery with other men so he can buy his right to fool with their wives. Most of us are pretty solid about this. You just say "No" with your actions. Sometimes it may be unnecessarily hazardous to say so with your mouth, so you can legitimately adopt all the evasive maneuvers that Rahab used on the spies of Jericho or the midwives of Israel used on Pharaoh. In this case your husband is in the same category as any other non-Christian persecutor, and can be treated as such.

The Chain of Command. These cases were extreme. Most of our day-to-day conflicts with our husbands revolve around life-or-death matters like whether we should have a Christmas tree this year or who is going to paint the garage. People in the working world have conflicts like this all the time, only they have the benefit of a socially respectable chain of command to resolve them. If the boss says paint, you paint. You aren't considered a doormat for obeying him. You also aren't forbidden to share your reasons for thinking that someone else should do the painting, assuming they are legitimate reasons and that the corporate culture in your company is not so tyrannical that all suggestions are penalized.

The Bible says that we do have a chain of command in the home as well. Just as in the working world, the boss is not necessarily the person most qualified to boss. The plant manager might be brighter, better educated, and socially more astute than the CEO, but the company owner will still take a dim view of the plant manager ignoring the CEO's orders and doing whatever he likes. If the owner wanted the plant manager to be the CEO, he would have made him the CEO.

Jesus Christ is the owner of your family. He decided that husbands should be family heads for reasons that seemed good and sufficient to him, including but not limited to the delicate interplay between male and female that is supposed to illustrate the relationship between Christ and the church. He also decided that wives should be home managers, with a semi-autonomous sphere of authority of our own. The husband is supposed to supervise but not overcontrol the wife's operation at home. Like a good company head, he would be wise to solicit her input before making decisions, and get her consent where possible. There will be times, however, when she will just have to go along with decisions she dislikes. That's real life, and it's no big deal.

The feminists at *Executive Female* print articles about how to deal with bad bosses. They have never yet suggested that you simply shout down the boss and demand your own way, for the very simple reason that it does not work in the workplace.

SOME PARALLELS BE-TWEEN BUSINESS AND MARRIAGE:

☐ Job security produces greater loyalty to the company.
☐ Employees appreciate being given an opportunity to contribute creatively.
☐ Employees respect a boss who is honest and encouraging.
☐ The most satisfied employer is one who knows his employees share his goals.

It doesn't work in the home, either. Moreover, it's foolish and unnecessary. A few good books on management will teach you more about how to get along with a difficult boss (husband) or obstreperous lower manager (wife) than all the marriage books on the market put together. The reason is that businessmen like their businesses to keep going and to make money, whereas the more families fail the better marriage experts like it.

Go a step higher. Some indecisive bosses will move only under pressure from above.

— Melanie LeMay
"Working with a Wishy-Washy Boss"
Executive Female
January/February 1989

What Happens When Women Pray. Now let's look at one technique for influencing upper management I have never see written up in *Executive Female* : Prayer.

The Bible highly endorses prayer as a means for middle management to influence upper management. Your husband is failing to do his job, or interfering with yours? Take it to The Boss. God runs the company. He can, if He finds your case has merit, pass His orders down the line to your husband—who, whether he knows it or not, is answerable to Him.

Karen Rhodes of Virginia shared a wonderful example of how "taking it to the top" really works in a recent issue of *HELP*.

"I have been interested in home schooling for years," Karen said, "but whenever the subject came up, my husband was very negative about it. As the time drew near for our first child to enter school, the discussion grew more vigorous and I began to become quite depressed. I was as sure that it was God's will for us to home school as I was sure of anything, but my husband said, 'We are *never* going to do that. You might as well get it out of your head.'

"I began to wonder why God would give this conviction to me but not to my husband, and then tell me to be submissive! I began to feel that God had aimed His bolt of conviction at my husband and missed!

"Finally I had to say to God, 'I believe you want us to do this, but I cannot convince or nag my husband into this, so if it is really your will, you must convict him of it.'

"Then I told my husband, 'I believe home schooling is what God wants, but you are the leader of our family and God speaks through you—so you decide how our kids should be educated. I will go along with whatever you decide.' And I meant it—I felt I could get to know his teachers personally, visit his classroom, work with him at home, etc., if it came to that.

"But once I said that to my husband, it *freed him* to stop arguing with me and really seek out answers. Once I stopped doing so much talking, he could hear the voice of God telling us to home school. He is now a committed home schooler, and cannot even remember being against it! He takes a big part in teaching our son, and I learned a lesson in faith and waiting upon the Lord."

Getting the Kids on Your Team

I am really tempted to say something about how well prayer works for husbands, too—but I'll let Bill say it all in his book on family management for husbands, which I hope he will write someday! Let's just move quickly to the real test of management strategy: kids.

Again, let's start by getting our goals straight. If all we really want is for the kids to go away and stop bothering us, that can be arranged. Just buy them a houseful of toys and spend a fortune on babysitters and, later, psychiatrists. But if we are serious about wanting them to end up as godly adults, that means we will have to do some serious training.

A well-organized household, by definition, has family members who act like a team. This does not come about by accident.

Businesses spend millions of dollars studying how to get their employees to practice teamwork. The key is to get the workers to "own" the goal—to care about reaching it. So the question facing moms and dads everywhere is clear: how do we get our children to act like members of a family instead of guests in a hotel?

When other women in my church look at my life they often say . . . HOW DO YOU DO IT? They don't realize how much help I have from my family and how long it took me to learn how to do what I do now. If you asked my husband what our house looked like when I had only two or three children, he would probably roll his eyes and hope he didn't have to remember too clearly! Our house spent weeks at a time looking like the health department could close it down. It took me years to learn how to prioritize work, to get rid of things that had to be cleaned but added little to the hominess of our house, and very importantly, to have children who were old enough to really give me help in tangible ways. A two-year-old who can set the table is nice, but a thirteen-year-old who can single-handedly (and voluntarily) scrub the bathroom from top to bottom is worth rubies and gold!

—Kim Jeffery, PA

173

Discipline is Habit-Forming. Kids are wonderful. But, like the rest of us, they are born with a sin nature. This means that they will fight furiously against what they really want at times, and want what they really shouldn't at others. Providentially, they are small enough upon arrival so that the energy they throw into rebelling can be easily diverted into productivity without too much trauma. If, that is, you know how to handle it.

So we arrive at that dreaded word: Discipline. The Bible says that if you discipline your son he will give you rest in the end, strongly implying what it says straight out in other places, that if you *don't* discipline him he will give you hullaballoo.

Discipline means instruction in a habit of righteousness. Today we tend to confuse it with physical punishment, which indeed is part of the process but is not the whole story. You want the whole story? Here it is, as best we can figure it out after years of child-training, and with the help of a few thousand other Christian parents: Discipline is promptly *encouraging what is good* and *punishing what is bad while encouraging the offender to do better* in such a way as to *instill the habit* of doing good and avoiding evil.

To this end, we have to carefully explain about good and evil—laying down the law at first to little ones, and giving more reasoned explanations as they mature.

After they have received God's law and our family rules, they are responsible to obey. Here is where a lot of parents fall down two ways:

■ Not promptly punishing *all* infractions. This encourages kids to gamble on your sluggishness and try to get away with things. Tipoff: You find yourself giving orders twice or more often, or raising your voice, or making threats. Even more obvious tipoff: The kids are driving you bats. If the children don't obey an order the first time it is given, you have to get up from your easy chair and deal with the culprits.

■ Not promptly encouraging good behavior. How easy this is to forget! Our attention is much more readily drawn to Suzy dropping her green beans on the dining room floor than it is to Suzy quietly sitting there eating all her green beans without being told. As uncomfortable as it makes some of us, it is our duty as parents to commend Suzy when she does well.

Now, some hints about how to do the punishing and encouraging.

Punishment That Instructs. When it comes to rebelliousness and foolishness, you have no choice. The Bible says to spank. But kids do lots of things that don't fall into these two categories. For example: Johnny gets into Tommy's room and busts his prize airplane model. Unless you told Johnny not to go into Tommy's room three seconds ago, this action was not primarily rebellious. It was mean, not foolish. Here another Scriptural principle applies: restitution. Johnny will have to either fix the model or buy a replacement. If he can't do either, Tommy can suggest some alternative way Johnny can make it up to him. If Johnny is utterly unable to make any kind of restitution, only then need you fall back on spanking.

What about a child who constantly misuses his toys, breaking them or losing them? Here the Scriptural principle in the parable of the talents applies. He who does not make use of what he has loses it. In this case, the parents can remove their child's toys to the attic for a while, or in extreme cases give them away, until he learns to appreciate them.

You can develop your own list of Scriptural principles for punishing sins from a study of the Bible laws and another study of how God, as a father, deals with His children. You will find God using all sorts of punishments perfectly suited to the crime, from withholding eye contact (the "light of his countenance") to letting the glutton have what he wants (enough to make him sick) to severe hidings. The design of each

Fathers, do not exasperate your children; instead, bring them up in the training and instruction of the Lord.

—Ephesians 6:4

Fathers, do not embitter your children, or they will become discouraged.

—Colossians 3:21

In June I ordered and received Richard Fugate's book *What the Bible Says About Child-Training.* I read it and my husband has been reading it aloud to the kids once a week. We're re-establishing physical discipline—spankings for the older boys (we had rarely spanked after age ten and tried to use other forms of discipline) for disrespect, foul language, physical fighting, lying, and defiance. I feel if we'd had the book a year ago, we'd probably still be home schooling. However, in the past, I've usually been the one to try to get my husband not to spank the children and use some other form of discipline instead. You can see the poor results. . . .

—R.H.

We have found that spanking a child through a tantrum to the point of grief is a relief for the child. This is not for the purpose of venting my own irritation (which I have done), but to reassure *them* that when their rage is boiling over and they can't control it, Mom can reestablish order and peace.

I think parents are mistaken when they merely spank a child until he/she is infuriated. When I have spanked to the point of grief (which is extremely draining to me) you know what? The child is happy after the tears are kissed away. When I haven't done this, I only want to get *away* from my child (the ultimate form of hatred).

Discipline that consisted of spanking alone would be a crime, of course!

Another area: sharing. We don't make our children share. We have few personal toys for them—mostly group stuff. Sharing enforced by me is usually to relieve my ears of the screaming done by the younger child. I've robbed the older child of the job inherent in spontaneous sharing.

—Kathy von Duyke, DE

punishment is to correct the sinner for his own good, not to vent your anger, even though you, like God, are allowed to be angry and say so.

One last word on this subject: punishment is for *sins*, not for normal childishness. Toilet-training failures, bedwetting, and a certain amount of forgetfulness are unavoidable parts of growing up. Every year a few pitiable children are beaten to death, usually by the mother's live-in boyfriend, for inability to potty on command. Your child might not understand what you are saying or may be physically incapable of consistently obeying. Be *very* sure that your child understands your command (hint: have him repeat it back to you) and that he is *consistently* capable of doing what you ask before punishing him for failing.

Encouragement. I come from Massachusetts, and we Yankees don't believe in praising people. We don't trust people who smile too much. We tend to assume all encouraging words are flattery until proven innocent. So it wasn't until I ran across a tape series by Robert Doman, head of the National Academy of Child Development, called *The Miracles of Child Development*, that I ever realized how much children need praise.

Without endorsing every single thing on those tapes I can honestly say Mr. Doman was absolutely right about insisting that parents should praise their children. Think of it. Who wants to stay in a negative environment? If all your children ever hear from you is, "Cut that out. You're being bad. Why don't you ever do this? Why do you do that?" the kids in the school drug clique are going to look pretty good in comparison.

Our homes should be our kids' favorite place to be. If we are warm and encouraging, they will be.

Mr. Doman shared another valuable thought in that series. He talked about praising kids with *frequency*, *intensity*, and *duration*. Frequency, of course, is how often you do it. Intensity is how strongly you do it. Duration is how long you do it. Of the three, intensity is the most important. You can throw out praise frequently, but if it sounds like you are bored or not really thinking about it, it won't do much good.

Two more things I will mention that I don't recall Mr. Doman saying:

- Kids can tell the difference between honest praise and flattery.
- Furthermore, praise is not the same as encouragement. Encouragement means telling children how they could do better when needed and remarking upon their accomplishments whenever honesty allows. You are trying to instill confidence and a desire to do better.

Rewards That Motivate. Policy analyst Charles Murray, in his wonderful book *In Pursuit of Happiness and Good Government,* includes a chapter on enjoyment, self-motivation, and intrinsic rewards. Citing the research on what kind of rewards motivate people, Murray points out that

- Enjoyment is directly related to an appropriate amount of challenge. If a job is too easy, it's boring. If too hard, it causes worry and anxiety. The major researcher in this field knocks enjoyment down to three elements: "a feeling of creative discovery, a challenge overcome, a difficulty resolved."[1]
- The kind of motivation that allows people to enjoy their work gives information about how well the job was done while allowing them to do the job creatively. Rewarding people for *how* a job is done (as opposed to *how well* it is done) undermines motivation. Perfectionist rewards that always push the worker to work harder next time also sap motivation, as do rewards not based on the value of the work (e.g., paying children to solve jigsaw puzzles).

Forgetting to praise your child discourages him and can lead to fatal bitterness. The Bible warns fa-

Countenance everything that is good and praise-worthy in your children and servants. It is as much your duty to commend and encourage those in your family that do well, as to reprove and admonish those that do amiss; and if you take delight only in blaming that which is culpable, and are backward to praise that which is laudable, you give occasion to suspect something of an ill nature, not becoming a good man, much less a good Christian. . . . Most people will be easier led than driven, and we all love to be spoken fair. . . . Smile upon them when you see them set their faces heavenwards, and take the first opportunity to let them know you observe it, and are well pleased with it, and do not despise the day of small things. . . . Let them have the praise of it, for you have the comfort of it, and God must have all the glory. Draw them with the cords of a man, hold them with the bands of love; so shall your rebukes, when they are necessary, be the more acceptable and effectual.

—Matthew Henry
"A Church in the Home:
A Sermon Concerning
Family-Religion"

To date, the only combination of rewards and feedback that seems to improve intrinsic motivation over the baseline condition of no reward at all and no feedback at all is performance-based extrinsic rewards (rewards that depend not only upon doing the task, but upon how well it is done) plus information feedback.

—Charles Murray
In Pursuit of Happiness and Good Government

Observation: Intellectual parents tend to reward intelligence regardless of how it is handed to them—even when it is clothed in deceitfulness. Overwhelmed parents tend to make as few standards as possible so as not to have to hold themselves accountable to follow up with discipline. We must always bear in mind that the parents' behavior is on trial as much as the child's.

—Laurie Sleeper, WA

thers that they are particularly prone to this sin (Colossians 3:21).

Praising a child dishonestly destroys his judgment and endangers his soul (Romans 12:3, Proverbs 29:5). Mothers frequently fall into this trap.

You want to aim for the golden mean—giving your children honest, loving feedback on how they are doing.

Celebrating Achievement. Beware of playing carrot-and-stick with goals that are dropped for new ones the second a child reaches them. How to tell if you are overpressuring your child: When was the last time you celebrated one of his accomplishments? Achievements *should* be recognized, and if they never are, it's time to change. We go so far as to throw a family party when one of our children finishes a grade of home school. Lesser ceremonies uplift lesser occasions. An unexpected present of a typewriter when your son learns to type, or a beautiful storybook when your daughter learns to read, go a long way to enlisting your children on God's team. Even just a word of praise and a loving look when your child is trying hard helps him a lot to keep going.

Try this for a while. Whenever your children are being good, tell them you have noticed it and that you appreciate it. Avoid coupling your praise with exhortations to do "even better"; dwell on what was achieved, not on what you hope will be achieved next time. At first, if you have not done this before, they may act embarrassed, but after a while they will begin to obviously enjoy it.

This is not a manual on how to solve deep-seated problems of teenage rebellion that have been fed and watered for fifteen or sixteen years. Even so, a little consistently unselfish encouragement of the good and punishment of the bad goes a long way. If your kids can believe you really are training them *for God's sake and not your own*, they will feel like part of the team and not part of the opposition. The key is to be honest with God and them. Admit your failures and ask forgiveness, but don't go too far and start groveling. Your ultimate goal must be the good of their souls, not the pleasure of their company, or you will only be allowed to enjoy the pleasure of their company on very degrading terms.

How Our Own Family Does It

We have combined the children's need for training with our need for help. I still almost never pick up any of their toys. Whoever messes up, picks up—down to the one-year-old (he loves it!). Ted (age nine) does the dishes and Sarah (age five) sets the table. Joseph (age seven) vacuums the kitchen and loves to clean the bathrooms —the appeal of the squirt bottles, no doubt! They all help with baby-watching (I am nearby, of course). When Magda was two, she even took off her own diaper in the morning, wiped up, and changed into her training pants! Now that the children are so responsible, my domestic workload is actually *less* than before I had children!

Earn and Learn. Now . . . how do we get them to do all this? Do we beat and threaten them? Well, we *have* been known to spank when someone absolutely refused to do his or her job. But that is unusual. Following the business principle that "the worker is worthy of his hire" we have instead a family system of pay and praise. Nobody gets paid for cleaning up after himself; however, actual work not of the child's own making does get paid. We don't subsidize not-working with an allowance that gets paid regardless of the child's output, but we recognize his or her labor as valuable. We often schedule small tasks just before mealtime or some other desired activity and announce that we will eat (or whatever) when the job is finished. And, speaking of motivation, pay is *doubled* for work done with a cheerful attitude (!!!).

I try to pay fair wages, e.g., less than I would have had to pay an outsider, but not completely ridiculous wages like 5¢ for washing a whole family's dishes. Ted has already earned enough to purchase a used

I don't make charts, stars, and all that. We have work periods—a big one before school, before dinner, and before bed. Some afternoons are times to *learn* a job. The kids do what I ask in those periods—if I forget something I make a note of it for the next time period. I keep a chart of chore needs in my notebook so I don't forget stuff.

I don't get paid for making my bed—my children need to know that work is part of everyday living. My son who just turned eight has earned a lot of money outside the home, saved it in a bank account, and is trying to think of a business idea. He has my admiration! I think that is the best incentive I can give him.

For poor attitudes about chores—we do not spank. This is childishness, not rebellion. They get *more chores.* That way they have more opportunities to practice having a good attitude!

—Kathy von Duyke, DE

I trained the children how to post Accounts Receivable, etc., and I even paid them extra for doing this. None of ours had an allowance. Our youngest, now twenty-two, tells me this allowance idea does not teach how to manage money—"It just teaches you how to spend without working for it!"

—Martha Pugacz, OH

HOW TO DELEGATE

☐ Each task should be clearly defined.
☐ Find the right person for
   the job.
☐ Provide careful instruction.
☐ Make sure subordinates
   understand what they're
   being asked to do.
☐ Follow up.
☐ Never stifle employees.
☐ Never delegate just the
   "dirty work."
                    —Lin Grensing
       Office Systems '89, February

See how pertinent manage-
ment theory is to
child-training?

electric typewriter (his own choice). Joe doesn't have that much, since he has been fined at times for destroying things (usually in fits of creativity, like the time he cut holes in his brand-new wool blanket so he could pretend it was a tent and look out of it. . . . That time he wasn't fined, but he has to live with that holey blanket for a while!). The little ones pick up on the older ones' example. I have noticed each child starting to help picking up at an earlier age.

Cheerfulness. I have also always made a special effort to be cheerful about my work. Consequently, the boys could hardly wait to learn to do the dishes and mop the floors. When it's housecleaning time, everyone around here is working, even our just-barely two-year-old, who can be spied valiantly plying the vacuum wand amid the chair-leg forest in the eating area.

All of this energy disappears when adults really dislike the work they are doing. Then kids start sneaking out the back door to avoid being trapped into it themselves. That is why it is *so* important to avoid complaining about your chores.

Make Chores a Game. Besides exhibiting a cheerful attitude, we also try to make work a game (play basketball with the rolled-up socks and the laundry basket after folding the clothes), and stay on top of inspecting and rewarding it. Refusing to enforce your orders is always fatal, and causes much more stress and unquiet. "Discipline your son, and he will give you peace" (Proverbs 29:17).

All we have done is take Biblical management principles and apply them to our home. It's Biblical to make work into a game, doing it "heartily as unto the Lord." It's Biblical to inspect the children's work and reward them if it is done well, or assign more training if it is not. It's Biblical to be cheerful about our own work and never assign a task we wouldn't be willing to pitch in and help with (if needed) ourselves. It's especially Biblical to frequently share our goals with the children and thank them for helping us reach them.

Our children know that someday they will be adults with (God willing) children of their own. We are trying to help them become excellent at their future jobs, and they know it. Because we take our fatherhood and motherhood very seriously, they know we are preparing them for something very important. It's not all that odd that they should cooperate with us.

The more important you can feel your home calling is, the more seriously the children will take it, assuming they are not immersed in counterchristian culture.

You will know you have succeeded as a Two-Minute Manager on the day your children start bringing you *their* ideas about how to reach your family goals. And what could inspire them more to have ideas than a nice little family business of your own—as we'll see in the next chapter.

A Nice Little
Family Business

12

*L*et's talk business. *Real* business—Your Family, Inc. We've looked at investment strategies that prepare you for independence. We've looked at how to develop your personal skills and knowledge. We've even seen how you can improve your management skills and shape the whole family into a productive team. It's time now to put it all together into a family business and ministry of your very own.

"Wait a minute! What's this about family business and ministry getting mixed together?" I had a reason for putting them together like that. We are not going to talk about family business in conventional terms: what type of business will make the most money. Instead, we are going to resurrect the ancient Christian concept of your *calling*, or as it is sometimes known nowadays, your *ministry*.

Opportunity Calling

Our Christian forefathers believed that God loved His people and that He had a wonderful plan for each of His children's lives. (Sound familiar?) They believed in the verse in Ephesians that says we are "God's workmanship, created in Christ Jesus to do good works, which God prepared in advance for us to do" (Ephesians 2:10). In other words, God has some special work just lined up waiting for you and your family to do it!

Today we tend to equate that special work God has prepared for us with some church function we can fulfill. Our fathers and mothers, though, didn't limit God's special work to church offices. They spoke of a person's *calling* instead of his "job" or "career." The idea was that God has gifted us each in unique ways and has also chosen the best way for each of us to use his or her gifts. Our job is to find out God's plan—our calling—and follow it faithfully.

THE FREEDOM CHART

E — Master/Mistress
F
F — Contractor
O
R — Hired Servant
T
— Slave

(EFFORT arrow pointing up)

IT TAKES EFFORT TO RISE, BUT IT'S WORTH IT!

THE FREEDOM CYCLE

1. HIDDEN ART develops skills
2. CALLING emerges
3. INVESTMENT
    + diligence
    + prayer
    REWARD
4. INDEPENDENCE
5. BLESS OTHERS

Sounds good, but how do you do it? If you want to start immediately without going through any preliminary steps, I admit you have a tough row to hoe. But once you have followed the steps of the Omega Strategy, put in your Cinderella apprenticeship, and absorbed the lessons of the Two-Minute Manager, your family's special business and ministry will emerge *naturally*.

Let me explain how this works. Take a look at the Freedom Cycle chart on the left. You will note that the first step is labeled "Hidden Art" in honor of Edith Schaeffer's book by that name. She first opened our eyes to the idea of doing the humble things of life with zest as an offering to the Lord. Her book is a marvelous idea-generator for how to do such things as gardening, decorating, cooking, and hospitality "unto the Lord."

By doing the humble work God gives you as well as you can, you cultivate the skills for your business. You also give God a reason to open the door of opportunity for you. Remember, opportunities are not the product of either chance or of diligent effort. *God* is the one who decides whether to open or shut the door of opportunity. And God's rule is to give to the person who is already making the best use of what he has. "For everyone who has will be given more, and he will have an abundance. Whoever does not have, even what he has will be taken from him" (Matthew 25:29).

To use one very personal example: I always loved to read while I was growing up. One of my first desires was to be a writer. But I always heard that only tremendously talented people could become authors, and authors never made any money, and besides you had to suffer through years of far-out liberal arts courses, etc. Besides, I had nothing to write *about* (a major problem!).

Years later, as a young Christian, I found myself desperately wanting to express the truth of Christianity to various friends and loved ones. Just at this point I read *Hidden Art* for the first time. Mrs. Schaeffer was quite forceful with her advice to would-be writers. "Write letters. Rewrite those letters until you think they say what you are really trying to say. Decorate your letters with art and other personal touches. Write letters to the editor. Don't think you have to wait to write a book! Write *little* things, the things at hand." That was the essence of her advice, and I took it. I would write, and rewrite, and re-rewrite letter after letter, mostly to people who never wrote back.

Then I started seeing magazine articles discussing the death of motherhood, and suddenly I had something to write about! I followed Mrs. Schaeffer's advice again, writing letters to the editor and gradually working my way up to an article or two.

I read books on writing and did all the exercises. Eventually I wrote a book, and it got published. So did other books. Then Bill, who had been learning a lot about the writing and editing process as I went through it, came out with *his* first book. Now our family income is mostly derived from the business of writing—a business some would say we fell into, but that we can see we were *led* into when we tried to be faithful in the "little things."

I must emphasize that not everyone who tries to write good letters ends up writing a book. Neither has my effort to bake good bread ever turned into a home baking business. The point is that while you are trying to become excellent at everything you do, one of your tasks will emerge as your calling.

Choosing Your Calling

OK. You prepare for your calling by hidden art, doing the little things faithfully and well. So how do you figure out what your calling *is?*

Here's a little test to discover your family's calling.

■ *What do you like to do best?* List as many things as you can think of, even those that don't at first blush seem to have much socially redeeming value (like playing soccer) or much money-making potential (like eating cookies).

It's not the number of your employees or your title that makes you free, but your

☐   Time
☐   Control, and
☐   Flexibility.

187

Q: I could also use some help in how to schedule time for a home business. I'd like to do sewing, but feel like it may be more than I can handle. How to involve the family?

A: If you have four kids, ages nine to two, you don't *need* a home business! I know . . . I have one! Maybe a better idea would be for the kids to start *their* own business. It keeps them busy and happy, is good character training, and you can serenely supervise and advise without contending with extra deadlines of your own.

■ *What are you best at?* Be honest. If this part is hard to answer, go back to the Cinderella chapter and try, try again!

■ *What bothers you the most?* What are you always complaining about and wondering why someone doesn't do something about it?

Question Three really tells the tale. Almost everybody thinks the best way to find a business is to assess your skills and likes and pick something based on those. That's a fine way to be comfortable and selfish, but no way to find your ministry. The way to find the business that is your calling is to ask, "What is burning inside me? What do I want to change or improve? What drives me crazy?"

You see, the reason you are wondering why everyone else is so selfish/ignorant/apathetic/or whatever about the issue burning in your heart is that God has given this issue to *you*, not to them. You can either spend your time complaining about it, or get to work doing something about it.

This applies just as well, by the way, to more traditional church ministries. If the lack of a family Sunday school class drives you nuts, try to figure out how you could make such a class possible. If it's impossible to get your kids from a late Sunday lunch to an early Sunday supper and they are always starving during the evening service, perhaps this is a signal for you to volunteer to prepare light snacks that people could eat before evening service so they could afford to have a leisurely supper at home afterward. If you can't understand why your suburban church doesn't have a ministry to the inner city, it's probably because you are the only one whose cultural background qualifies you to start up that ministry. Do what you can to help something good happen, without condemning everyone else who isn't doing the same thing you are, and suddenly people who used to duck when they saw you coming will be anxious to help!

The Gripe List

☐ What do you LOVE?
☐ What BUGS you?

Most of us have gripe lists, whether we are aware of them or not. The difference is that few of us take the initiative to do something about them. For example, here are a few of my gripes:

■ Why can't I find a modest swimsuit?
■ Why does most clothing for children feature ads for cartoon characters or media idols?
■ Why do I have to get so much junk mail?
■ Why is newspaper coverage so slanted against Christian causes?
■ Why are houses so expensive?
■ Why is it so hard to find information about home-schooling programs and resources?

Turn it around, and you have a list of family businesses.

■ Modest swimwear. This could expand into a whole line of modest clothing, as fashion gets weirder.
■ Simple clothes for kids without those idiotic ads all over them. This is the premise of the very successful Hanna Anderson clothing company.
■ A mail-sorting service for people who hate junk mail. This may be hard to pull off, but I know of at least one person who'd sign up!
■ *World* magazine and its associated children's newsweeklies are an example of a response to someone's heartburn over the mainstream media's attitudes and coverage.
■ Innovative architectural design, engineering, and components design are all possible answers to the problem of expensive housing. We had to search and search in our area for a builder whose houses were large enough for our family and whose price was small enough for the same. Lots of other people appear to be searching for the same thing, judging by this family-owned firm's success.
■ The last gripe actually led to our own home business. I started buying and analyzing educational materials for the sake of my own children, and this grew into what will soon be five books on

ALL THE WAY HOME

For we are God's workman-
ship, created in Christ Jesus
to do good works, which
God prepared in advance for
us to do.

—Ephesians 2:10

*GOD HAS A SPECIAL JOB
FOR YOUR FAMILY!*

home schooling and home-schooling resources,
plus a bimonthly magazine column.

You see how the principle works. Write down the
problems, but don't quit there. Go on to the next step
and start *brainstorming some answers.*

Don't forget to pray for insight, especially insight
into whether this is "your" problem or not!

Directions for Your Calling

At this point it helps to be aware of the different
directions your calling could take.

In her excellent book *Homemade Money*, Barbara
Brabec lists four different kinds of home businesses.

(1) Products you make yourself. This includes
products whose manufacture you farm out to others.
Examples include paintings, crafts, food, kits, patterns, newsletters, and clothes. You stock the inventory, usually, although sometimes the manufacturer will
hold inventory for you.

(2) Products made by others.

    (a) You buy wholesale and resell. Example:
        books. You keep an inventory.

    (b) You take orders only. Inventory expenses
        are minimal; usually just a sample kit. Ex-
        amples: Discovery Toys® party hostessing.

(3) Services sold to individuals. Example: hairdressing.

(4) Services sold to business. These tend to be
more highly paid. Example: computer typesetting.

Mrs. Brabec's listing goes on to include services
that you can sell *from* your home, but not *in* your
home. These fall into the same categories: "to individuals" or "to business." These are not appropriate
businesses for a mother, but might be fine for a husband's venture.

**Advantages and Disadvantages of Different Types
of Businesses.** All the business categories above are not
created equal. When you can, *you are much better off creating and marketing your own product* than reselling other
people's goods. The reason is that out of each $1 the

customer pays, you have to pay the wholesaler around 50-60¢, and even more (usually) when dealing with high-ticket items. When you manufacture an item yourself, your only cost is for its ingredients and your labor. Even when you farm out manufacturing, you can expect to pay only about twenty percent or less of the end-user's price, assuming you set a wise price.

Services, in contrast to products, have usually very little overhead. You have no inventory costs, except for the few supplies you need to provide your service. They are easy to start up also, requiring little advance capital. This explains why service businesses are among the fastest-growing areas of the economy. Service businesses depend much more on the uniqueness and quality of your skills, though.

Sales. Now you have to decide how you are going to sell what you are offering. This comes as a rude shock to many people who picture themselves idyllically ruminating over their favorite hobbies with money raining down on them from the skies. But the unvarnished truth is that *all* businesses are in the business of selling. No matter what you create, it's not a business until someone buys it, and nobody's going to buy it unless you tell them about it.

The reason why canny business owners as a rule of thumb price their products at five or even eight times what it costs to produce is that they know they will have to spend several times the price of the product on locating customers who might want that product. People who don't know this, but misguidedly feel they should serve their customers by selling their wares at just a smidgin more than it costs to make them, quickly go out of business, thus depriving their customers of *all* their products!

Focused advertising, in contrast to mass-market advertising, does not attempt to create new wants but to let people who might be interested in your product know what you offer. If they don't know you offer it, they can't buy it.

Your choices are:

Owners of businesses have more kinds of incomes. They have wage income, which is many times higher than that of the average wage earner [ed. note—*sometimes!*] and they also have dividend income. Then, they have another advantage: In periods of economic growth, they enjoy large profits that may be used for further capital investment, which will provide additional profits at a later time.

Workers, whether blue- or white-collar, have only one income source: wages.

—Jerry Mander
Four Arguments for the Elimination of Television

One of the great advantages in starting up a mail-order business is that you *can* start part-time. . . .

Furthermore, it is usually *wise* to start part-time. . . .

And you have an *advantage* if you start part-time. . . . One of the most important skills in mail order is to be able to move fast on the basis of skimpy evidence. Part-time operators don't need to move so fast, and therefore they can move more surely.

—Julian Simon
How to Start and Operate a Mail-Order Business

■ Retail sales direct to consumers. If you are serious about having a *home* business, such sales opportunities are not great, except by telephone. Exception: Rural home businesses in well-traveled areas, where you can hang out a shingle for customers.

■ Mail-order sales. Mail-order is great for home business, but requires that you either write good advertising copy yourself and deal frequently with printers or find someone to do these chores for you. Julian Simon's *How to Start and Operate a Mail-Order Business* is considered the Bible of mail order. It explains how to handle every aspect of mail order professionally.

■ Wholesale sales. You sell to distributors (whether local shops or national catalogs) and they take care of selling individual items to consumers. You can wholesale to local shops, like the noble wife in Proverbs 31, or you can try wholesaling to national distributors. The latter type of wholesaling is a high-flying business typically involving trips to trade shows and calls on major customers. You can hire a sales rep to do this work, but you had better not consider this route unless you have a mass-market product and major capital behind you.

Switch-Hitting. You can switch back and forth between sales styles, just as you can switch back and forth between offering products and services. Often your business experience leads you to develop expertise in an area you would never have considered a year earlier.

Our first home business venture was a little spiral-bound home-school curriculum buyer's guide. We promoted it through offering review copies to state home-schooling organizations. These told readers of their newsletters where to buy it and how much it cost. By these means, we were able to sell about 700 copies. The rest we wholesaled to a friend with a ministry to home schoolers, who sold them at retail.

Emboldened by this success we put together a small list of books, lined up accounts with publishers and wholesalers, and copied off some sheets offering these books. When I look now at the dot-matrix print, not at all improved by copying, I am surprised that anyone ordered from us. But we kept on merrily sending brochures out to small mailing lists of our kind of customers, and the orders kept trickling in.

Our next step was a nicer computer and printer. We started producing much fancier brochures, mailing more often, and getting bigger orders. The business still was nothing anyone else would get excited about, but we were having the time of our lives. I would enter and fill orders on our computer accounting system, and Bill and I would talk over business strategy in the evenings after he came home from work.

Around this time I started writing for a few magazines, and took my pay in free advertising in the magazines and their associated card decks. The trickle of orders was becoming a stream by now, so we moved up to a bigger computer with a laser printer. Our copywriting and design had improved quite a bit; we had a catalog and a newsletter to practice on.

Next came the big step: Bill came home. The business was showing real promise, enough to justify his full attention. At first we felt every day like we were going to go under, but we stuck at it and the Lord blessed us. Now our business, Home Life, although not setting any world records, makes as much as Bill's old job. Home Life has also bought us a good chunk of equipment, each item of which is a multitude of potential businesses, should times get worse. And Bill is following his calling, instead of just earning money working for someone else.

Why Wait?

So you've decided on a calling and a direction for that calling. After that, the next step is spelled w-a-i-t. Don't rush off half-cocked to save the world. Sit on your idea a bit and see if it hatches. The devil is the

As many as ten million people operate home businesses now, according to IRS figures, and the U.S. Labor Department predicts that half the American work force could be working at home in 10-15 years.

—Barbara Brabec
Homemade Money

193

one who likes to get us rushing wildly about without forethought, not the Lord. "God is not the author of confusion, but of peace" (1 Corinthians 14:33).

As a general rule, we like to wait before making *any* business decision. If the great deal will evaporate if you don't sign up this very second, *don't sign.* God can and will hold the deal for you if it is really that great. You show your trust in Him by giving Him the chance to veto it.

We have never regretted taking the time to calm down and pray through things, but we have had several occasions to regret "great" deals put together in haste.

Take the time between your choice of a business and your entry into that business to master the books listed in Resources for this chapter. Consider subscribing to a home business newsletter as well. These will open your eyes to the real processes involved in business: research, invention, purchasing, learning to use new equipment, manufacture, inventory control, pricing, promotion, sales, fulfillment, accounting, hiring (maybe), and managing. Barbara Brabec's book covers most of these areas, but you will have to get a few more to fill in the gaps. Not that you have to perfectly master everything about business before going into business; but it does help to know where to find the answers!

How to Succeed in Family Business

You have found your calling. You have a product or service you are eager to offer the world. You have discovered this product or service by the God-ordained route of faithfully doing the little jobs that come your way every day. You have boned up on business skills. Now what?

Here come the business experts. They will tell you what to do. "Mortgage your house and leverage the debt." "Make the rounds of your friends and family and line up capital for your venture." "Put together a business plan and try to interest venture capitalists." "Run market tests, set up an ad campaign, and plan for national roll-out ASAP." "Go for it!"

Can you tell what is wrong with this advice?

I'll give you a hint. Here's a Bible verse: "He who gathers money little by little makes it grow" (Proverbs 13:11). Here's another one: "A stingy man is eager to get rich and is unaware that poverty awaits him" (Proverbs 28:22). Here's another: "Do not wear yourself out to get rich; have the wisdom to show restraint" (Proverbs 23:4).

Forget the headlong rush toward wealth promoted in the business magazines. Your first step is not lining up OPM (other people's money) or even YOM (your own money). You are not going to zoom out into the market, make a killing, and cash out. Not if you do it God's way, that is!

You are going to . . .

- grow slow
- be generous
- and reinvest in your business.

Slow But Steady Wins the Race. "Cast but a glance at riches, and they are gone, for they will surely sprout wings and fly off to the sky like an eagle" (Proverbs 23:5). Your business plan should not gamble on quick profits. You are not trying to jump in and grab fifty percent market share, elbowing out all the competition. Instead, like a Christian, you are going to look for *what is not being done* or *what is being done badly* and take that as your niche.

Let's talk a bit more about this subject of business competition. Today's business world looks like some surrealistic war zone. Company gobbles up company, while business leaders swarm like piranhas to fasten onto any business that shows signs of faltering. The sign of great executive leadership is knocking a competitor out of the marketplace and throwing several thousands of people out of work. The way to the top is littered with the broken dreams of other men and the broken bank accounts of their former employees.

Some companies do deserve to die, and in a robust economy workers can get new jobs. But breaking a competitor for the sheer joy of winning a war game is

Do not wear yourself out to get rich; have the wisdom to show restraint.
—Proverbs 23:4

The goal is not WEALTH, but FREEDOM

not a Christian way to do business. Growth is not to be pursued for its own sake at the expense of others.

The Bible warns us not to get into this kind of competition. "Better a little with the fear of the Lord than great wealth with turmoil" (Proverbs 15:16).

Since you aren't trying to hog some huge profitable market, you have a much better chance of being left alone and allowed to grow. The better you do your job, meanwhile, the less incentive anyone will have to raid your territory.

Superfast growth is usually funded by cancerous debt. Expect to see a lot of today's fast-growth companies go down the tubes when the next recession hits. If you're smart, yours won't be among them.

Remember the childhood song: "There were ten in the bed and the little one said Roll Over." Start small with whatever you have on hand and roll over your profits to finance more growth. This is the way to get a kitchen-table business growing and keep it going.

Be Generous. If you forget the poor and needy, God will forget you. Take care: it can happen quicker than you think when you get immersed in pursuing growth (Matthew 13:22).

Reinvest in Your Business. If all you want to do is cash out and go lie on a beach for the rest of your life, why start a company? Hop on the next flight to Waikiki and go straight to work as a beachcomber. If, like most of us in our saner moments, you would like to go on being useful to God and man, reinvest most of your share of the profits back in your company. Don't spend it all on promoting your goods and services to new markets, either. Invest in making your product and service better. This not only satisfies customers and enhances your word-of-mouth reputation, but discourages any piranhas that might be floating about.

Employees. Employees are not an issue for the vast majority of home business startups. If you do need extra help, try:

Almost everything in the market now is short-term in its orientation. It is a reflection of a society that thrives on immediate gratification. . . .

All of this buying, selling, and dumping to create ups and downs has its effects not only on the small shareholders but also on the employees of the firm whose future is being manipulated. One of the prime ways of making a company more efficient is to lay off people. . . .

I certainly do not impugn bad motives to the LBO [leveraged buyout] operators. I do see a different worldview than some of them.

—Richard Chewning
Business ethics professor
World
November 21, 1988

- Paying the kids. You would be giving them a great chance to learn business skills. If you have not incorporated there is no tax advantage to keeping track of these payments and deducting them, though, since you will just have to add them back in to the family income.
- Paying an outsider to come in and help you out now and then. If this is not regular work, your outside helper can get business cards and make out invoices for his work, which in theory makes him a contractor instead of an employee. IRS publication *Circular E—Employer's Tax Guide* explains how to determine if a person working for you is a contractor or an employee. Generally the contractor has to work for other people besides you, or he is considered an employee. The advantage here is avoiding the endless forms and taxes associated with employees. You only have to fill out IRS Form 1099. You still have to recruit this worker, though, which may be tough. People generally want regular hours, even if they are part-time. And you will not be able to take the easy route of hiring temporary help from an agency if you work from home unless your home office has a separate entrance of its own, I was informed by a temporary service in my area. This is because of provisions in the temp service's liability coverage. Zoning laws also may strangle your chances of employing outside help, in which case a possible out is to find a live-in employee, unless the zoning laws forbid *that* as well.
- Many home businesses prosper well enough for the husband to come home and work full-time at the business. Once your husband is involved, you have the option of renting office space and hiring employees in the normal way.

Paul and Sarah Edwards' book *Working from Home* lists several other sources for business help: contract-service companies, bartering or exchanging services, pooling talents with others, and asking for support (equipment, assistance) from those you work

SOME RULES OF THUMB FOR DEALING WITH EMPLOYEES

☐ Pay as much or more for the job than non-Christian employers in your area. (Exception: apprenticeship programs—by whatever name—where you are investing a lot of time in training the employee.)
☐ Pay wages *promptly* and *frequently* (Lev. 19:13).
☐ Have the goal of letting each employee earn a piece of the business, or learn to start his own business. Share this goal with him.
☐ When a long-term faithful employee is ready to start his own business, help him out (Deut. 15:12-15).

A GOOD EMPLOYER respects his employees.

A GREAT EMPLOYER helps them grow and sets them free.

FREEDOM AND USEFUL-
NESS IS WHAT COUNTS,
NOT JUST HAVING YOUR
OWN BUSINESS

The Lord gave my husband
an idea for a courier service
serving the smaller towns
surrounding San Antonio.
After much research and
plenty of encouragement
from local businesses, we
took our $10-$11 thousand
savings and dove in. [My
husband] is very creative,
very professional, and quite a
salesman. We bought just
what we could get by on and
still look like a serious business. The Lord provided a
number of things free. We
even got a large van for
$2,000 or $3,000 under its value. Several days I prayed for
new accounts or sufficient
work and God answered
specifically in response to my
requests. . . .

Interestingly, at the end of
seven months, the Lord has
nearly shoved [my husband]
into a job (using other believers) which he would not
have considered, but now
knows is perfectly suited for
him. When we got our first
paycheck, aside from a little
cash in our wallets, we had
$0.00. . . . All this is to say,
God does not *always* bless
home business.

—Lynn Nobles, TX

for. These are mostly too complicated for a startup to
consider, with the possible exception of bartering.

The Good Master. Now your home business has
become your family's income and you are your own
boss. Take care you are not a hard one! Life will continue to swing along at a great pace with all sorts of
projects leaping at you. Determine to *always* take time
to spend with the Lord and your family and to smell
the roses, no matter how frantic your deadlines.

When we were starting our home business, I was
not used to deadline pressures. I'd work and work,
neglecting myself, certain that once *this* project was
over I'd have some free time to take it easy. Four
years later I know that free time never comes unless
you drag it in by the heels. So even if I have a book
due in two days I will still take some time every day
for personal relaxation above and beyond the time I
spend playing with the children.

You didn't start a home business to make a pile of
money and go crazy, after all. You wanted to find the
right outlet for your creativity and provide a bit more
financial independence for your family. You also
wanted to spend time with your family. When a business—even one that is a ministry—starts eating you
up, it's time to hire help, scale back, or sell out.

All this business philosophy may sound simple
and common-sense (which it is), but believe me, it is
worthwhile studying these pages again and again.
The most common trap in starting a small business is
to work without thinking about why you are working.

A business with no clearly defined mission or
policies is like a mad dog; it staggers about, bites its
owner, and sooner or later falls down dead. After you
have launched a big advertising campaign that is
flooding you with orders it's too late to start thinking
about whether you want to hire help. After the kids
have burnt down the house it's too late to think of a
better place to keep the matches. You want to see
where you are going *before* you get there.

Making money is fun. I won't deny it. But a family who just piles up loot together is missing out on what Jesus said is the greatest blessing of all.

Even if your business is a ministry, God still has some church and community ministries for you as well. We'll see what they are in the next chapters.

Family Practice
(Church Growth from the Bottom Up)

13

"That afternoon, Pollyanna went to the church where she attended Sunday School and, today, the Ladies' Aid was having a meeting. She begged them to find a home for Jimmy Bean, just as she remembered her father had asked for help from their Ladies' Aiders back home. Unfortunately, the Beldingsville ladies had pledged all their money to help children in a faraway country and had none to give for the support and education of Jimmy.

"Jimmy was keenly disappointed that the Ladies' Aid were giving all their money to children in a faraway land and could not help him.

"'But wouldn't it be fine if somebody 'way off somewhere wanted *me?*' said Jimmy.

"Pollyanna clapped her hands. 'Why, Jimmy, that's it! . . .'"[1]

When Eleanor Porter, decades ago, wrote her famous children's book *Pollyanna*, already the church had fallen into the habit of helping those far away and passing over the needy close to home. Foreign missions were in their heyday. Missionaries challenged congregation after congregation to turn their interest and dollars away from the rich U.S.A. and spend them on the benighted heathen. "Here in America we have one pastor for every thousand people! The rest of the world has only one for every million!" mission leaders thundered. Too, the U.S.A. didn't have the pressing social problems of other countries: rampant immorality and drunkenness, broken families, corrupt government. Christians all over America itched to send their help "where it will do the most good."

And we did it. We sent floods of earnest young men and women who would have been barely qualified to run a family of their own, let alone lead a

CHRIST'S LAST WORDS ON EARTH

But you will receive power when the Holy Spirit comes on you; and you will be my witnesses in Jerusalem, and in all Judea and Samaria, and to the ends of the earth.
—Acts 1:8

NOTE THE SEQUENCE:
1. Your own town (Jerusalem)
2. Your own country (Judea)
3. A nearby culture similar to yours (Samaria)
4. Foreign cross-cultural missions ("to the ends of the earth")

Thread, or Thirteen Resolved to Evict All Dealers, has operated for more than a year on East 13th Street in Manhattan's East Village. It is a racially mixed group of residents that formed in the face of the same problems that afflicted Restaurant Row. "A year ago, you had to step over bodies to get out of your building," says Richard Behar, an associate editor at *Forbes* magazine who founded the group. . . .

Although police may express concern over violence arising from the actions of such groups, Behar says: "That's what they say publicly. Privately they say, 'Break their stems.'" . . .

"People say we are lawlessness," says Behar. "But we exist because of lawlessness. The system has broken down."

—"Neighbors Join to Roust the Criminals in the Street" *Insight* November 28, 1988

whole tribe or nation to Christ. We sent tons of aid. Mountains of clothes. Shipfuls of food. Heaps of medicine.

Now, what do we have to show for it?

Is the rest of the world now rescued from heathen darkness?

This Present Darkness

What actually happened is that the U.S.A. and other "sending" nations now have pockets of heathen darkness of our very own. Our inner cities look like Third World nations (I'm just repeating what astute journalists are saying). We, too, now have hordes of ragged people in the street, jails stuffed to the brim with violent prisoners, and millions of children weeping hopelessly for their daddy or mommy who never will come home. And as for preachers with a vigorous gospel message—they are one in a million.

Nor have all those nations blessed with Western missionaries embraced the cross of Christ. One after another they have fallen to either renascent paganism, communism, Islam, or voracious Hollywood materialism. The tribes where our missionaries witnessed are at each other's throats. They are drowning in blood and wine—and much of the bloodshed started *after* years of Christian missions.

We have all seen fund-raising letters boasting about tremendous revivals in Africa and the "new openness" of every ethnic group under the sun. All those great new opportunities have been paraded before us again and again. But can we trust the figures showing so-called revival—especially when we consider the fruit of these "revivals"? Mass murder, warfare, and the African AIDS epidemic are not the normal fruit of salvation.

The foreign missions point to statistics to prove Christianity is gaining great ground in the countries in which they operate. Well, we in America have census figures and Gallup polls that claim over 80 percent of all Americans are Christians—but if anyone believes that 80 percent of Americans have really repented of their sins and surrendered to Christ, I have a nice bridge in Brooklyn I'd like to sell him.

The fact remains that after spending billions (maybe trillions) of dollars and millions of man-years, Western missions have not produced anywhere near the effect that you see in the book of Acts.

Is it because these are the End Times and we can't expect anything better?

Nope. The End Times are a result, not a cause. When the worldwide church apostasizes, that will be The End—but the Christians of that time won't be able to claim they just couldn't help it, the world was so wicked, etc.

We need to face facts—our Christian missionaries went out from a world that was less wicked and came back home to a world that was more wicked.

Obviously they did not have the effect our forefathers hoped for and preached about. Who ever preached a missions sermon like this: "We know our missionaries won't lead very many people to Christ, and those people they lead to Christ will have no positive effect on their society—in fact their society will get worse—so now dig down deep in your pockets and give generously to this great cause"?

We founded schools and orphanages and medical clinics because we expected to make a difference. We didn't know we would be educating the next crop of communist leaders. But that's what we did.

Why did it happen? Because our missionaries did not (with some noteworthy exceptions) understand the principles of leadership that we are going to see in the next chapter. The reason is that this kind of leadership is learned through leading your family—and too often Western mission boards despised, mangled, and destroyed the missionaries' families.

How Careerism Destroys Missions

Western missions *invented* modern careerism. The idea was to make sure every adult supported by mission funds was doing what the mission thought of as gospel work: teaching, preaching, and working in in-

While chatting not long ago with a religious superstar, I learned that he sent his youngest child, a small boy, to a day-care center. His older children were all in school. His wife didn't work outside the home, and he was home a great deal of the time, but still the boy was sent to the center. Being naturally nosy (and extremely tactful), I inquired why the child was booted out of the house five days a week.

"Because my ministry doesn't allow me to spend much time with the children."

Oh. Good reason.

That comment reminded me of the following quotation from the great Reformer, Martin Luther: "Though I am an old doctor of divinity, to this day I have not got beyond the children's learning—the Ten Commandments, the Apostles' Creed, and the Lord's Prayer—and these I understand not so well as I should, though I study them daily, praying with my son John and my daughter Magdalen."

—Dr. W. David Gamble
American Reformation Movement newsletter, February 1989

Before 1890, Burundi had been an independent Tutsi monarchy for almost a thousand years.... They took over the land for their cattle and made the shorter Hutus their serfs....

Missionaries Prepared the Way for Revolution
The seeds for change were planted in the mission schools where Hutus learned the biblical teaching of equality and acquired skills and trades. After World War II this long trodden-upon majority began asking for equal rights....

Belgium was willing to grant independence. But the restless Hutus in Rwanda could not wait. In November, 1959, they massacred thousands of Tutsis and took over the government.

In 1963 an unsuccessful Tutsi invasion from Burundi provoked the Rwandan Hutu army to go on a rampage against Tutsis in Rwanda....

In Burundi a coup brought a new Tutsi government into power....

In 1972 a rebel faction tried to overthrow the Tutsi ruler. The Tutsis quickly put down the revolt, then began a systematic slaughter of Hutu leaders and university students ... two to three hundred thousand killed in less than three months ... the leadership of hundreds of congregations decimated....

—James and Marti Hefley
By Their Blood: Christian Martyrs of the 20th Century

stitutional charity settings. Single workers were more desirable than married, and childless more desirable than those with children. Heedless of the need to show the Biblical marital pattern that Paul says demonstrates the proper relationship of Christ and His church, mission boards encouraged every married missionary to act as if he or she were single and childless. Wives were supposed to be "missionary wives, not missionary's wives." Motherhood was considered wimping out on your Christian duty to be 100 percent dedicated to the mission. You could *have* babies, but you couldn't *raise* them. That would be selfishly preferring your children to the cause of Christ! Once family planning became more scientific, you couldn't even freely have children, as Christian mission boards today widely discourage large families, and at least one I know of even now *refuses* to send out missionary candidates who have more than two children or support more than four children on the field.[2]

Those missionaries unwittingly set about destroying the tribal patriarchal patterns and substituting their own increasingly egalitarian and feminist model. The old, structured society was replaced with hordes of people clamoring for their "rights"—leading, naturally, to revolutions (see the sidebar). These brave new societies promptly expelled Christian missionaries, wherever feasible, and let the rest remain only if the mission agreed to act as a civil service branch of the government by providing literacy programs, health services, and so on. So now we have the spectacle of so-called "Christian missions" whose sole job is to teach English to communists or provide medical care for Muslims, while they are *forbidden by law and by the agreements they have signed with the government* to openly evangelize (see the sidebar on the next page for an example).

We call this work "missions," but it bears no resemblance to hearty straightforward evangelism. Careerist concentration on out-of-the-home evangelism has led to that kind of evangelism becoming *impossi-*

ble in country after country. And the countries most "blessed" with careerist missionaries have followed the missionary leaders' examples in quite unpleasant ways. China, the favorite country of Western missionaries, where the immensely influential China Inland Mission sent all missionary children to boarding school at age two, now repels missionaries and slaughters its own unborn (and sometimes born) children in a grotesque quest for the missionaries' dream: a One Child Family, with the child raised by professionals.

Careerism and the Church

The same principles that have shackled Western missions have been carried over into the pastor's family, other church leaders' families, and finally *all* our families. They can be summarized like this:

(1) God's work conflicts with family life.

(2) God's work comes first.

(3) Therefore, children are a burden that gets in the way of ministry.

(4) So children should be shuffled off to boarding school (if you are on the foreign field), or the nursery, babysitters, or a program of their own (if you are at home) to get them out of your hair.

Let's not waste time deploring this. Let's state exactly why it is wrong, point by point.

(1) God's work does not conflict with family life. Family life is where men are trained to be elders (1 Timothy 3:4, 5) and where their wives are trained to be the "older women" of Titus 2:3 and 1 Timothy 5:10. The family is where new souls are brought into being and discipled in the most intensive way possible, while their disciplers learn by experience through this relatively easy job how to manage tougher disciples. Family life *is* God's work.

(2) God's work of begetting and training children comes before the institutionalized programs, nowhere found in the Bible, which take up the bulk of most churches' efforts.

(3) Therefore, children are not a burden but the

Dr. M'Baissouroum Mouanodji, a Chadian cardiologist currently in Abidjan, Ivory Coast, worked from 1985 to 1987 with World Vision in Mauritania. As a member of a mobile medical team providing food and health care to Mauritanian children, he traveled extensively in the southern regions of the barren, sun-baked country.

"It is forbidden to engage a Mauritanian in a discussion about Jesus Christ," Mouanodji explained, "but if someone asks a question a Christian has the right to explain his faith." . . .

"In general," he added, "you encounter no problems if you respect their culture, their laws, and their religion —and if you don't evangelize."

—Richard Nyberg
World, February 6, 1989

Most churches find children a nuisance. Churches were the first to have day-care centers and nurseries. We believed in worshipping together as a family from the beginning. Mark has gone to church every Sunday since he was four days old! He's our youngest and always tells me, "Don't ask or plead with me to do anything. Just tell me—that's what I'm here for." Would the world believe this? ? ?

We never believed in terrible twos, troublesome threes, etc. We always told ours how wonderful they are—and this is how they all turned out! The power of life and death are in the Word. . . .

—Martha Pugacz, OH

very soil in which church leadership grows. Not only do their parents gain spiritual capital by taking this job seriously, but children brought up in such a household have a tremendous head start on converts from other backgrounds.

(4) So if we really want our churches to grow, we should stop shuffling our children into corners and start helping parents to train their children in God's ways themselves.

Church Growth Through Child-Training

In *The Way Home*, I pointed out that although "Christian" kids today are ignorant of the Bible, uncommitted, and prone to sins of the flesh (43 percent involved in sexual intercourse by age nineteen!)[3] they really can do a lot better than that. New Testament Corinth wasn't exactly Disney World either, what with pagan cults and prostitutes and all manner of lowlife behavior, but the Christians of that day didn't lose their children to the world like we do.

What can we do about it?

Proposed answers take two forms:

- Many people today make their living cleaning up after the unwed mothers, junkies, and teen prostitutes that too many kids raised in "evangelical" homes have become. This is mopping up the water as it continues to flow over the rim of the bathtub.
- Others, more visionary, have started producing programs to explain to kids why they should not engage in premarital sex, take drugs, drop out of school, and so on. These are attempts to shut off the faucet.

I propose that neither approach gets at the root of the situation. We need to *stop looking at Christian kids as problems to be solved* and see them as what they are—*the single most obvious source of church growth*. We should be able to count on the vast majority of them (like 99 percent) continuing as genuine Christians, rather than the vast majority of them dropping out of the church the minute they leave home.

I discussed why we have a right to these expectations in *The Way Home*. Now, here is how we can go about it. We have to ask two questions:

—*What* do we want our children to learn?

—*Who* do we want to teach them?

Once we have answered these two questions satisfactorily, the answer to the third question,

—*How* should they be taught?

becomes obvious.

I Don't Wanna Get Adjusted

What do we want our children to learn? "Uhh . . . we want them to learn to forgive each other." That is a pretty typical goal for a Sunday school class. There it is, right in the Objectives for the lesson: "The children will learn to forgive each other."

So we get incredibly smarmy lessons about how Robert is slapped by Freddy, but refuses to fight, whereupon Robert's teacher leads the class in an epiphany of praise for Robert, who is demonstrating the fruit of forgiveness right in front of Freddy, who falls down before Robert and cries that he is sorry and he, too, wants to become a Christian so he can be like Robert, who immediately tells him to pray to "receive Christ" without any instruction at all in who Christ is or counting the cost or other silly little Bible doctrines that the apostles thought so important. Our kids sit and listen to this stuff for years and years, sometimes being forced verbally to assent to it and other times allowed to push it from their minds by the fun games and handwork with which it is always accompanied, and as soon as they get the chance flee the church, hardly ever to return.

Weldon Hardenbrook, author of *Missing from Action: Vanishing Manhood in America*, blames a feminized Sunday school for the widespread defection of men from the Christian faith. Pastor Hardenbrook is right. He should only have gone one step farther. Sunday school has also contributed to the widespread rejection by women of Biblical Christian faith. These women, unlike the men, remained in the

The opening and proliferation of Sunday Schools dramatized the ministerial and feminine struggle for possession of sacred territory. Sabbath Schools, begun in England in the later eighteenth century as a means of educating and controlling lower-class children, spread rapidly in America in the early nineteenth century. . . . From its inception, the Union was funded largely by businessmen, but the most active promoters and organizers were ministers and women.

—Ann Douglas
The Feminization of America

I believe that every boy is being subjected to powerful feminizing forces inherent in the current structure of the elementary schools and Sunday schools of America. . . .

My friends and I *hated* Sunday school. We thought it was worse than public school because we didn't have recess! . . .

I'm not thankful for the negative influence a feminized Sunday school had on me and my male friends. As I write, I can think of only a handful of friends out of a hundred or more children whose faith in Christ survived those early years. . . .

All too often the end product of the American school system is a feminized young man who is unequipped to handle the responsiblities of mature manhood.

—Weldon Hardenbrook
Missing from Action: Vanishing Manhood in America

Since the American Revolution and disestablishment, the Protestant clergy have tended to be feminized (Douglas, 1977). Terman and Miles (1936) found clergymen to be more feminized on tests of masculinity than the general population of males. Sexton (1969) showed how mass, compulsory schooling tends to create academically successful males that are feminized.

The consequences of this are that many institutions are losing their vitality because of the influx of feminized males into positions of authority. Those Protestant churches that have gone to the extreme and "ordained" women have lost members, while those Evangelicals marked by robust, dynamic and masculine leaders are growing in influence and members. Also growing in membership are Eastern Rite churches. In these institutions, the priests are even required to wear beards.

—George Kocan
Homiletic and Pastoral Review
October 1987

church and went on to teach the next generation in the Sunday school classes they ran.

What we have now, under these women who have become *de facto* teaching elders, is a sentimentalistic Sunday school concept of "changing lives" to *make people happier* rather than the Biblical doctrine of fighting sin and Satan *because they are bad.*

Nothing and nobody, in most Sunday school curriculum, is ever bad. Mistaken, maybe. Misunderstood, perhaps. The victim of an unhappy background, certainly. The "bad" characters never need to admit they are bad and need to be saved from deserved hellfire. They just need their attitudes adjusted.

And your kids need *their* attitudes adjusted. They don't need to study any *facts*. Even when studying Bible stories, the questions focus on values rather than on content.

TEACHER: Was Miriam brave to stay near Moses in his basket, Suzy?
SUZY: I guess so.
TEACHER: What does that teach us, class? [Silence while the class strains to guess what answer the teacher wants.] We should always be brave, shouldn't we?

Never mind giving the children any *information* about Miriam and Moses. The lesson objective says "Teach bravery," so bravery it is. (And sometimes the lesson objective can ludicrously miss or even pervert the very point of the passage far worse than in this example here.) Every teacher an unordained and unqualified preacher. Every lesson a sermon accompanied by handcrafts. Every head empty of facts while the teacher strains to adjust the child's attitudes in a knowledge vacuum.

Where did this idea of attitude-adjusting come from?

What's Affecting Us?

Churches today have, almost universally, fallen into the trap of "affective" education. Affective education was invented by a fellow named Edward Thorndike and a colleague of his named John Dewey. You might remember Dewey as the father of the Humanist Manifesto. Dewey, a fervent anti-Christian, believed it was more important to manipulate a child's values than to teach him anything. But Dewey was not stupid enough to trust this method himself. Once he was philosophy professor at Columbia Teachers College, he made sure every one of his students was taught the content of his philosophy. These students fanned out and took over public education, with the results you see today.

The problem is that while Dewey's disciples were overruning colleges of education everywhere (which train the certified teachers sent to public schools), the church was getting a yen for respectability. Academic degrees were becoming desirable. Very desirable. So when the dust settled, people who had been trained in the latest teaching methodology were installed as heads of Sunday school curriculum houses.

Which is why, even today, Sunday school curriculum is heavy on sentimental sermonettes and almost totally lacking in any systematic Bible training.

How many Christian children do you know who can recite the entire *Westmister Shorter Catechism*? Or who know a key verse from every book of the Bible? Or who can find any verse you call out in two seconds flat? Or who know the Greek and Hebrew alphabets and how to use the reference tools? Or who can fill in the kings of Israel and Judah on a timeline, and get them right? Or who have listened to or read the whole Bible through so many times that they know the "valley of dry bones" is in Ezekiel and Leviathan is in Job? Or who know the Ten Commandments and the Sermon on the Mount by heart?

These should be the *minimal* requirements for any Christian child over the age of ten. I say they are *minimal* because when our forefathers the Puritans decided to take training their children seriously, they did far better than that. The results persisted down even to the early 1900s, when a youth who could not in-

Educational achievement consists, not in strengthening mystical general powers of the mind [e.g., memorizing facts and understanding them], but in establishing connections, binding appropriate responses to life's situations, "training the pupil to behavior" ("behavior" being the name we use for "every possible sort of reaction on the circumstances into which he may find himself brought")....
—Edward L. Thorndike
Colleague of John Dewey

Ultimately, Thorndike's goal was a comprehensive science of pedagogy on which all education could be based.
—Lawrence Cremin
The Transformation of the School

The theory of evolution, applied to the mind, was used by Thorndike and other psychologists as a basis for building a new theory of learning by conditioning. Children were to be considered as animals—for, after all, man was nothing more than the "king" of the animals, as Thorndike put it—and the classroom was to be transformed into a laboratory providing the optimum environment in which learning by reflex conditioning could take place....

While Thorndike developed and formulated the psychological basis for progressive education, John Dewey formulated its social aims....

—Samuel Blumenfeld
NEA: Trojan Horse in American Education

At our church's Christmas program this year, Tim (age three) recited the Christmas Scripture from Luke 2:1-14. All of the other children recited inane little "speeches" or poems, and all but two read their lines instead of memorizing them. I'm not talking about just the other nursery-class students, either—*all* of the children, up to twelve years old, were participating.

Later, Keith said to me, "I wonder if those other children felt bad when they heard Tim saying his Scripture?" And I replied that if anyone should feel badly, it is the *parents* of those other children, for not taking time to help and encourage their little ones in learning their parts. But the attitude of those others is that Tim is exceptionally smart, when in reality any of those children could have done the same thing.

My mother-in-law told me later that several years ago she was responsible for organizing the Christmas program and had suggested that the elementary-age children memorize the Christmas Scripture and recite it as a group, and parents and grandparents had called her on the telephone, angry that she would place such a burden on the children!

It seems that no one expects to have children who are inquisitive, with a thirst to learn, nor do they expect their children to be obedient, and they certainly don't expect raising them to be even a pleasant experience, let alone a joyous one.

—Liz Messick, DE

stantly recognize any Biblical allusion, no matter how obscure, would have been thought culturally illiterate.

Our children need to know *facts*. Bible religion is based on words. Those words need to be studied and learned. Then they will have a basis for real wisdom.

Every church everywhere ought to give top priority to developing a list of verifiable knowledge goals for its children and adults. I say "verifiable" because it must be possible to see whether anyone is actually learning these things. Unlike the curriculum objective of "learning to forgive," which can't be measured with a class pre- and post-test, learning the names and identities of all the prophets is testable. You know it or you don't.

We waste umpteen million hours of so-called "Bible study" time each year on *not* studying the Bible. The Bible is the very bedrock of all Christian growth. You have to know what it says before you can apply it. So let's get serious about learning what it says.

Training the Trainers

Now we come to the second question: who is supposed to teach the children?

The answer to this question has profound implications for church growth strategy.

Presently the church tends to shuffle children off to be taught either by volunteers or (preferably) by paid youth ministers. Not only is most of this teaching touchy-feely nonsense mixed with fun and games, all from the hand of John Dewey, as we have seen, but this whole setup is in error.

Parents do not need to be liberated from their children so they (the parents) can do the important work of the church. Parents need to learn to teach their children so they (the parents *and* the children) will be fit to do the important work of the church.

The Bible's structure for church growth works like this:

■ Every man who has not disqualified himself has the goal of becoming an elder.

- Every woman, ditto, wants to be an "older woman" qualified to teach the younger ones.
- Every child wants to become a full-fledged adult member of the church.
- Even those who are disqualified from the official offices of elder and deacon should be desiring to learn to rule their households well and develop a family ministry.

Each elder should be discipling the men under his care into future elders. Each elder's wife and other qualified mature women should be doing the same with the women. Each set of parents should be training their own children. Everyone has the goal of becoming a leader "qualified to teach others" (2 Timothy 2:2, Hebrew 5:12).

The church is set up to meet these goals. People are to be evangelized, then discipled, which means trained until they are able to be trainers themselves. That is what the church is for. It is *not* an infirmary for permanent spiritual cripples, or a playground for permanent spiritual babies. We are not merely consumers (beyond our initial spiritual babyhood) but producers! We have a *mission*, each and every one of us!

The church's role in the Biblical education of the children of Christian parents ought to be to *encourage the parents*, not to do their job for them. The more crutches the church hands out, the less likely its members ever will walk on their own.

Towards this end, I suggest the church might do well to install a set of rewards for parents and children who *together* demonstrate knowledge of specific Biblical items the church wants them to know. (You are not rewarding just the children for learning, but the parents for teaching.) For example: How about handing out merit badges for Bible memory work? Or for learning the Greek alphabet? Or for being able to recite the Bible books in order? I can just see these rewards being handed out after every morning service. What a boost that would give to all the parents who want to train their children!

One marked difference between the faith of our fathers as conceived by the fathers and the same faith as understood and lived by their children is that the fathers were concerned with the root of the matter, while their present-day descendants seem concerned only with the fruit.

—A. W. Tozer
The Root of the Righteous

Discipling is not limited to elders and their wives. Other spiritually mature men and women should disciple others—they just don't have the same binding authority as elders.

—Pastor Phil Lancaster, MO

We have no certainty as to what the morrow may bring forth, any more than do our more cautious neighbors, but we are sure of this, that the constant challenge and spur of increasing responsibilities and necessities have been fundamentally good for us. If we ever amount to anything—socially, financially, and particularly as to character and worth—my husband and I are agreed that we shall blame it on the children.

—Marjorie Wells
Writer and mother of ten
North American Review
March 1929

The poor condition of the churches today may be traced straight to their leaders. . . .

A number of factors contribute to bad spiritual leadership. Here are a few:

1. *Fear*. The wish to be liked and admired. . . .
2. *The economic squeeze*. The ability of the congregation to turn off the flow of money. . . .
3. *Ambition*. . . .
4. *Intellectual pride*. . . .
5. *Absence of true spiritual experience*. . . . For many ministers this explains their failure to lead. They simply do not know where to go.
6. *Inadequate preparation*. The churches are cluttered with religious amateurs culturally unfit to minister at the altar. . . .

—A. W. Tozer
God Tells the Man Who Cares

Think about it: Isn't it odd that the church has no structure set up to reward parents who do their job properly? Handing out roses to every mother on Mother's Day or a plaque to every father who attends a Father's Day banquet is not the same as rewarding actual *achievement*. Doesn't the Bible say we are supposed to "encourage one another daily"? Why, then, does the church not encourage parents who do their job?

We parents cannot be expected to do our job when the leadership never tells us what it is. Nor are parents given by God to become teacher's aides, drilling children in assignments passed out by unordained Sunday school teachers (perhaps on top of assignments for Christian school or home school). The idea should be to reward families for achieving *at their own pace*, whatever that pace might be, rather than adding guilt and frustration as parents are judged by teachers as to whether their children have their assignments done "on time." The parents' authority over their children also must not be challenged by unordained outsiders who take it upon themselves to tell the parents what to do when with their children. The assignments should be developed by the church leadership as a team based on their understanding of what is most Scripturally edifying, made known to the membership, and rewarded whenever completed as publicly and enthusiastically as possible.

Children need to learn much more than Bible knowledge, of course. They need to learn to witness, to face temptation, to choose wise companions, and a million other things. Some of these things are well-suited to formal instruction; others God meant to be taught through day-to-day example and "teachable moments." As much as possible, the leadership should make it its business to *teach the parents* what they want the children to learn—and *teach the parents how to teach* the children. The parents in turn should teach the children how to teach, so they can teach *their* children someday. Everyone should be growing and learning, and knowing *what* they are learning and *how* they are growing.

This structure gives both men and women godly scope for their ambitions. The men can look forward to becoming leaders; and so can the women. If you become holy and wise, you will have greater opportunities for ministry to members of your own sex. (The only exception: pastors are allowed to teach the *older* women.) If you teach your family well, you will be allowed to teach others. Men would not be encouraged to neglect their families, as is now the case. Children would be looked at as future citizens of the church, rather than as nuisances to be packed off so the adults can "minister" to each other. We would finally have a system where we could measure what we are doing in a way Scripture approves.

The net impact of this system is a church that can flex and grow to meet any situation. If revival hits, the church will find it easy to generate many new leaders in a short time. If revival *doesn't* hit, so many new leaders will have been produced that there won't be enough followers for them, and they will have tremendous motivation for praying down and working toward revival! But actually this church training structure *produces* revival. Not that man can force God to send revival, but God has made it clear that when the hearts of the fathers are turned to the children—meaning that the fathers are taking their job of training up godly children seriously—when God "visits" His people He will bring a blessing, not a curse.

Church growth begins at home. *Your* home! The next chapter shows how you and your family can start right now preparing for leadership.

Here is a trustworthy saying: If anyone sets his heart on being an overseer [bishop, elder, church leader] he desires a noble task.

Now the overseer must be above reproach, the husband of but one wife, temperate, self-controlled, respectable, hospitable, able to teach, not given to drunkenness, not violent but gentle, not quarrelsome, not a lover of money.

He must manage his own family well and see that his children obey him with proper respect. (*If anyone does not know how to manage his own family, how can he take care of God's church?*)

—1 Timothy 3:1-5

The Church in Your Living Room

14

"*J*oseph and Magdalene, start picking up the living room. Sarah, start looking over the Greek alphabet cards. Ted, find the Greek New Testament and bring it to me while I poke up the fire. First we'll all go over the alphabet cards together, and then we'll try figuring out a sentence or two of Bible Greek."

"OK, Daddy!" "Yes, sir!" "I found the New Testament first!" "Here, let me look at those cards!"

What in the world is going on here?

This was a peek into a Sunday afternoon at our house. We have an advantage over other Christian parents in that we both studied Greek on our own before having children. And we fully intend to pass on that advantage to our children. It's supposed to work that way—each generation building on the knowledge and achievements of its predecessors.

Other parents are mighty in memory work, or heavy on Bible history, or powerful in prayer. Each of us should know our strengths and make sure our children inherit them. At the same time we have to poke around for resources to help us build new strengths.

We have discovered three main times ideally suited to instructing our children in the things of God. These are daily family worship, after church on Sunday, and during the Sunday service itself.

Family Worship

Although Scripture never specifically commands parents to have a daily devotional time with their children, the Bible symbols of the morning and evening sacrifice and the example of millions of faithful Christian families throughout history commend family worship to us. It is clear that we parents are supposed to teach our children the Bible *somehow,* and human nature being what it is, a structured time of teaching helps.

"Aquila and Priscilla salute you much in the Lord, with the church that is in their house," 1 Corinthians 16:19.

Some very good interpreters, I know, understand this of a settled, stated, solemn meeting of Christians at the house of Aquila and Priscilla, for public worship. . . . But others think it is meant only of their own family, and the strangers within their gates, among whom there was so much piety and devotion, that it might well be called a church, or religious house. Thus the ancients generally understood it. . . .

In this sense I shall choose to take it: from hence to recommend family religion to you [he means family devotions], under the notion of a church in the house.

—Matthew Henry
"A Church in the House:
A Sermon Concerning
Family Religion"
Complete Works, Volume 1

You must read the scriptures to your families, in a solemn manner, requiring their attendance on your reading, and their attention to it: and inquiring sometimes whether they understand what you read. . . .

When you only hear your children read the Bible, they are tempted to look upon it as no more but a school book; but when they hear you read it to them in a solemn, religious manner, it comes, as it ought, with more authority.

Those masters of families who make conscience of doing this daily, morning and evening, reckoning it part of that which the duty of every day requires—I am sure they have comfort and satisfaction in so doing, and find it contributes much to their own improvement in Christian knowledge.

—Matthew Henry

I would stress the need for the *man* to *take charge* of family worship. Even if he can't read he can be the leader and question the children on the passage read by Mother at his request, etc.

—Pastor Phil Lancaster, MO

The great Bible commentator Matthew Henry likened family worship to a "church in the house." Henry, the son of a father eminent for piety and himself the father of zealously Christian children, listed four elements of successful family worship: hearing, teaching, praying, and singing.

Hearing the Scriptures Together. Matthew Henry considered leading family worship to be normally the father's job. Henry believed the Bible itself would hold a child's interest; he didn't include any suggestions for alternative readings for the young children. I personally stand with Henry, having small fondness for Bible storybooks. God's Word is not improved by bowdlerizing it, nor yet by dressing it up with un-Biblical imaginations.

Even the smallest child can sit still long enough for a parable or a short story from Bible history. Slightly older children are ready for the wisdom literature. Precepts are next in order of difficulty, and finally the prophetic literature rounds out the picture. This is not a rigid order, but might help a young family just starting out.

We have discovered that when a family gets into the habit of family worship, the babies respond to the quieter atmosphere of Bible reading even if the subject matter is far over their heads—and if they don't, they can be carried out and put to bed!

Those who are not yet loose enough to read aloud, or who have some physical ailment preventing it, can "read" by playing a cassette tape. Many recorded versions of the Bible are available.

But do we read the Bible, the whole Bible, and nothing but the Bible? Matthew Henry suggested that those whose Bible knowledge was weak might also read aloud from a good commentary, to supplement the Bible reading, and in this way increase their own understanding while instructing their families.

Henry also pointed out the importance of checking to make sure the children are listening and understanding what is read. He suggested you ask them questions. To this I would add a few more suggested feedback methods:

- Have the children retell the story (or saying, or precept, or prophecy).
- Let them do it as an impromptu play, verbally taking the parts of the characters.
- Ask them to act out the story. One son might be Balaam; the other, Balaam's donkey. Little sister stands in the way as the Angel of the Lord, holding a serving spoon to represent a sword. This method instantly wakes up and energizes sleepy children.
- Pull out the crayons, or paints, or colored pencils, or whatever, and have them draw pictures of the action or subject.
- Get out clay and have them model the action or subject. Example: the animals going two by two into the Ark.

You will have noticed that each feedback method on this list takes more effort and materials than those before it. In our own family, we frequently ask questions and have the children retell, dramatize, or act out what they have heard. Art and sculpture usually is reserved for Sunday afternoon, when we all have more time.

I do not recommend that you adopt these methods for *teaching* the Bible. The great flaw of "family devotions" books is that they make teaching so complicated. You do not need finger puppets, bean bags, costumes, flags, bells, or whistles to teach kids God's Word. You do not need to hunt for magazine pictures for collages, buy packages of dried peas for the object lesson, or sit up late at night making flannel pictures. All this stuff just distracts from the content of the message and wears you out. Unless you have energy to burn and can keep the presentation from looking silly when adorned with these trappings, skip it. The naked Bible has enough power on its own.

Teaching and Learning Doctrine. Christians who belong to confessional churches have a built-in cur-

FAMILY WORSHIP IS:

1. Hearing the Scriptures together.
2. Teaching and learning its precepts.
3. Praying together.
4. Singing psalms, hymns, and spiritual songs.

AS A *REGULAR, DAILY* ACTIVITY

riculum for Bible doctrine: the catechism. I strongly recommend developing a reward system for this kind of memory work. Perhaps I should have said "recognition system," since the idea is not to bribe the student but to acknowledge his genuine achievements.

The recognition system can be very simple. We have used a largish sheet of posterboard for each child, ruled into numbered squares (one for each catechism question) with a gold star applied when a question was learned, and a scratch 'n sniff sticker for every ten questions and answers memorized. As Matthew Henry wisely said, "Wisdom also will direct you . . . not to make [learning the catechism] a task and burden, but as much as may be, a pleasure to those under your charge."

Some families do Scripture memory drills during family worship. Others do memory work during home school, or at breakfast or supper. Whenever you do it, you have a golden opportunity to instruct your children in the *meaning* of the passages they are memorizing. This will add greatly to the usefulness of the daily Bible reading.

Family Prayer. "You must not only as prophets teach your families, but as priests must go before them, in offering the spiritual sacrifices of prayer and praise. . . .

"And it is good . . . ordinarily to dwell most upon the concerns of those that join in their family capacity, that it may be indeed a family prayer, not only offered up in and by the family, but suited to it." Matthew Henry speaking again!

The elements of family prayer are:

- Acknowledging the family's dependence on God for salvation, life, health, money, food, etc. and praising Him for who He is.
- Confessing our sins privately to God as needed.
- Thanking God for mercies received.
- Submissively petitioning God for our family needs and wants.

■ Intercession for those outside the family: relatives, neighbors, friends, the church, the unsaved, and those in power in various social positions (government, media, education, medicine, etc.).

Some people seem to have a real gift for prayer and for teaching their families to pray. I must confess that we have had to learn as we go.

We have discovered that family worship is *not* the best time for instruction in how to pray. For us, that is better done when we can give it more time and emphasis.

Learning to Pray. My friend Prudence shared some refreshing wisdom with me on how she and her husband, Will, have taught their spirited little children to pray (all but sweet red-haired baby Christopher, who is still at the coo-and-gurgle stage!).

"Will prays with our girls individually by each one's bedside before bed, and we have seen them learn to pray through this nightly exercise. It also provides time for individual burdens or sharing.

"This is a separate time from our Bible reading times, which are at the breakfast and supper table.

"All of our four girls are comfortable and able to express their thoughts to God directly, because of this practice.

"Learning to pray happens by *doing* it, not by reading books on it!"

The Prayer Album. It helps to keep a Prayer Album.[1] This can be just a photo album where you place pictures of people you are praying for, letters they have written you, or other memorabilia, along with a list of prayer requests and a column for Date Answered and How Answered. We have also tried making up index cards with our prayer requests on them and drawing cards to pray for. Doing this we discovered a whole new range of things to teach our children about, as the list of movements we are spiritually battling requires a lot of historical explanation!

The Prayer Diary. The best published prayer resource I have been able to find is Youth with a Mission's *Personal Prayer Diary/Daily Planner.* Designed like

Someone made the statement, "When man works, *man* works; when man prays, *God* works." . . .

Only through the prayers of the saints will God's purposes be carried out (Rev. 5:8 and 8:1-5). The seventh seal, the final one, is unusual! Why was there silence in heaven for half-an-hour? It was not just for dramatic effect, or the silence before the storm. It was because God would not act until His people prayed. Once their prayers had risen to the throne, God poured out the fire from the altar upon the earth.

The fire of the Spirit comes in answer to prayer (Acts 1:4, 14; Acts 2:1-8), but so does the fire of judgment! James and John wanted to call down fire from heaven on the Samaritans (Luke 9:54), but in rebuking them Jesus did not *deny* they could! . . . We now have that awesome authority as we pray in the Spirit. Let us use it.

—Patrick Johnstone
*Operation World:
A Day-to-Day Guide
to Praying for the World*

Under this head of family-worship I must not omit to recommend to you the singing of psalms in your families. . . . This is a part of religious worship which participates both of the word and prayer; for therein we are not only to give glory to God, but to teach and admonish one another. It is therefore very proper to make it a transition from the one to the other. It will warm and quicken you, refresh and comfort you; and perhaps if you have little children in your houses, they will sooner take notice of it than of any other part of your family-devotion, and some good impressions may thereby be fastened upon them insensibly.

—Matthew Henry

a business planning diary with yearly, monthly, and week-at-a-glance planning sections, it lists a Bible selection for each day and a cultural group to pray for. So far, no big deal—but this diary also gives in-depth write-ups of several major cultural groups each month, maps, and a Countries of the World section that details what progress the gospel has made in each land and what difficulties the local Christians are facing. The beginning sections on worship, quiet time, intercessory prayer, prayer for the nations, meditation, and memorization are about the best how-to information on these subjects I have seen. You can easily use this with your children as a starting point for developing a Christian worldview, as well as a prayer tool.

Operation Worldview. And speaking of developing a Christian worldview, here is a book that will take you where no secular encyclopedia has gone before. *Operation World* by Patrick Johnstone is an incredibly rich fund of information on every country in the world from the point of its prayer needs. You'll find information on the country's ethnic and religious groups, the growth or decline of the gospel in that land, the history of mission work there, its current cultural and religious climate, and detailed prayer needs. It's all arranged in geographical order with each area or country assigned a sequential date for prayer. And you can get a set of coordinated prayer cards too, each showing a country's location and a brief rundown of its condition and prayer needs, plus a world map, for only $10, from Send the Light (see Resources). Savvy home schoolers use this set to teach their children prayer, geography, cultural anthropology, and Christian worldview all at the same time.

Singing Together. Mary Ann Froehlich, in her book *Christian Music Education in the Home,* points out that making music as a family and teaching our children how to sing is not an "option."[2] The Bible commands us to do this.

Happily, this command is not at all burdensome. Kids often like this part of family worship the best of all!

In our own family we use *The Book of Psalms for Singing* for family worship. The Psalms are God's own words, and a pretty compelling case can be made for sticking with them, as some of our Christian forefathers did. For less formal sing-alongs our little children just adore *Wee Sing Bible Songs*. Finally, those of you who like to keep up with contemporary Christian music might want to subscribe to Al Menconi's *Media Update*. Al covers all angles of the Christian music scene, plus the gruesome happenings in secular rock. He and his staff review recordings, report news, and try to analyze music from a Christian perspective. Menconi Ministries also has cassette and videotapes and curriculum covering what's good, bad, or ugly about secular rock and Christian music today. You can also order the Praise Company Christian music discount catalog from Menconi Ministries.

Sunday, Sunday

My husband Bill, in his book *Flirting with the Devil,* pointed out that "the number-one, grade-A, best training ground for learning to be joyful in the Lord is keeping the Sabbath." Bill was discussing the famous passage from Isaiah 58 which says,

> "If you keep your feet from breaking the Sabbath
>   and from doing as you please on my holy day,
> if you call the Sabbath a delight
>   and the Lord's holy day honorable,
> and if you honor it by not going your own way
>   and not doing as you please or speaking idle words,
> then you will find your joy in the Lord,
>   and I will cause you to ride on the heights of the land
>   [or "the earth"—the Hebrew can mean either land or earth]
> and to feast on the inheritance of your father Jacob."
>   The mouth of the Lord has spoken.

As Bill says, "We have a *promise* in this passage, not a command." Bill then proceeded to list some of what happens when you start to keep Sunday as a holy day:

SUNDAY IS FOR:

- ☐ Testing your love for God.
- ☐ Renewing your perspective.
- ☐ Preventative maintenance.
- ☐ Spiritual practice.
- ☐ Spiritual power.

Sabbath, properly under-
stood, is rest from the
bondage of work. God, ever
a Liberator God, is concerned
about our freedom. . . . God
gives us fifty-two Sabbaths,
or seven and a half weeks, of
vacation time a year!—time
during which we are to do no
work. As Thomas Aquinas
put it, each week one goes on
ad vacandum divinis—a day of
vacation with God.

—Karen Burton Mains
Making Sunday Special

"First, the Sabbath is a test of whether you love God or not. . . . Second, the Sabbath is a day to get away from the devil and his messengers and get a true perspective on the world. . . . It is also preventative maintenance time for our spiritual armor. . . . Sunday gives us time to practice our sword play and shield work before we test them in the world. . . . Finally, those who keep Sunday as a Sabbath, not as a legalistic attempt to earn salvation but as a day to enjoy God, will be blessed with spiritual power."

Could your family use a bit more spiritual power? Hmmm?

If so, then here are some ideas for making Sunday special.

- Special toys, games, and books. These should all have Christian content of some sort, and be *saved for Sunday.* If your special Sunday toy is available for playing with all week long, it loses its specialness. *Sacred* means *set aside,* so set aside some goodies for Sunday!
- Start breaking your TV habit by keeping the electronic idol shut off on Sunday (Psalm 101:3).
- Sing! We have wonderful songfests at our house on Sunday afternoon (Psalm 9:11, 21:13, 30:4, 32:11, 33:1, 47:6, and a host of other verses).
- Make music! Sunday is also a great time to get out the guitar, harmonica, recorder, or whatever, roll down the piano lid, and play some hymn tunes. Even the baby can rattle a tambourine. Amen, brother (Psalm 27:6, 33:2, 81:2, etc.)!
- Rewards. Now is the time to tell each child how he or she has especially pleased you this week. Give out rewards for verses memorized or other achievements. After all, the Sabbath is supposed to be a foretaste of our eternal reward in Heaven (Hebrews 4:9, 10)!
- Remember. Look back over the week's accomplishments and thank God for them. Every Sunday is Thanksgiving!
- Feast. Sunday is also a foretaste of the Marriage Supper of the Lamb. So at our house on Sunday

we have special treats that we don't get the rest of the week. We want to connect our children's memories of Sunday with happiness. Sunday is the day we get to do special things and eat special food, so there is no need to feel we are "doing without" by disconnecting the outside world for a day.

■ Rest. The neo-Puritans loved to tell their congregations that, in spite of what the Bible said about the Sabbath being a day of rest, it was not for "carnal rest," i.e., putting your feet up and snoozing. Oh yes, it is! If you work hard all week, getting to take a nap on Sunday is a treat.

■ Celebration in community. If God has provided you with a church home, you go to church!

Children and Church

Sunday morning worship! The Christian community celebrating the resurrection of our Lord together! Well, all of us except the babies in the nursery. And the little kids in the toddler room. And the older children in children's church. And the teenagers babysitting in the nursery. And all the other people running the nursery, the toddler room, and children's church.

At a typical American church service, bunches of people are in the building but missing the meeting. That's because we have developed an attitude that church, like all other group activities, is for *adults*.

Keeping the kids out of grownup church provides the following benefits:

■ Daddy doesn't have to teach his children to behave in public.

■ Daddy doesn't have to admit his children don't know how to behave in public.

■ The preacher can use big words and abstract concepts without anyone embarrassing him by admitting they don't understand a word he's saying.

■ Mommy doesn't have to jog up and down in back of the sanctuary to keep the baby quiet. She can do this at home in the middle of the night for the next two weeks after the baby picks up a flu bug in the church nursery.

Do we need Sunday school for the children of ungodly parents? No, in fact our church has never allowed underage children to attend church without their parents. An underage child is supposed to be under the authority of his parents. His parents have the responsibility for religious training. If we preach to the child and not to the parent we set up a tension in the child. . . .

Children's church does a disservice to the child's parents. It allows the parents, both godly and ungodly, to avoid their responsibility to teach their children. If they want their children to get some religious teaching we should help and guide them but never do it for them.

"But what if they don't?" If they don't—they don't. God will call their children some other time in some other way and they will answer to God for their lack of obedience. But we will not have helped them not obey.

—Donnajean Meahl, CA

I felt then, and still do, that leaving an unhappy baby in the nursery or anywhere has a lasting impressing and effect on them. To this day it really bothers me to hear babies crying in the church nursery, when all they usually want is for them mom to hold them.

—Judy Pickens, CA

We have gradually become more and more certain that we wanted to have a Sunday school class for the whole family. Now that is happening, but on a trial basis. We are so excited about it!

Out of the blue, the man in charge of adult Sunday school was sharing with Ferd his dilemma—the need to devise a three-year plan for the adult Sunday school. However, as he studied the Word, he just kept seeing how the parents are charged with the spiritual training of their children. Of course, Ferd was happy to share our dream with him; then he with the elders; so now Ferd and I are administering a family Sunday school class for five families.

The common views are that the class cannot possibly appeal to all ages, that Mom and Dad won't be getting the challenge they need spiritually, that they already have family devotions (so that is enough), etc., but the class is going very well.

We give each family a folder each week that outlines some projects that could be done that week, specific to the theme (Fall, Flood, Abraham, Joseph, etc.). The first week we also listed some ideas that could be used for any theme. So part of our class time is spent reporting on the various projects from each family. This is really great for the children to have such a supportive and interested audience.

—Linda Rivas, OR

■ Mommy and Daddy can fall asleep much more comfortably, since they have no squirming children on their laps.

Segregating the children also has its disadvantages:

■ The children learn that they are not expected to act like grownups.
■ A number of adults have to miss church regularly in order to "minister" to other people's children.
■ Some babies (quite a few, in my experience) hate being left in the nursery. They worry that Mom and Dad will never come back. They cry and scream and learn to *hate* church.

Even those churches who don't believe in segregating children feel pressured to provide nursery and children's church for the benefit of visitors who expect these services. If you are in this situation, resist it. The Christian church is not here to give the world what it wants, but what it *needs*—and what it needs right now is age integration and discipleship.

We *must* help our children *quickly* mature into independent adults. There is no reason why a nine-year-old can't be mighty for Jesus (Psalm 8:2, 112:2) , and there are lots of reasons why we are foolish to keep him a spiritual child. For one thing, in our current legal climate Christian parents' right to raise our own children according to God's law is hanging by a fragile thread. I don't know about you, but I want my children to be adults spiritually, standing before God and man on their own, as soon as possible.

Therefore we should include our children in all spiritually edifying activities as much as possible. Adults today aren't so spiritually astute that a sermon understandable by children would insult their intelligence. Nor are children unable to appreciate prayer and testimonies. And kids *love* to sing! Even a fussy baby will calm down where everyone is belting out a hymn.

Now, how to accomplish this goal? How can we put children and church together without children's church?

Here are a few suggestions:

- **The Dry Run.** This helps even if your children are already attending Sunday service with you. Play "church." Get out chairs, have everyone sit in rows, and tell them how they are to behave. No turning around and staring at people behind you. No talking, loud whispering, or screeching unless the church catches on fire. Have them practice sitting up and paying attention. Impress on them that church is for worshipping God, and that we owe Him reverence.

- **Proper seating.** Families with young children should have an escape route planned if the baby messes his diaper or the three-year-old needs to be disciplined for pestering his sister. This means sitting in the back or near a side door, usually. Don't embarrass yourself by having to walk past everyone in church with your crying baby! Churches can help if they want to by considering the needs of young families in their seating plans. At the very least, the last rows in the church can be roped off for families with young children.

- **Leave the bribes at home.** The only reason for having your children with you in church is that you want them to become spiritually mature. If you have to keep them supplied with a constant stream of coloring books, sweets, and presents for good behavior, they are not getting the idea. Direct them to the spiritual joy you find in the Lord! (If you *don't* have all that much spiritual joy, you might want to get a copy of my husband Bill's book *Flirting with the Devil*.)

- **Keep 'em moving!** Until it's time to sit down, find a place where your young children can run about a bit and let their steam off. It's great if the church has an area, such as a gym, where kids can move around between church and Sunday school.

- **Swift discipline.** Your yes should be yes and your no, no. If you tell Junior to stop talking and Junior ignores you, it's time for Junior to know you mean what you say.

I thought I would tell you about the various ways I've seen and tried having young children in worship service with you. Dutch families use long-lasting, very sticky candy balls—seems to work best with two-year-olds as long as no dentists go to your church. In England most families bring books (special Sunday books or quiet books) or coloring books or pencils and paper. In Kenya, the noise level of the service was higher, people coming and going and moving around, so children could wiggle and whisper questions or run outside to the bathroom without disturbing others or adult wrath falling upon them. In India, men and women sat on opposite sides of the room and children could move between, leaf through the Bible, watch bugs, and (because services were often three hours long) doze off.

My children have sat through sermons in Hindi, Swahili, German, Dutch, Persian, English, and American and truly have learned about God in all of them—either from whispered questions or other adults' loving responses, from comments in the sermon that caught their attention or leafing through their Bibles. Sunday is their favorite day. Having children in the worship service in this culture is often difficult but worth working at. I find most of the problems are with me, not to try to impress other people and to demonstrate to my kids how to worship in a body of believers.

—Marcia Jones, FL

I hear and feel the pain from many people who have been so hurt by careless, nosy, and unloving people who have said and done cruel things. Our family, too, was in a very painful church situation almost two years ago. . . . We finally had to resolve our situation by leaving that assembly, and we now home church with several other families. Our final decision to leave was made for our children. We did not see how we could teach certain truths at home and have the children see and hear a much different line of preaching at church. This left us with the choice of either saying nothing so as not to undermine authority in their eyes or to correct as best we could, but give the impression of encouraging a "do as we say, not as we do" attitude toward spiritual and church policy matters. We are more thankful every day that the Lord gave us the strength to leave when we did, as it was a very difficult thing to do, to say the least. Things do get better over time, and an awful lot of the hurt is gone now.

—A Massachusetts mom

- **Encouragement.** Smile at the children and let them know you are proud of them when they are behaving well.
- **Act proud of your children.** When Mrs. Jones congratulates you on how well they have behaved, say, "Yes, they are good children," instead of, "Well, they may have been good today, but you should see them at home!" Or if Mrs. Snideley gives the children a dirty look when they sit down next to her, inquire pleasantly if something is bothering her. Maybe it's just her sinuses acting up. If she does have something nasty and unfair to say about your children, gently try to straighten her out. If there are too many Mrs. Snideleys around, you might want to consider another church—or, as my pastor recommends, stay around and let Mrs. Snidely be the one to leave!

Home Church v. Church Church

Speaking of considering another church, in all fairness we must look at the question of home church versus church church.

Some Christians have become so burned out with the anti-family attitudes in their local churches that they have withdrawn entirely from communal fellowship. They have started to worship at home with their families.

Now, there is nothing wrong with having a church in your home. Priscilla and Aquila did. But is worshiping with your family really *church*?

After having looked at this issue from both sides, Bill and I have drawn some conclusions.

Not everything that calls itself a church is a church. Flagrantly liberal "churches" that preach about God the Mother (horrid blasphemy!) and promote New Age occult spiritual tactics obviously are not Christian churches. But there are apparently conservative churches that also deny the gospel, preaching Jesus the Need-Meeter rather than Christ the King.

Should you attend such a church?

It depends on (a) whether the leadership is committed to an un-Biblical position or is holding it in ignorance and (b) what your position is likely to be in the church.

Some people preach that we should attend church not for what we can get but for what we can give. They take this to mean that we can join anything that calls itself a church and work to change it for the better, forgetting that the Bible tells us to have no fellowship with those who preach a false gospel. Infiltrating and secretly working to change a church is Satan's method, not Christ's.

On the other hand, if you are called as the church's pastor, or if someone from the church asks you to join and take over the Sunday school, they have become your disciples. In that case, go right ahead!

Not every home is a church. It's not a church without outreach, true preaching, discipline, and the sacraments. Worshiping at home may be necessary in cases of geographical isolation, or handicap, or total spiritual burnout. But the true Christian has a yearning for communion with the Lord in the community of His Body. We should be seeking to recover from burnout, or transcend our handicaps, or reach out beyond our isolation.

A church in the home can become a real church if its leaders emerge from the "wilderness" experience ready to reach out to and learn from others. This is hard for some, I know, especially those who have been rejected before. All the same, the Spirit won't let you alone until you start gathering together to work for Christ's Kingdom with other Christians. As the Bible says, "Let us not give up meeting together, as some are in the habit of doing, but let us encourage one another" (Hebrews 10:25). This does not mean that you can never withdraw yourself from a misguided fellowship and be between churches, but that you should desire the encouragement of fellow Chris-

As nature makes families little kingdoms . . . so grace makes families little churches; and those were the primitive churches of the Old Testament, before "men began to call upon the name of the Lord" in solemn assemblies, and "the sons of God came together to present themselves" before him.

Not that I would have these family-churches set up and kept up in competition with, much less in contradiction to, public religious assemblies, which ought always to have the preference: "The Lord loveth the gates of Zion more than all the dwellings of Jacob," Psalm 87:2, and so must we; and must not forsake the assembling of ourselves together, under color of exhorting one another at home.

—Matthew Henry

Unhappy contests there have been, and still are, among wise and good men about the constitution, order, and government of churches; God by his grace heal these breaches . . . .

But I am now speaking of churches concerning which there is no controversy. All agree that masters of families who profess religion and the fear of God themselves should, according to the talents they are entrusted with, maintain and keep up religion and the fear of God in their families "as those that must give account," and that families as such should contribute to the support of Christianity in a nation. . . .

This way of instruction by catechising, doth in a special manner belong to the church in the house; for that is the nursery in which the trees of righteousness are reared, that afterwards are planted in the courts of our God. . . . As mothers are children's best nurses, so parents are or should be their best teachers. Solomon's father was his tutor, Proverbs 4:3, 4. And he never forgot the lessons his mother taught him, Proverbs 31:1.

—Matthew Henry

tians. Conversely, if you are getting *no* encouragement to live the Christian life where you are now (which is the case in an unhappily large number of modern churches), you would not be "in the habit" of giving up meeting with other Christians to abandon such a false fellowship to recoup your energies, even if you could not immediately find a trustworthy church to attend.

And by the way, encouragement to live the Christian life does not mean constant unconditional praise and acceptance, but rebuke for our sins and joy in our righteousness; so a trustworthy church is *more* uncomfortable for some people than a bad one! We shouldn't pick a church just for its level of comfort, but for its level of commitment to Christ and His Word. Don't flee the surgeon just when he's about to operate on your cancer!

"Two are better than one and a cord of three strands is not quickly broken" (Ecclesiastes 4:12). The church is God's army, not a one-man operation. Neither you nor I is a spiritual Rambo. Even David had the Israelite army behind him when he faced Goliath. The desire of my heart, even today, is to see the Christian community united and fearlessly confronting the evil of this world. "This is a sign to them that they will be destroyed, but that you will be saved—and that by God" (Philippians 1:27, 28). There is no virtue in sheer numbers, but when the troops are mobilized under leaders chosen by God, then let Satan tremble!

Family Church and the Church Family

As we saw in the previous chapter, God has set up a definite hierarchical structure for His army. Parents lead the children; husbands lead wives; and elders lead the families under their care. Whether the Bible shows any more complicated church structure than this, wise men have debated for centuries—but no one has ever successfully argued against the elder-to-heads of households-to-children line of authority.

The church can reinforce this natural authority structure or undermine it. Of late, the church has been undermining it, with the sorry results we see today. Abortion. Broken homes. Children running wild. Lawlessness. A government that thinks it owns us all. But all these problems *can be reversed* if the church will just commit itself to building up the family's authority.

You notice I said, "Building up the family's *authority*," not, "Building up the family." We have been infested with plagues of so-called family-building programs that just fragment the family further and make it more dependent on outsiders for its normal in-house functions. What is needed now is for the church to take its hands off the family's jobs and just *encourage* and *expedite* these jobs.

Each church, as we saw in the last chapter, should have a well-defined set of goals that families are expected to reach *on their own*, with the only help offered being rewards for achievement in reaching these goals and on-demand instruction in how to reach them more effectively.

Here are some of our goals:

■ That every one of our children be able to recognize any Bible passage, tell where it comes from , associate it with other passages on the same subject, and apply all that to his life and his world.

■ That none of our children be exposed to corrupting evil, whether of so-called lifestyle or doctrine or language.

■ That all of our children be "arrows in the hand of a warrior," trained and sharpened to confront the evil in this world in their specific callings.

■ That they all be able to distinguish good from evil without confusion.

Or, on a bigger scale:

■ That the medical profession be humbled and brought back to its proper role of medical servants.

■ That the media no longer be monopolized by counterchristian viewpoints.

Matthew Henry lists six reasons for starting a "church in your house":

☐ Closeness to God—"God will come to you, and dwell with you in them."

☐ Safety—"God will make them little sanctuaries."

☐ Protection from infiltrating evil—Satan will not have a seat there.

☐ Comfort—Your home-life will be pleasant.

☐ The future—You will leave your children a good spiritual inheritance.

☐ The present—"A church in the house will contribute very much to the prosperity of the church of God in the nation. Family-religion, if that prevail, will put a face of religion upon the land, and very much advance the beauty and peace of our English [Canadian, American, Australian, etc.] Jerusalem."

- That the entertainment industry be greatly diminished and purged of its current vileness.
- That the gospel be preached clearly and not censored by the state, the media, the educational establishment, or any other agency.

These may seem large goals, but we either accomplish them or undermine them every day. Each of us has one vote politically, and also one vote in the areas of medicine, entertainment, education, and so on. If I don't subscribe to cable TV, that's one vote against cable. If I don't go to see *The Last Temptation of Christ*, that's one vote against blasphemy. If I cancel my subscription to *Parents*, that's one vote for babies!

One of the church's jobs is to coordinate our votes and make sure they don't cancel each other out. Right now we are too frequently canceling each other out. The reason is that we are not being trained as a spiritual army. The church has become a counseling center instead of a military base. We need to get organized—not as some sort of cultist top-down pyramid, but as a grass-roots network of individual families empowered to do our job and held together by our churches.

The church can get stronger in the world by encouraging us to be stronger in our living rooms.

So what can we do for the world from our living rooms? How can one family make a difference? How can you expand your one cultural vote to be worth 1,000? The answer is in the next chapter.

"It's Superfamily!"

"I just had to write you to pass on this story that recently happened to me and my children. I had to go to Children's Hospital here in Knoxville to get a blood work-up on my three-month-old daughter. As usual, I packed up the troops (three boys ages 7, 5, 2¾, and baby Julie) and off we headed.

"Upon arrival, there was all kinds of paperwork and computer work to take care of (about thirty minutes' worth). My boys behaved as I expected them to—good little guys. Julie sat calm and relaxed in my arms. Before our departure for the lab, one of the receptionists said to me, 'Your children sure are well-behaved; most that come in here aren't.' I thanked her and off we went.

"At the lab, a technician came out and told me she'd sit with my three boys while I went in with Julie. I did not know this, but while I was in the lab this girl was talking with my children and, finding out that they were home schooled, asking my seven-year-old to read to her, etc. As I came out of the lab I heard her say to another technician there, 'Not only does this lady have four kids, she teaches them at home! You should hear him read!' The technician I walked out with said, 'Not only does she have four kids and teach them at home, her baby doesn't even cry when we put a needle in her!' We all laughed and then several other technicians going on a lunch break all started asking questions. One lady thought home schooling was 'just wonderful.' Another woman was really probing with her questions—'Is that *really* legal?,' etc., etc. They asked questions for about ten minutes. It was an opportunity for me to share things these women had never thought of before, all because my children had been under control. The girl that had watched my boys for me thanked me for letting her watch them and said, 'They didn't need me, though.'

So how do we approach the task of getting such a culture [as ours] first to admit the legitimacy of allowing a "religious" point of view, and then of using that point of view for themselves?

My guess is that critical as the political front is, it may not be the place to focus our main energies. Politics does not so much shape public life as it reflects it. Before a Godly perspective will ever be seen in public policy matters, a Godly perspective will need to become a constant habit in the lives of tens and hundreds of thousands of people at the grass roots.

—Joel Belz
World, November 14, 1988

237

We seem to have a lot of influence because we have
well-behaved children and a
happy family. Henry is such
an example as a father, husband, and provider, not using the excuse of college to
shirk his responsibilities. He
is well-known and liked in
our church and work sphere,
so who knows how God will
use this. As for me, I'm the
Area Coordinator of Leaders
for La Leche League of
Arkansas/Oklahoma and a
lot of people are watching
me. Our joy about our family
is evident, and although
some think we're crazy, I
think they secretly admire us
for taking a stand and following God's perfect will in
this day.

—Charlotte Siems, OK

"I went home and promptly called my husband to
share the events of our exciting morning. As I recalled all that had transpired, he said, 'Yes, it's *Superfamily!*' We laughed, but it really was an encouragement to us as I hope it is to others as they read this."

I really enjoyed this cute story that Betsy Michalik
of Tennessee shared with the other readers of my
newsletter, *HELP*.

Her story illustrates an important truth—the family
that governs itself is given opportunities to influence
others.

You want to win friends and influence people?
You want to change this world for Jesus? Here are the
steps to power God has given us.

Family Government

"He that is slow to anger is better than the mighty;
and he that ruleth his spirit than he that taketh a city"
(Proverbs 16:32 KJV). If we want to "take a city," that
is, have influence over our culture, we have to start
by governing ourselves: our appetites and deeds. Parents are supposed to teach our children this great lesson first of all. In the process, the parents learn to
govern their families. When the family governs itself,
it is no longer dependent on others. According to the
Bible, this family self-government causes our daily
lives to win the respect of outsiders (1 Thessalonians
4:12)—just as you saw in the example that opened
this chapter.

Family self-government gives us more than respect and a chance to influence others. The family is a
government of its own. The home is our own little
world in which we are the rulers, the artists, the educators, the entertainment media, the business leaders,
and so on.

If we want to make our culture Christian—its
laws, art, education, entertainment, business, and so
on—we can do it by making our homes Christian.

Typically, Christians who want to influence a culture strain their brains thinking of ways to affect it
from the top down. They meet legislators and press

the flesh, give news conferences, start universities, and found groups called something like "Winners for Christ" to target top athletes, students, and other present or potential leaders with the gospel message. I'm not saying this all is wrong—although I would dearly love to see someone name a group "Losers for Christ" for a change! It's just that working from the bottom up is so much more effective in the long run. In fact, spreading Christian culture from the home out is the *only* method that works in the long run. God is the one who blesses or judges nations, and His evaluation begins with "the household of God," including our literal households (1 Peter 4:17).

Make Your World Christian

Look around you. This is your world. You control your home. You make the rules, choose the furnishings, and decide what books and magazines are brought in. You manage the citizens, settle their disputes, and reward or punish them.

Now comes the $5 billion dollar question: *Is this what you want the world to look like?*

I have often felt a sense of unreality reading about the degenerate world outside my home. Inside these four walls there is no such thing as pornography, drug abuse, bad language, punk rock, abortion, euthanasia, unwanted children, juvenile delinquency, sexually-transmitted disease, murder, rape, embezzling, and so on. If you went down the list of federal bureaucracies, you would find that not one does any business with my family. I say this not to boast, but to encourage you to do the same.

Inside my home we are building a Christian culture. We don't have to guess and wonder about deep political theories such as theocracy *v.* pluralism *v.* natural law *v.* who-knows-what. My home *is* a Christian nation. We have Christian rulers (Mommy and Daddy), Christian laws, and Christian enforcement. We have Christian media: Christian books, magazines, and videos. Not all of these are produced by Christians, but they fit in with our Christian world-

The word holy means "set apart for God." The basic goal of Christian parents is to make the home holy, set apart for God as far as possible in the areas that matter. . . .

Ultimately, children reared thus may find themselves very successful in the world, in their education or career. Despite the glamor of the rock culture, after all, those who take it seriously and emulate its lifestyle are more likely to end up digging ditches than designing the plans.

—Connie Marshner
Decent Exposure: How to Teach Your Children About Sex

THE FAMILY THAT
GOVERNS ITSELF IS:

1. Not causing problems.
2. Not funding or supporting
   problems.
3. Providing solutions.

"An election that is about
ideas and values," President
Bush said last August in New
Orleans, "is also about philosophy. And I have one. At the
bright center is the individual.
And radiating out from him
or her is the family. . . . From
the individual to the family to
the community, and then on
out to the town, the church,
and the school, and still echoing out, to the county, the
state, and the nation—each
doing only what it does well,
and no more."

And then he spoke of the
need for all those components
to make their respective contributions, shining together as
a thousand points of light
against the enormous darkness.

—Joel Belz
World, January 30. 1989

view. We have Christian art on the walls—not Biblical
scenes, but paintings with a Christian spirit of peace
and enjoyment of the creation. We have Christian entertainment, Christian conversation, Christian standards of dress, Christian relationship, Christian business practices, and Christian medicine. If someone
snatched away the outside world and plunked us
down in the middle of a New Christian Earth, the little children might not even notice the difference.

Jesus said we are supposed to be *in* the world but
not *of* the world. He meant that the world should
come to us—*on our terms*, and we should go to it—
also *on our terms.* These were the rules He played by.
Christ always controlled His environment. He acted
like a King, not like an average Joe taking whatever
the culture dished out!

We might or might not be able to change the composition of the Supreme Court, but we sure can
change the world starting at ground zero right here.

Let me tell you how it works.

The Law of Exponential Returns

A certain famous public man recently gave a
speech suggesting that we replace overblown government with "1,000 points of light." Let's take his 1,000
lights and translate them into 1,000 Christian homes.
Let's assume that each of these 1,000 homes is actually living out its Christian principles in the area of law,
economics, art, medicine, entertainment, and so on.
Let us further assume that each such family finds two
other families every year, shares the gospel with
them, and shows them how to live like this. The new
families then turn around and do the same, each finding two new families the next year.

In Year One, you have 1,000 families.
Year Two you have 3,000 families.
Year Three—9,000 families.
Year Four—27,000.
Year Five—81,000.
Year Six—243,000.
Year Seven—729,000.

Year Eight—2,187,000.

Year Nine—6,561,000.

Year Ten—19,683,000.

These families each have two adults and (we presume) quite a few children. By Year Ten the "Christian culture" voting bloc is more than six times as big as the government employee voting bloc.

Now let's lay aside voting for the moment, and calculate the effect that this number of Christian homes will have on public policy just by existing. Take day care, for example. We can assume that families who welcome children as blessings will receive some, so let's peg the day-care-aged child population of these families at a conservative forty million—only about two apiece. In our model, the parents ardently desire to train their young children themselves at home. Since the entire U.S. day-care-age child population as of 1989 was less than fifteen million, you can see that the political viability of a massive federal day-care bureaucracy would have disappeared well before Year Ten.

Or take public school. The school-age children of these families (all enrolled in home school or Christian school), another forty million or so, would come close to the entire public school population in size, thus curbing the influence of the NEA and similar groups.

The effects on the mass entertainment industries, magazine industry, book industry, medical industry, and so on can hardly be imagined.

This is *already happening*. The home-schooling movement is at about Year Ten growth level right now, assuming a rate of yearly doubling rather than tripling as in the example above. If you went back ten years, you wouldn't have found many more than a thousand home schoolers. Each year the movement has doubled in size, now reaching the half-million-families mark.

Your Choices Matter

Let me talk to you personally for a minute. You are not a statistic. But you are a reader of this book!

The "thousand lights" image is hardly new. The apostle Paul pre-dated Bush's use of it when he told the Philippians to "shine like stars in the universe" as they held out the word of life in a crooked and perverse generation.

—Joel Belz
World, January 30. 1989

Therefore go and make disciples of all nations, baptizing them in the name of the Father and of the Son and of the Holy Spirit, and teaching them to obey everything I have commanded you.

—Our Lord Jesus Christ
Matthew 28:19

Can parents seize control of the youth culture? That's a question of major proportions. Are there enough motivated and concerned parents in our nation to change the viciousness of the youth culture? . . .

All of us as parents, however, are responsible for how the culture is allowed into our homes. While we cannot seize control of the entire culture [this I disagree with!], we *can* prevent our chilren from being sucked into it. We can limit its incursions into our homes. This is essentially playing a defensive game; if we are starting when our children are young enough, we can play more of an offensive game and create a genuine Christian culture in our homes.

—Connie Marshner
Decent Exposure: How to Teach Your Children About Sex

Let's say you decide to create a Christian kingdom in your home, and start spreading books like this one around to your friends and family. You might feel isolated at first, but if as many other families start doing this as read the first edition of *The Way Home*, in six and a half years or so you will be part of a twenty-million-family movement.

By that time you will have made connections with other likeminded families, besides the ones you jump-started (even sooner if you subscribe to my newsletter!). And since under God the whole is always greater than the sum of the parts, you will very likely have access to a tremendous amount of spiritual energy, far more than you have ever known before. It's called Revival, and it's what happens when God checks up on His people and finds them busy at work building His kingdom.

We need to learn to make choices by the right rules. These question should not be, "Is choice X cheaper . . . or easier . . . or less confrontational than choice Y?" We should be asking, "Which one develops Christ's kingdom in my home?"

What you have in your home, you get in the world. If we welcome sleazy novels and TV shows, drop-kick the kids into the Youth Culture, fail to govern our families, and surround ourselves with the culture's vision and artifacts, what we see will be what we get. But if our homes are full of sensible rules, wholesome homegrown entertainment, Christian kids with team spirit, and uplifting art, we can reasonably expect this to spill over on the world.

This Little Light of Mine

We've been crunching numbers. Now let's think about the potential ministries of all those revitalized families. Once our homes are under control, we will discover that we have the leadership skills and other resources to actually be "points of light" in our culture. We will be able to do more than encourage others to come home. We will be using the resources of our homes to reach out.

Les and Penny Gioja of Illinois, whose fascinating family ministry we will be reading about in a minute, explain how self-governed families just naturally develop important ministries. As Les wrote:

"'Ministry' is a frustrating word for many Christians—especially those with small children, and especially the mothers of those children. We think we should be serving God by ministering to others, but we just don't have the time or energy to get involved in ministry programs.

"The real problem, however, is that we set up getting involved in these programs, rather than ministering to others, as the goal. Jesus does not want us to be inseparably linked to some committee with that committee's survival as our goal, but rather to love God with all our heart, mind and soul, to love our neighbor as ourselves, and to minister out of this love. (See 1 Corinthians 13.)

"Ministry is simply loving and helping other people with the physical and spiritual resources God has given us in order to assist in bringing them closer to God. Period!!

"You do not need much money to give to the truly needy nor do you need a degree in evangelism to lead someone to Christ. It does not even take much time and energy to make someone else's day special. You merely have to stop, identify the needs of those around you, and match your available God-given resources to their needs. For instance, if your neighbors are old and unable to handle heavy loads, and you take a little extra time to shovel their walk while you shovel your own, you will have ministered to your neighbors, your spouse (for whom you are shoveling the walk), and your children (who will be blessed by your example) while spending a minimal amount of time, money, and effort.

"Ministry is fun and rewarding! When we can give to someone else out of our abundance, we feel great because we are truly doing what God wants us to do. Do not forget your children, either. When they see you minister to someone else, you are helping

We recently started changing our regular type of visiting to Work Weekends or Work Days. We started doing this with one family once a month. We go to one or the other's house and help with projects. Example: I needed my refrigerator cleaned, she needed mending done. Women pitch in and work on that project. Men did wood cutting with their chain saws. Girls worked on a quilting project. Little guys had play—but we are planning some projects for them next time. We also used this as an opportunity for our home-schooled children. In the evenings they give oral reports of the month's work, give a recitation, sing songs, or whatever. What great fellowship around a working-together theme!

I really have a hard time just having fellowship as the family gets bigger, and there is so much work that needs doing. This idea grew out of the desire to keep on working while having fellowship. "In all labor there is profit, but talk leads only to poverty."

—Laurie Sleeper, WA

There is nothing mysterious about why people become atomized in modern urban settings. Individuals are drawn to community affiliations and attach themselves to them in direct proportion to the functional value of those organizations. . . . Take away the functions, and you take away the community. . . .

To enable people to pursue happiness, good social policy consists of leaving the important things in life for people to do for themselves, and protecting them from coercion by others as they go about their lives.

—Charles Murray
In Pursuit of Happiness and Good Government

build their character. They even become moved by the Holy Spirit to minister as well."

We've already talked about how to organize and train your family to work as a team under the Lordship of Christ. Now let's look at a few practical steps you can take as a family to influence your neighborhood, community, and world for Christ.

Serving Your Neighbors

Here are some ways you can reach out to the neighbors:

- Helping the neighbors keep their own places nice also helps. Restoring trash cans that have rolled away to their proper location or helping the little old widow lady next door rake her leaves establishes you as a good neighbor.
- So does volunteering to work on common land (putting a flower bed in, perhaps).
- Your family can sponsor a block party or backyard barbecue.
- You can hang out Christmas decorations with a Christian message.
- You can have a Good News Club or other evangelistic outreach in your home.
- You can keep an eye on the neighbor's property to protect it from burglars; take in their mail when they are away; water their lawn when they are on vacation.

Children can have a special ministry to neighbors. In this day when children are widely perceived as liabilities, a house full of helpful, respectful children who will shovel snow, rake leaves, take in trash cans, and perform other chores for the neighbors (even for pay if appropriate) can help change people's anti-child attitudes. Good children make the difference between a neighborhood and a bunch of houses or apartments.

Charles Murray in his book *In Pursuit of Happiness and Good Government* stresses that neighborliness is the bottom-line defense against community disintegration. When people stop being neighborly, the criminal element find it easy to take over. Even when they have taken over, a revival of neighborliness can send them packing. You may not have realized you are accomplishing all that by planting flowers in front of your house and talking to the neighbors, but you are!

Serving Your Community

Good neighbors often graduate into positions of influence in the community. We tend to equate community service with politicking, but really it is a work of charity and cultural influence. For example:

- Tutoring adult illiterates, or immigrants, or inner-city youth.
- Donating land or goods to community causes (parks, community celebrations, the State Fair).
- Donating services (hanging Christmas lights, cleaning sidewalks, rototilling community flower beds.)
- Joining community agencies: the foster care review board and other watchdog groups. If you really want to help foster kids, or help stem the tide of judicial corruption, this is the place to start.
- Volunteering to help an established charitable group (candy-striping, fund-raising, membership drives, and so on).
- Taking the kids to visit a nursing home, or sing carols around the community, or help clean up the park.
- Being chosen to head a community group which you have served as a volunteer. Example: Serving as a La Leche League leader.
- Starting your own group to meet a community need instead of begging the government to step in and take over. The church is not responsible for all the charity work in society; some of us need to get busy and tackle it with church backing but without taking the church's precious teaching and evangelism time for it.

We have tried to involve our children in any "church work" that we have done, but not always with great success. We have cleaned the church a few times as a family, but I ended up with a twenty-pound baby in a backpack while I ran the vacuum and tried to interest the three-year-old in putting toys away—and Ferd had to clean the bathroom with the twins trying to help him. We sure were tired after that!

The children have also helped to select and deliver food to families that have contacted us for help, and that is usually a good activity for showing kindness and help to others. Recently we prepared some soup and a meal for a family whose mom was sick with the flu. The girls and Davey covered a box with colorful wrapping paper while I was assembling the food. Then we all delivered our cheerful package.

—Linda Rivas, OR

If Christians who have been sitting at home for years only knew the blessing they would receive by taking their children or grandchildren to a rest home! If they did, there would be fewer lonely people in our country and a lot more fulfilled people who know what it means to give to others.

—Florence Turnidge
Quoted by Mark Cutshall
Focus on the Family
March 1989

Serving Your Legislators

Once you have achieved a position of some community influence, you may find political types ap-
proaching you for help. Yes, *help!* Our legislators are
normal human beings who need help. And, as always, he who would influence the legislature must be
servant of all!

First of all, your legislators need help getting
nominated and elected. You can join the local committee of the Republican, Democratic, Libertarian (or
whatever) Party and find out who you'd like to support for office. Then the fun begins. Coffees. Printing.
P-R. Door-to-door. Phone calls. Mailings. Children
can help with all of this. I know, because my father
trained me to do it all before the age of ten! He had
me covering one side of the street tucking flyers into
people's doorways while my sister covered the other
. . collating and stapling mailings and stuffing envelopes . . . standing in front of the Stop 'n Shop supermarket wearing a red, white, and blue sash and
passing out brochures . . . and lurking out in front of
the polling place with a sign that exhorted voters to
choose our candidate. He got elected, too!

Once elected, your legislator needs even more
help. As the title of a book by California State Senator
Bill Richardson says, *What Makes You Think We Read
the Bills?* In this age of messianic government, legislators are constantly being asked to enact more laws
than they have time to read. You can perform a valuable service by researching particular bills in your
area of concern and summarizing them for your representatives. This service does require special
gifts—and if you happen to have this special gift, the
rest of us would really appreciate your doing this for
us!

Lobbying really just boils down to giving your
representatives the reasons you are for or against a
bill. Point out the unintended negative consequences
of a bad bill (these days, almost all are bad!). Explain
how they could affect you personally. Take your children to visit the state capitol and meet your legisla-

tors. Let the kids themselves lobby a bit. This could be the first step Junior needs to propel him to the Governor's Mansion someday. If you teach him to rule wisely by training him for Christian leadership in the home, who knows what God could use him for?

Living-Room Missions

We must not rule out the possibility that Junior is destined for even greater things than the governorship of your state. If you have taken on your Biblical role of training Junior into a Christian leader, your family can *right now* start ruling spiritually in your community. "He who wins souls is wise" (Proverbs 11:30), and may well stand in greater honor in the kingdom of heaven than he who administers the state's laws.

The Nation at Your Doorstep. A small but growing number of churches in various denominations are beginning to see the potential of your home as an evangelistic and discipleship center.

In fact, the era when "church" meant "the large building our congregation is always paying for or adding to" may just about be over. With today's skyrocketing real estate and construction prices, congregations are finding it harder and harder to find good locations and build facilities large enough to accomodate the entire church body. I myself can without any difficulty think of not one, but two churches in my immediate area that are both stalled in this holding pattern, unable to relocate and unable to handle any more numerical growth in their present location.

The use of homes as shepherding centers, where parents teach their children from day to day and each elder periodically instructs a small number of families under his personal care, unlocks the church's potential for growth. Not only does each child and adult now have a clear training goal in mind and at least one person who is personally responsible to help him achieve it, but far more of the church's financial resources and energy can go directly into evangelism

The New Testament Scriptures point out the importance of the house church as the earliest method of Christian fellowship and worship. Jesus used houses as centers for mission activities. The early church used houses for teaching purposes. And Paul's letters refer to specific private houses that were centers of activity for teaching and preaching. . . .

Four basic functions of the house church have been identified: (1) prayer, (2) fellowship, (3) evanglism, and (4) a meeting place.

The Biblical examples of house churches can be a model for restoring community, evangelism, and growth in Churches of Christ during the 1980s. Christians can be encouraged to follow this model as they strive to evangelize an urban population. . . . Evangelistic teaching often takes place in the personal sharing of a disciple with a person who desires to be a follower of Christ. The houses of Christians in the 1980s are as personal in atmosphere as the homes of the early church. From a Biblical and practical standpoint, the use of houses as places for sharing the message of Jesus makes sense.

—Verlon Harp
House Churches Among the Churches of Christ During the 1980s

As a member in the body of Christ of several years' standing, by [now] you should be a teacher. You may feel there is no need for you to teach inasmuch as you feel there are "enough teachers already for each of the classes at church." This reflects a vastly different definition of teaching than what we have in mind. It also indicates a view that what teaching there is to be done is to be at the church house. But look again at your Bible. *Where was the classroom then?*

—Alvin Jennings
How Christianity Grows in the City

The house church in the 1980s can be an evangelistic center for growth in smaller sections or neighborhoods of the city where it is located. As evangelistic Bible studies grow and divide, the house church becomes larger and soon is large enough to divide into two smaller ones. This process of growth is working [as detailed in the descriptions of several churches that operate like this provided in the book I am quoting] and suggests a working model for any congregation that seriously desires successful growth in the future. The atmosphere can provide adequate training and experience for effective ministry and leadership in the mission field.

—Verlon Harp
House Churches Among the Churches of Christ During the 1980s

and discipleship under this system. As Alvin Jennings, author of *How Christianity Grows in the City*, says, "In congregations whre the one man 'pastor system' prevails, or where the bulk of preaching and teaching is by 'the preacher' whose labors are centered in a church-owned building, a large portion of the contributions must go to the purchase of the land and building and its maintenance. It requires from 150 to 200 members of the body of Christ to support one full-time minister on an average where a church property is involved. A full-time worker is supported by only 27 members in one religious group where no church-owned property is involved."[1]

Mr. Jennings, who is also the president of Star Bible Publications, proposes we readopt the New Testament scheme of using the homes of qualified church members for the basic work of the church, with occasional large-group meetings in rented facilities. Most denominations are already trying to revitalize themselves with some kind of home meetings (typically home Bible studies and fellowship groups). In cases where a new church is starting, or the church is in a poor neighborhood, or an old church just has to expand, some kind of mix of home church meetings (supervised by qualified leaders) and use of existing facilities would seem to promise optimum growth possibilities.

Star Bible Publications publishes a fascinating little booklet titled *House Churches Among the Churches of Christ During the 1980s* which summarizes the experience of some churches that have for one reason or another begun using a "house church" setup. Author Verlon Harp "discovered thirty-three congregations of the Church of Christ that currently use house churches." The most obviously successful of these was a church in Lexington, Massachusetts. Set up as a "normal" church, in 1979 it had shrunk to forty members. In six years after adopting a format increasingly reliant upon home churches, it had increased to 1800 members and was renting the Boston Opera House for congregational meetings. "Elders, evangelists, deacons and other trusted teachers lead in thirty-one 'house churches' (Philemon 2) throughout the metropolis under the supervision of the elders."[2]

According to Verlon Harp, "Every congregation [of the thirty-three Churches of Christ he interviewed] listed several advantages to house churches. These included: (1) increased number of baptisms, (2) spiritual growth among members, (3) stronger relationships in the groups, (4) an atmosphere for meeting needs, (5) informal discussion periods, (6) association of many different age groups (there were two churches that did have teen house churches, while most of the congregations promote a mixture of all ages in each house church), (7) an enthusiastic setting for all ages, (8) growth among leaders, (9) better organization and accountability, (10) greater responsibility and concern among members, (11) an emphasis on individual talents and gifts, (12) opportunities for all to be with children, (13) more individualized attention and encouragement, (14) appealing setting for visitors, and (15) less building-oriented ministry."[3]

Once your home is operating as a reasonably credible pattern of Christ's kingdom, you can multiply it *rapidly* with a structure like this. You can reach out to neighbors, friends, and even total strangers, all under the direction of more seasoned leaders. Instead of fishing for souls with a pole, bent paperclip, and worm, you can start scooping them in with a net!

I might be wrong, but I am going to predict that if God chooses to "visit" His people with a blessing in the decade of the nineties, we will see an explosion of churches using some house-church principles. You and your family will have tremendous opportunities to evangelize! So get ready—and don't forget to get your church leaders copies of those great books from Star Publications while you're at it!

The World at Your Doorstep. And finally, if you set up Christ's kingdom in your family, you have a chance to change not only your country but the whole world.

BENEFITS OF THE SHEPHERDING APPROACH TO EVANGELISM AND EDIFICATION

1. Provides intimate shepherd-sheep relationship (John 10:1-14). . . .
7. The heavy expense of purchasing real estate is eliminated.
8. Teaching the Bible to children is the main responsibility of the parents, thus strengthening the family unit while inciting more Bible study and discussion on a day-to-day basis. . . .
11. Younger men have greater awareness of their need for leadership participation, and they can much more easily identify with the teacher or preacher in this setting as a pattern within reach for their imitation. . . .
13. New places of assembly (in homes) can be arranged without a consideration of the financial abilities of those being taught. . . .
17. The number of "pulpits" opened through this method can accomodate the needs of . . . even hundreds of capable ex-preachers and ex-teachers in getting back into actively spreading the Word. . . .
20. There is no way to outgrow facilities. . . .
23. Conforms to every known Biblical and practical principle.

—Alvin Jennings
How Christianity Grows in the City

It has often been said that all Christians can have a part in foreign missions by praying, most by giving, but that only a few could do the going. However, God has now made it possible for virtually every Christian in the United States to actually be a foreign missionary.

How can we possibly estimate the potential effect of these millions of international [students] on the whole missionary enterprise around the world in the next twenty-five years? Most are destined in the next twenty-five years to occupy one-fourth to one-half of the world's top positions of leadership—politically, militarily, economically, scientifically, academically and socially. Less than half a percent of all the Protestant missionaries in the world are working among these people, and yet it is one of the greatest missionary opportunities of the century.

—Mark Hanna, former International Students Inc. staffer, quoted by Lawson Lau, author of *The World at Your Doorstep*

The World at Your Doorstep: A Handbook for International Student Ministry is the name of a book by Lawson Lau (InterVarsity Press, 1984) that shows how your family can have an international missionary outreach—all from your living room!

As *The World at Your Doorstep* points out, international students are much easier to reach than overseas non-Christians. They speak English, are here in our climate wearing our type of clothes and eating mostly our type of food. You don't need a visa. They appreciate your friendship and hospitality all the more, being cut off from their own families. And as the book says, "It is rare to find any of them who do not love children."

Your warm family life is your greatest asset in dealing with these students, according to those who have this ministry. International students are not searching for "programs" to attend in a building, but for a family to belong to.

Les and Penny Gioja of Illinois describe the mission in their home in just these terms.

"Our family's personal ministry is in hospitality and friendship evangelism. The Lord has provided us with a campus full of international students (but other groups would work just as well in developing your own ministry). Statistically, 80 to 90 percent of the international students in the United States never see the inside of an American's home. They frequently have no friends here and greatly desire companionship. Many are also very interested in learning all they can about Jesus and Christianity. So the need is great.

"In using our available resources, we have made good friends with the International Student Affairs Officer on campus. He calls us up when a student is coming in after hours. We pick him or her, and maybe their family, up at the airport and take them to our house for the night or the weekend.

"Meals are nothing special, unless the student makes them; we just set out an extra plate whether it's lasagna or leftovers. We just share what we have and they really appreciate it.

"We also help them find an apartment and move in. We take their names and phone numbers and either befriend them ourselves or assign someone else who would like to do it.

"These students love shopping in grocery stores, attending weddings, going to the park with the family, travelling with us on vacation, painting our house with us, and almost anything we might have occasion to do. We also have some special outings, but we go as a family and have an enjoyable time together while ministering to our friends.

"It seldom takes long for our friends to ask us about Jesus. We give them a Bible in their own language, if they want one, and answer their questions. They usually draw the gospel out of us with their questions, and a few will become Christians. It is really wonderful to see the Holy Spirit working in this way. And it takes only a little more time for us, because we invite them to do things we would do anyway. And our children receive as much benefit from our actions as our international friends.

"Since we started three years ago, we have ministered to approximately 150 students from over thirty countries. Half a dozen or so have become Christians, and nearly all have heard the gospel at least once. There are approximately fourteen other families or singles working with us so that our total ministry has reached many more. Think of the impact you can have!

"Don't be scared off by the numbers. We are no more 'superstars' than you are, believe me! We have four children, I work full-time outside the home, and my wife works full-time in the home home schooling, housecleaning, cooking, and taking care of a day-care baby. We don't have any extra time, either, but everyone has twenty-four hours a day as a resource. We just ask others to share in some of our everyday activities and thereby use our available resources for our own little worldwide ministry. And so can you!"

The Taussigs began in a small, hesitant way. There was no grandiose plan, no master strategy, no knowledge of other international student ministries, no training program for American volunteers. There was only a couple who wanted to do something for international students, especially Nigerians, at Kansas State University. They have certainly made an impact. . . .

After several years of prayer for and service among international students, the Taussigs said they are grateful to God for the opportunity to go to eighty countries without having to leave Manhattan, without needing a visa and without having to learn a foreign language. At Kansas State they have the world at their doorstep.

—Lawson Lau
The World at Your Doorstep

A worldwide home ministry like the Giojas' doesn't happen overnight. I don't have one like this yet, though I hope to someday! But as we learn to create happy homes for our children, get them on our team and train them, rid our homes of obstacles to ministry, and start practicing the arts of charity, service, and hospitality, we prepare the way of the Lord to visit His people with tidings of great joy.

God is not bound. He can still spiritually visit His people, find us faithfully at work, and bless us with great power and authority. Our faithfulness in the little things leads to authority over bigger things. Great things still can happen.

Come home and help us make them happen!

A Note to the Reader

I would love to hear from you with your own stories, ideas, and comments about the topics in this book, so I can pass them on to the readers of my newsletter, *HELP,* or use them to improve future editions of this or another book. You can contact me directly at the Home Life address (see Resources).

Please help me make the most of your letter by

- Including permission to quote it. Please don't be shy about this! Even if you don't think you have said anything worth repeating, I might very well disagree with you—and it saves me writing a separate letter asking for permission.

- Tell me if you need a personal response to your letter. If all you want is to know that we received and read it, you can include a stamped self-addressed postcard. This is a big help!

- Write or type (typing is also a real help!) on *one* side of the paper only. This makes it so much easier for me when I photocopy your letter for my files.

- Put each topic in your letter on a separate page. For example, if you write about breastfeeding and ideas for family celebrations, put the comments about breastfeeding on one page and about family celebrations on another. And, if you could, please put your name and state on each page. This helps me tremendously with my filing.

Patience is a great virtue, and anyone who writes to me will likely have an opportunity to exercise it. Bill and I do read every letter, though, even if we aren't whizzes at answering them pronto!

Thanks so much, and we look forward to hearing from you!

Footnotes

Chapter 1
Marriage for Mortals

1. Barbara Gordon, "How to Win the Younger-Woman-Old-Man Game," *Bottom Line Personal*, January 15, 1989, p. 12.

2. "During a 12-month period that ended in March [1988], 1.16 million couples got divorced and 2.39 million couples got married, almost a 1-2 ratio, according to the National Center for Health Statistics." Charlotte Low Allen, "Planning for Failure with Prenuptial Pacts," *Insight*, August 15, 1988.

Chapter 3
Bring on the Babies!

1. "Fewer U.S. Couples Are Able to Have Kids, Study Shows," Cleveland *Plain Dealer*, February 11, 1985, p. 1-D.

2. *Ibid.*

3. Germaine Greer, *Sex and Destiny: The Politics of Human Fertility* (New York: Harper & Row, 1984), Chapter 2, "The Importance of Fertility."

4. "Infertility Problems Reported On Rise," *St. Louis Post-Dispatch*, April 13, 1985, p. 2-A.

5. "Fewer U.S. Couples Are Able to Have Kids, Study Shows." *Op. cit.*

6. George Grant, *Grand Illusion: The Legacy of Planned Parenthood* (Nashville: Wolgemuth & Hyatt Publishers, 1988), p. 34.

7. "Infertility Problems Reported On Rise." *Op. cit.*

8. *Ibid.*

9. "Who Keeps Baby M?," *Newsweek*, January 19, 1987, p. 49.

Chapter 5
The Good Birth

1. Stephen Goode, "A Mother's Body, a Fetus's Fate," *Insight*, June 27, 1988. Interestingly, the Georgia Supreme Court ruling in 1981 that established the precedent of allowing a doctor to enforce an unwanted cesarean at the point of a court order was obviously a mistake. "The court granted the order, but the mother refused to comply, going home to deliver. Both mother and baby survived with no complications."

2. Mary Pride, *The Child Abuse Industry* (Westchester, IL: Crossway Books, 1986), p. 115. Consider this quote from Dr. Burton White of the Center for Parent Education, made at an Education Workshop at the Governor's Conference on Children and Youth in Jefferson City, Missouri on December 7 and 8, 1981—"Sending a new parent home with a six day old baby as we do now in this country is insane" (*Child Abuse Industry*, p. 117).

3. The U.S. 1987 cesarean rate was 24.4%, representing nearly one million cesarean births. Figures from Cesarean Prevention Movement (address in Resources).

Chapter 6
The Three Little Hassles

1. "School Daze Obscures View of Motherhood Duties," *World*, March 21, 1988.
2. *Ibid.*

Chapter 8
Is There Life After TV?

1. Tamra B. Orr, *Not on the Newsstands* (Warsaw, IN: Priority Parenting Publications, 1988), p. 59.

Chapter 11
The Two-Minute Manager

1. Charles Murray, *In Pursuit of Happiness and Good Government* (New York: Simon & Schuster, 1988), p. 145.

Chapter 13
Family Practice

1. Eleaner H. Porter, *Pollyanna* (New York: Grosset & Dunlap, 1960), adapted and abridged by Iris Vinton, pp. 34, 36.
2. The Christian and Missionary Alliance.
3. Survey conducted by Barna Research Group for Josh McDowell, as reported in *World*, February 15, 1988, p. 5.

Chapter 14
The Church in Your Living Room

1. We got this idea from Gregg Harris's *Family Restoration Workshop*. See Christian Life Workshops in the Resources.
2. (Westchester, IL: Crossway Books, 1989). Reviewed in manuscript.

Chapter 15
"It's Superfamily!"

1. Alvin Jennings, *How Christianity Grows in the City* (Fort Worth, TX: Star Bible Publications, Inc., 1985), p. 119.
2. *Ibid.*, p. 141.
3. Verlon Harp, *House Churches Among the Churches of Christ During the 1980s* (Fort Worth, TX: Star Bible Publications, Inc., 1987), p. 28.

Resources

This resource list is a catalog of the best helps for your family. These are arranged by chapter, so each topic discussed in the book has its own list of resources. Under each chapter heading you will find at least some of the following:

- Books to read
- Organizations to join
- Periodicals that tap you into what's happening in that field
- Training courses to sharpen your skills
- Suppliers of helpful materials appropriate to that chapter.

At the end of some listings you will notice an italicized business name, e.g., *Home Life*. This means that the book or product is available from that business. Usually the business mentioned will be listed in that chapter's Resources. A few businesses carry materials spanning several chapters; these are listed at the end of the Resources, along with a few periodicals of general interest.

Elizabeth Baker. *The Happy Housewife.* Wheaton, IL: Victor Books, 1975. This wonderful little book helped straighten out a lot of things for me when I was a new Christian. Elizabeth Baker gently points out deep truths about how to handle marriage, sex, entertainment, children, devotions, and so on in a deceptively simple style. *Out of print* (wouldn't you know it!).

Weldon Hardenbrook. *Missing from Action: Vanishing Manhood in America.* Nashville: Thomas Nelson Publishers, 1987. Every man in America should read this book. It shows how men have run away from an active role in their families, how this has thrust women into the leadership role in home and society, why this is a disaster, and how men can quit shoving off their job on social institutions and turn things around. A great read with eye-popping insights on every page. *GCB.*

Chapter 1
Marriage for Mortals

Mary Pride. *The Way Home: Beyond Feminism, Back to Reality*. Westchester, IL: Crossway Books, 1985. The female counterpart to *Missing from Action*. Builds a Biblical basis for home-centered (as opposed to institution-centered) living, working, and playing, and shows the consequences of either obeying or neglecting the role of "homeworker." *Home Life*.

Edith Schaeffer. *What Is a Family?* Tappan, NJ: Fleming Revell. Lively, thought-provoking, practical look at what families can accomplish in this world. *GCB*.

Nick Stinnett and John DeFrain. *Secrets of Strong Families*. Boston: Little, Brown and Company, 1985. This intriguing book developed out of research into the question, "What makes some families strong?" Lots of true-life stories and practical suggestions from the interviewees. *GCB*.

Chapter 2
Holy Sex

Connie Marshner. *Decent Exposure: How to Teach Your Children About Sex*. Brentwood, TN: Wolgemuth & Hyatt Publishers, 1988. Could have been called *How to Teach Yourself About Sex*. Here is a wide-lens view of sex that ranges far beyond the usual discussion of technique. Technique, in fact, is not discussed at all. Has great insights into the real nature of the Youth Culture and prescriptions for reintroducing Christian culture in the home. *Home Life*.

Chapter 3
Bring on the Babies!

George Grant. *Grand Illusions: The Legacy of Planned Parenthood*. Brentwood, TN: Wolgemuth & Hyatt Publishers, 1988. George is not only a fabulous writer with a keen eye for the drama of the story he unfolds, but a meticulous researcher. Find out where today's anti-baby propaganda comes from though the twisted history of PP and its philandering founder, Margaret Sanger. *GCB*

Sheila Kippley. *Breastfeeding and Natural Child Spacing*. Cincinnati: Couple to Couple League, 1989. Second revised edition. The classic study on this subject. *Couple to Couple League*.

Mary Pride. *The Child Abuse Industry*. Westchester, IL: Crossway Books, 1987. This book tells you what you need to know about the laws, regulations, and mindset governing children and family service departments. Read it before deciding to adopt a child through a government agency or become foster parents. *Home Life*.

ORGANIZATION
Couple to Couple League
P.O. Box 111184
Cincinnati, OH 45211

John and Sheila Kippley, a Catholic couple who have authored several major books on natural family planning (NFP) and ecological breastfeeding, started Couple to Couple League to teach the sympto-thermal method of NFP. Their work has branched out to include all aspects of godly family life, including chastity education, birth, bonding, child-training, and support for home schooling. $15 a year gets you six issues of the newsletter. Their mail-order bookstore carries all the books you will ever need on NFP and related subjects.

Gail Sforza Brewer, with Tom Brewer, M.D. *What Every Pregnant Woman Should Know:The Truth About Diet and Drugs During Pregnancy.* New York: Random House: 1977. The one book about nutrition every pregnant woman should read. *NAPSAC.*

Coalition for the Medical Rights of Women. *Safe Natural Remedies for Discomforts of Pregnancy.* San Francisco: Coalition for the Medical Rights of Women, 1981, rev. 1982. Order from 2845 24th St., San Francisco, CA 94110 (415) 826-4401 for $4.

Rahima Baldwin. *Special Delivery: The Complete Guide to Informed Birth.* Berkeley, CA: Celestial Arts Press, 1979.The very best book on preparing for and going through a planned home birth. Ignore the tiny bit of California-esque mysticism and concentrate on the excellent practical information. *NAPSAC.*

Nancy Wainer Cohen and Lois J. Estner. *Silent Knife: Cesarean Prevention and Vaginal Birth after Cesarean.* Bergin and Garvey Publishers. What every woman should know about medicalized birth *before* it happens to her. Caveat: some New Age philosophy is noticeable in the chapter on grieving. *NAPSAC.*

Robert Mendelsohn, M.D. *MalePractice: How Doctors Manipulate Women.* Chicago: Contemporary Books. Most readable introduction to the arguments for home birth. *NAPSAC.*

Chapter 4
Let's Enjoy Pregnancy (As Much As Possible)

Chapter 5
The Good Birth

David Stewart et. al. *The Five Standards for Safe Childbearing*. Those five standards are: good nutrition, skillful midwifery, natural childbirth, home birth, and breastfeeding. Dr. Stewart and his guest authors present an irrefutable case for each of these standards (based on numerous actual validated studies of childbirth outcomes). If you are only going to read one book about childbirth, start here. Warning: Chapter Fifteen, "The Influence of Belief in Childbirth," has a bit of New-Age and evolutionary flavor (as indeed most of medicine does these days). *NAPSAC*.

————. *The Napsac Directory of Alternative Birth Services and Consumer Guide*. Help for those seeking a midwife, birthing center, or sympathetic physician. State-by-state listings. Invaluable section on what questions to ask a prospective birth attendant. Also list of national and international alternative birth organizations, midwifery training programs, and resources available mail-order. *NAPSAC*.

The Whole Birth Catalog. Janet Isaacs Ashford, ed. Trumansburg, NY: The Crossing Press. Comprehensive sourcebook for books, resources, teacher aids, organizations, and everything else pertaining to birth. Unhappily endorses abortion—this is because Crossing Press and Mrs. Ashford have not yet disentangled true feminism (e.g., women free to be women) from phony feminism (women trying to be men). *ICEA Bookcenter*.

The Womanly Art of Breastfeeding. Franklin Park, IL: La Leche League International, 1987. Fourth edition. Practical information on how to breastfeed in a wide variety of circumstances, plus true-life stories from breastfeeding moms. *La Leche League*.

ORGANIZATIONS
Cesarean Prevention Movement
P.O. Box 152
Syracuse, NY 13210

One-year membership $25 US, $27 Canada, $30 overseas. Over 60 chapters in all 50 states. Newsletter, the *Clarion*. Information and support for cesarean prevention and vaginal birth after cesarean (VBAC).

International Childbirth Education Association
P.O. Box 20048
Minneapolis, MN 55420
(612) 854-8660

"ICEA unites people who support family-centered maternity care [FCMC] and believe in freedom of choice based on knowledge of childbirth alternatives." Founded in 1960, ICEA has over 11,000 members, including a number of professional childbirth educators. Operates childbirth educator teacher certification program, provides info on FCMC alternatives in your area and how to introduce more of same. Breastfeeding, cesarean birth resources. Conferences. Publishes many periodicals, from general to technical.

La Leche League
P.O. Box 1209
Franklin Park, IL 60131-8209
(312) 455-7730

LLL, an organization founded to promote breastfeeding, is one of the few organizations that still strongly supports at-home motherhood. It has support groups all over the USA and other Western countries, offers a certification program for professional lactation consultants, has conventions, and sells a variety of books and products by mail order. Unfortunately LLL confuses spanking with child abuse, and offers teaching and books that promote this error. LLL has also recently promoted *Mothering* magazine to its members, even though two LLL leaders wrote to the leadership asking them to reconsider this action in view of *Mothering*'s increasing New Age outlook. So you will have to exercise discrimination in your use of LLL support groups and resources.

NAPSAC
Rt. 1, Box 646
Marble Hill, MO 63764.

NAPSAC stands for InterNational Association of Parents and Professionals for Safe Alternatives in Childbirth. It is a wonderful organization, with support groups all over the United States and scattered about the Western world. The NAPSAC bookstore is a great source for information about home birth, or birth in general. To join, send $15 (U.S.) or $17 (other countries) in U.S. funds. Or send a large SASE for the free book catalog—a great selection of the best books on birth, home birth, bonding, breastfeeding, and other topics. Caution: some of the books in their catalog (by Alice Miller and Ashley Montagu, for instance) promote the mistaken view that spanking is abuse.

TRAINING COURSES
Apprentice Academics
3805 Mosswood Dr.
Conroe, TX 77302-1176
(409) 273-5175

Midwifery Home Study correspondence course. Established 1981. Free info pak.

Informed Homebirth/Informed Birth and Parenting
P.O. Box 3675
Ann Arbor, MI 48106

Correspondence course for certified childbirth educators designed by Rahima Baldwin, author of *Special Delivery* (see above). Encompasses both home birth and hospital birth. Over 1,000 teachers trained since 1977. Beware tinges of Eastern mystical thinking—the practical parts of this program sound good.

SUPPLIER
Spirit-Led Childbirth
6413 N. Lunar Court
Ft. Collins, CO 80525
(303) 226-5079.

A Christian "birthing and parenting supplies" catalog. Everything the midwife or home birther needs, from professional supplies to sitz bath herb mixes. Books and educational materials, too. Professional-looking catalog. Nice birth kits

Chapter 6
The Three Little Hassles and How They Grew

Gregg Harris. *The Family Restoration Workshop* (cassette series). This workshop contains a tremendous amount of Scriptural insight into our current culture. Among other things, Gregg is the only speaker I have heard confront the older generation for their partial responsibility for our present pickle. *Christian Life Workshops*

Connie Marshner. *Decent Exposure*. Most incisive analysis of the Youth Cult going. See Chapter 2 Resources.

Leonard Mogel. *The Magazine: Everything You Need to Know to Make it in the Magazine Business*. Second edition. Revealing look behind the scenes at how magazines are produced and marketed. Explains why advertisers are the magazine's *real* customers, and readers only the "product" delivered to advertisers. *New Careers Center*.

Olive J. Alexander. *Developing Spiritually-Sensitive Children*. Minneapolis: Bethany House, 1980. Excellent advice on this subject from a mother of older children. *Out of print*.

Al and Pat Fabrizio. *Under Loving Command*. Palo Alto: Sheva Press, 1969. A great little booklet that summarizes the principles of child discipline we must remember . . . and keep forgetting! *GCB*.

Richard Fugate. *What the Bible Really Says About . . . Child Training*. Tempe, AZ: Aleitheia Publishers. The first book you should read on this subject. From what I see offered in bookstores, this is possibly the *only* book you should read on this subject! *GCB*.

Marie Winn. *Children Without Childhood*. New York: Viking Penguin, 1983. In this revolutionary book, Marie Winn calls parents to account for throwing kids into the worst of the adult world for our own convenience. Her info on the Middle Ages is from sources that have been lately discredited—child rearing in the Middle Ages was not all that heartless—and her condemnation of Cotton Mather is unjust, but that is to be expected from a secular writer. Mrs. Winn points out the solution—protect your kid so he can enjoy being a kid. *GCB*

TRAINING COURSE
NACD (National Academy of Child Development)
P.O. Box 280012
Tampa, FL 33682
(813) 972-2025
On-site evaluations leading to home training and therapy programs for handicapped and gifted children. Every parent enrolling is asked to go through NACD's *The Miracles of Child Development*.This cassette-and-workbook course is available separately to non-NACD members as well. Free catalog.

Chapter 7
The Hassled Mother's Quick & Dirty Guide to Child Training

Chapter 8
Is There Life After TV?

Marie Winn. *The Plug-In Drug*. New York: Viking Penguin, 1985. Mrs. Winn makes a compelling case against television based not so much on the lousy content of the shows as what television keeps us from doing: raising our children, making our own entertainment, learning and teaching, and other little things like that. Lots of anecdotes and statistics. *GCB*.

Jerry Mander. *Four Arguments for the Elimination of Television*. New York: Quill, 1978. Mander proves that TV threatens our health, sanity, and liberties, and shows that its bad effects are the natural result of the technology. Caveat: His fourth argument drifts into some New Age thinking about the power of imagery. *GCB*.

ORGANIZATION
S.E.T. (The Society for the Elimination of Television)
Box 10491
Oakland, CA 94610-0491
(415) 530-2056

S.E.T. offers a newsletter (*News and Notes*), T-shirts, posters, and a speaker's bureau. The newsletter is a potpourri of clipped articles about TV, I-kicked-the-set stories, and editorials drawing linkages between TV use and unpleasant social phenomena. Subscription, $5/10 issues.

SUPPLIER
Animal Town Game Co.
P.O. Box 2002
Santa Barbara, CA 93120
(805) 682-7343 for info.

Source for family games. Free catalog

Chapter 9
The Omega Strategy

David Chilton. *Productive Christians in an Age of Guilt Manipulators*. Tyler, TX: Institute for Christian Economics, 1981. Second edition, revised, 1982. Chilton buries the case for "Christian socialism" with Biblical analysis and biting satire. Strong case for productivity. *GCB*.

Mary Pride. *The New Big Book of Home Learning*. Westchester, IL: Crossway Books, 1988. Product reviews and information for all basic areas of home schooling. Forty chapters, 382 oversized pages. *Home Life*.

———. *The Next Book of Home Learning.* Westchester, IL: Crossway Books, 1987. Companion to *The New Big Book.* Covers enrichment areas and special situations. Literature. Art, Music. Health. Home skills. Business skills. Languages. Toys and games. Etc. *Home Life.*

———. *Schoolproof.* Westchester, IL: Crossway Books, 1988. *Schoolproof* is about how to learn, how to teach, how to get rid of educational clutter, and how to have fun while doing it. *Home Life.*

John Pugsley. *The Alpha Strategy: The Ultimate Plan of Financial Self-Defense* . Los Angeles: Stratford Press, 1981.This ground-breaking book will change your thinking about money, economy, and the way government and big business cooperate. It also provides you with a bulletproof, productive use for your financial resources. Order from Commonsense Press, P.O. Box 471, Corona del Mar, CA 92625. $13.95 plus $2 shipping. Very highly recommended.

Luanne Shackelford and Susan White. *A Survivor's Guide to Home Schooling.* Westchester, IL: Crossway Books, 1988. The nitty-gritties you need to know. Humorous and fun to read. Great companion book to *Schoolproof* (see above). *GCB.*

Edith Schaeffer. *The Hidden Art of Homemaking.* Wheaton, IL: Tyndale House Publishers, 1971. Ways to create beauty in all areas of your everyday life. Written by a woman who has seen her "hidden art" develop into a worldwide ministry reaching millions. *GCB.*

Don Aslett. *Clutter's Last Stand.* Writer's Digest Books. More than a humorous book on how to de-junk your house. Don helps you distinguis between the beautiful and useful in your life and the useless clutter. If you have no time, no space, and lots of stress, this is the book for you! *Home Life.*

———. *Do I Dust or Vacuum First?* Writer's Digest Books. Don answers the 100 most-commonly-asked housekeeping questions. Only difference between this and other books is that this time you get the right answers! *Home Life.*

———. *Is There Life After Housework?* Writer's Digest Books. Here is the book that started it all. America's Number One Cleaning Expert explains how to eliminate 75% of your housework *and* have a cleaner house! Also available on a hilarious video. *Home Life.*

Chapter 10
The Cinderella Principle

————. *Make Your House Do the Housework.* Writer's Digest Books. How you can have a maintenance-free house, apartment, condo, or whatever. Find out what about your place is forcing you to work too hard, and eliminate it! Lots of simple, cheap solutions that can really improve your family's life. *Home Life.*

————. *Pet Clean-Up Made Easy.* Writer's Digest Books. How to clean up after every imaginable kind of animal mess—and even better, how to prevent odor, stains, and maintenance problems. *Home Life.*

————. *Who Says It's a WOMAN'S Job to Clean?* Writer's Digest Books. Don's simplest explanation of his no-work housecleaning system. Our kids love this book! *Home Life.*

SUPPLIER
Don Aslett's Cleaning Center
P.O. Box 39
311 S. 5th
Pocatello, ID 83204
(208) 232-6212 for questions or to order the catalog.
1-800-451-2402 for Visa, MC orders only.

All the nifty professional cleaning products and supplies Don tells you to use in his books. You used to have to go to a janitor's store in the grungy part of town and stand in line for two hours (not that these stores are so busy, but their service is rotten) to get these products—in sizes you couldn't use up in five years. I know, 'cause I've done it! Now that we can order these goodies from home, we have them all. This great catalog will make you *want* to clean your house! Cleaning tips included.

MY FAVORITE MAIL-ORDER CATALOGS
■ *Clothes*
Biobottoms, Box 6009, 3820 Bodega Ave., Petaluma, CA 94953. (707) 778-7945. Their telephone operators may not always speak English and their service speed is like that of the snail, but all the same this company sells some of the most long-wearing, pretty, sensible kids' clothes. We like their diaper covers, and find you can pass their playsuits down through four kids.

Hanna Anderson, 1010 N.W. Flanders, Portland, OR 97209. 1-800-222-0544. 7-6 M-Sat PST. I wince at the prices for these children's clothes, but they are exceptionally well-made, easy to wear, and like Biobottoms are free of advertising for culture icons. You can get your child two of these outfits per season (instead of more sets of cheaper clothes) and he will always look well-dressed and feel comfortable.

L.L. Bean, Freeport, ME 04033. 1-800-221-4221 24 hours, 7 days. Sensible, comfortable, sometimes even attractive clothes for active wear, plus a lot of outdoorsy gew-gaws you don't need. Bean models always look like real people doing real things—no sleazy expressions or poses, unlike almost every other adult clothing catalog. The L.L. Bean logo is creeping onto the outside of some of their clothes; I hope this trend reverses itself soon, as I refuse to wear advertisements on my body.

■ *Gardening*
Breck's, 6523 N. Galena Rd., PO Box 1757, Peoria, IL 61656. Widest selection of good-to-excellent quality bulbs, clumps, roots, and rhizomes. Beautiful catalog.

W. Atlee Burpee & Co., Warminster, PA 18974. The king of seed companies.

Gardener's Supply, 128 Intervale Rd., Burlington, VT 05401. 1-802-863-1700, 24 hours, 7 days. Composters, shredders, tools, seed-starting kits, and all sorts of fabulous gardening widgets. Good customer service.

Jackson & Perkins Co., One Rose Lane, Medford, OR 97501-9835. (503) 776-2400. *The* catalog for rose fiends, such as myself. The best and brightest in award-winning roses. The last one I received even smelled of rose perfume!

Miller Nurseries, West Lake Rd., Canadaigua, NY 14424. -800-826-9630. NY: 1-800-462-9601. Hardy trees, shrubs, roses, and berries. The stock I have received from Miller has consistently been superior to that from Stark Bros. and other mail-order nurseries.

Natural Gardening Research Center, Hwy. 48, P.O. Box 149, Sunman, IN 47041. (812) 623-3800. One-year guarantee. Natural remedies for insect pests and plant diseases. Bill and the boys like spooking me with the pictures of disgusting little critters eating even more disgusting little critters. Effective natural gardening for *Nightmare on Elm Street* types.

Nitron Industries, Inc. 4605 Johnson Rd., P.O. Box 1447, Fayetteville, AR 72702. 1-800-750-1777 for questions and technical help, 1-800-853-0123 for orders. Enzyme products, natural fertilizers, and soil enhancements. The new catalog has a bunch of other gardening stuff and looks Smith-and-Hawkenish.

Springhill Nurseries, 110 W. Elm St., Tipp City, OH 45371. Perennial flowers, bulbs, ground covers, shrubs. Absolutely lovely catalog. Excellent packing. Guaranteed.

Wayside Gardens, Hodges, SC 29695-0001. 1-800-845-1124. SC: call collect 223-1968. Credit card orders only; minimum $30. Ye upscale garden catalog. Gorgeous and uncommon plants in excellent shape for high prices. Strong in perennials, ground covers, shrubs, and ornamental trees.

■ *Gifts*
Childcraft, 20 Kilmer Rd., P.O. Box 3143, Edison, NJ 08818-3143. 1-800-631-5657, 24 hours, 7 days. Nice toy catalog. Many creativity-inspiring items. Decent prices.

Harry and David, Bear Creek Orchards, Medford, OR 97501.1-800-547-3033. The "fruit box" people. Lots of other food gifts. Nice prizes and presentation.

Mary of Puddin Hill, P.O. Box 241, Greenville, TX 75401. (214) 455-2651. Famous fruitcake (the packages of bite-sized ones are great for family or office gifts), cookies, and other gooey delights. All the sugar, all the calories.

Toys to Grow On, P.O. Box 17, Long Beach, CA 90801. 1-800-542-8338. L.A. area, (213) 603-8890. Very nice toy catalog. Age-graded. Focus on creative play.

■ *Sewing and Other Fabric Crafts*
Nancy's Notions, 333 Beichl Ave., P.O. Box 683, Beaver Dam, WI 53916. (414) 887-0690. Tools, notions, fabrics, patterns, and how-to books and videos from the TV sewing lady.

■ *Tools*
Harbor Freigh Salvage Company, 3491 Mission Oaks Blvd., Camarillo, CA 93011-6010. 1-800-423-2567. The handyman's dream come true. Two million customers buy from this catalog of "professional tools and new equipment" at rock-bottom prices. Everything from generators and garden carts to screwdrivers.

■ *Everything Else*

Sears, of course! Now that Sears finally has abandoned the decadent look, I am happy to recommend Sears as a source for general-purpose clothing (e.g., underwear), tools, appliances, and almost everything else except gifts. Their gift selection is still mindlessly consumeristic and iconistic. I'd walk a mile to *avoid* a "Strawberry Shortcake" sheet set or a "MacKids" shorts-and-shirt set, but the Sears gift section is mainly made up of items with celebrities, designers, or cartoon characters splattered all over them. Sears usually has fine quality at an excellent price, except for their clothes, which tend to be of only average quality. You have to pay for a catalog and establish a record as a proven Sears catalog shopper before you start getting regular catalogs.

Kenneth Blanchard and Spencer Johnson. *The One-Minute Manager.* New York: Berkeley Books, 1983. Management skills in parable form. Enormously successful book.

PERIODICAL
Executive Female
National Association of Female Executives
P.O. Box 1902
Marion, OH 43306-2002

I suspect these people put me on Planned Parenthood's mailing list, mainly because of the editorial slant I have detected of late (e.g., the phony magazine survey to determine if there is a need for federal day-care policy). This is a pity, because NAFE has a number of very helpful benefits to home businesswomen, including group insurance. Membership dues to NAFE ($29/year) include a subscription to the magazine.

Inc. Magazine
Subscription Service Department
P.O. Box 51534
Boulder, CO 80321-1534
1-800-444-1756 for the toll-free reader response line.

Inc. is not about how to start a home business. The editors are into "growth" companies—meaning debt capitalism. However, *Inc.* publishes very nice articles on management

Chapter 11
The Two-Minute Manager Comes Home

theory and excellently-written features on the trials and tribulations of actual businesses, and offers book reviews and lots of other useful info for the would-be manager. They also sell how-to-start-a-business videos and reprints of past articles.

Chapter 12
A Nice Little Family Business

Lynie Arden. *The Work-At-Home Sourcebook.* Only guide available to more than 500 companies with homework programs. Job descriptions, pay and benefits, how to get the job, and how to work like a pro at home. Very useful for those not quite ready to start their own business. *New Careers Center.*

Barbara Brabec. *Homemade Money: The Definitive Guide to Success in a Home Business.* The editor/publisher of *The National Home Business Report* covers a lot of ground in this book, from how to get free publicity for your business to how to avoid horror stories. Typical startup information; not-so-typical contributions by various experts (lawyers, tax accountants, etc.) that give more details. Invaluable listing of resources—other books, newsletters, organizations, and so on, that can help you make it. Regularly updated. *New Careers Center.*

Paul and Sarah Edwards. *Working from Home.* A big book that covers what you need to know about living and working under the same roof. Presenting a professional image. Zoning. Licenses. Laws. Home office. Marketing. A-Z listing of possible home businesses. The authors have somewhat negative attitudes about marriage and child-rearing; all their recommended reading on this subjects is from the Sickness Model. *New Careers Center.*

M. D. Jenkins, ed. *Starting and Operating a Business In . . .* What you need to set up shop in any state in the Union. Different edition for each state. Checklists, state forms required, condensed business overview, more. Updated annually. *New Careers Center.*

Bernard Kamaroff, C.P.A. *Small-Time Operator: How to Start Your Own Small Business, Keep Your Books, Pay Your Taxes, and Stay out of Trouble.* This book is Mr. Kamaroff's only title—but with a quarter of a million copies in print, he's not worrying! Best intro to the dreaded world of small business record-keeping. Sample forms, examples, upbeat explanations. Updated regularly. *New Careers Center*

Julian Simon. *How to Start and Operate a Mail-Order Business*. You've seen the ads for this hefty and expensive book and wondered "Is it worth it?" I could live without the lengthy quotes and lugubrious stories in the hardcover version, but Simon's step-by-step game plan for learning the mail-order biz is the best. No magic: Simon just points you in the right direction and tells you how to do your own market research. 99 out of 100 readers will be too lazy to follow his advice, which means *you* have a real advantage! An abridged, softcover version (*Getting Into the Mail-Order Business*) is also available. *New Careers Center*.

PERIODICAL
The Worksteader News. Edited and published by Lynie Arden, author of *The Work-at-Home Sourcebook* (see above under Books). Hundreds of ideas on how to start and operate a successful home-based business, where and how to get a home-based job, or how to move your present work situation home. Each issue features a pull-out section listing home work jobs, business opportunities, and new markets for your products if you're already in business. Mrs. Arden has worked at home for 20 years and knows the ropes. *New Careers Center*.

ORGANIZATIONS
The National Alliance of Homebased Businesswomen
Box 306
Midland Park, NJ 07432

The professional organization for home businessfolks. Workshops, seminars, discounted group insurance, newsletter. You don't have to be a woman to join.

SUPPLIER
The Reliable Corporation
1001 W. Van Buren St.
Chicago, IL 60607
Orders: 1-800-621-4344. Fax: 1-800-621-6002. Customer Service 1-800-621-5954.
Visa, MC, or open account.
Good service, guarantee, free shipping on most orders.

Reliable is . . . well . . . reliable. This company is your one-stop shopping source for office equipment and supplies, common office furniture, mailroom equipment and supplies, and so on. All discounted, by the way! Ask to be put on their list to receive monthly sales catalogs. Reliable has a separate Home Office catalog filled with more trendy designed furniture, colored paper clips, and other yuppie fancies. If you're serious about home business, you'll probably end up ordering from the regular catalog, but it doesn't hurt to request the other one too. Small businesses are Reliable's main customers, so don't be shy about ordering from your kitchen phone or applying for open account status.

Chapter 13
Family Practice (Church Growth from the Bottom Up)

Roland Allen. *Missionary Methods: St. Paul's or Ours?* Grand Rapids: Wm. B. Eerdmans Publishing Co., 1962. Written in the 1920s by an Anglican missionary, *Missionary Methods* proves Scripturally that St. Paul's missionary success is possible for us today if only we will readopt his methods (spelled out in this book). Places great stress on developing truly independent, self-sustaining, self-replicating churches and trusting in the Holy Spirit, rather than our bureaucratic controls, to keep the work alive and pure. Even more relevant today than when it was written. *Great Christian Books.*

Chapter 14
The Church in Your Living Room

Matthew Henry. *The Complete Works of Matthew Henry: Volume 2.* Grand Rapids, MI: Baker Book House, 1979. Matthew Henry was perhaps the most well-rounded, warm, balanced Christian who ever lived. The son of a distinguished English pastor, Matthew Henry had all the advantages of a Christian childhood nourished by parents who were intent on handing their spiritual capital on to their children. He became a pastor, a devoted husband and father, and the author of the most widely-read Bible commentary in the English language. If Christians today would read Henry and put what he says into practice, we could be giants for God instead of pygmies. His sermon "A Church in the House" is alone worth the price of the book. *Great Christian Books.*

Bill Pride. *Flirting with the Devil.* Westchester, IL: Crossway Books, 1988. I may be prejudiced, but I think this is a wonderful book for any family head who wants to lead his family to spiritual victory. Bill examines the temptations of Adam and Eve in the Garden of Eden and Jesus in the wilderness—the two times Satan came out from undercover with his temptations—and applies these lessons to today, with some surprising results! *Home Life.*

SUPPLIERS
Menconi Ministries
P.O. Box 969
Cardiff by the Sea, CA 92007-0969
(619) 436-8676 M-Fri 8:30-4:30 PST.

Donation-supported ministry that also offers books, tapes, and other helps for sale. *Media Update* newsletter, nicely produced, $10/six issues. The Praise Company discount Christian music catalog, $5 (also includes CD's and records). Al Menconi has a seminar on rock music that has been very effective in getting kids who are addicted to it to switch to Christian music. He certainly knows his stuff.

Reformed Presbyterian Church of North America
Board of Education and Publications
7418 Penn Ave.
Pittsburgh, PA 15208-2531
(412) 241-0436

Publisher of *The Book of Psalms for Singing* (available in hardback and looseleaf). Should have its new Psalms-on-cassette teaching tape series ready by the time this book is out. Free catalog. Quantity discounts, wholesale discounts to retailers.

Send the Light
P.O. Box 28
Waynesboro, GA 30830

Operation World, $7.95. Prayer cards, $2/set. Colorful world map, $2. All three, $10. Free postage on prepaid items.

Youth with a Mission
Box 55787
Seattle, WA 98155
1-800-922-2143 Visa, MC or inquiries, 7-5 PST M-Fri.
WA: (206) 771-1153.

Missions group with numerous overseas ministries. Publisher of *Personal Prayer Diary/Daily Planner* ($13.95 postpaid). Also sells Christian books and tapes on witnessing, prayer, spiritual warfare, and missions.

Chapter 15
"It's Superfamily!"

Verlon Harp. *House Churches Among the Churches of Christ During the 1980s.* Fort Worth, TX: Star Bible Publications, 1987. Little booklet contains pioneering research work based on questionnaires sent to churches that use "house churches." $1.50 from Star Bible Publications, P.O. Box 181220, Fort Worth, TX 76118. 1-800-433-7505 M-F 8-4:30 CST.

Alvin Jennings. *How Christianity Grows in the City.* Fort Worth, TX: Star Bible Publications, 1985. Tremendous little book on how "house churches" are being used in modern cities to grow the church faster, stronger, and more Biblically. $3.95 from Star Bible Publications, P.O. Box 181220, Fort Worth, TX 76118. 1-800-433-7505 M-F 8-4:30 CST.

Lawson Lau.*The World at Your Doorstep: A Handbook for International Student Ministry.* Downers Grove, IL: InterVarsity Press, 1984. All the information you need to get started in this ministry: how to do it, how *not* to do it, organizations that can help, statistics, true stories, etc. *GCB.*

Charles Murray. *In Pursuit of Happiness and Good Government.* New York: Simon and Schuster, 1988. 303 pages plus index. This book clearly and cogently makes the case for voluntarism as opposed to statism. It's fun to read, if you like "thinking" books, and even if you don't Chapters 9-13 will open your eyes. Every Christian leader (and I'm including pastors, Sunday school teachers, Christian school teachers, and all heads of households) should read this book. *Conservative Book Club.*

Recommended
Periodicals

Above Rubies, P.O. Box 500, Broadbeach, Qld. 4218, Australia. Lovely, glossy, colorful "magazine to promote family life" that really does! Unabashedly pro-baby, pro-life, pro-marriage. Strong evangelistic message, but no nasty sinner-bashing. About 180,000 copies are printed of each issue, many going as bulk subscriptions to churches and Christian organizations.No back issues are available—all have been snapped up! Printed 2-4 times a year, depending on finances. I strongly suggest that you get these in bulk for your church. Editress Nancy Campbell suggests the following rates (send Australian currency bank draft) if you would care to cover the cost of the publication (please do!):

Quantity	Sea Mail price	Air Mail price
1 magazine	$.47 Australian dollars	$1.20 Australian dollars
3-5	1.00	3.90
6-10	1.85	7.45
11-20	3.70	14.85
21-48	7.25	25.25
49-60	9.15	53.65
61-100	11.05	46.05

HELP. Our own newsletter. Quarterly. Freewheeling discussion of all topics covered in this book plus a few more. Resources, ideas, tips, many contributed by readers. Dedicated to providing readers with the tools to build Christ's kingdom in their homes. Subscription (4 issues) $15. Back issue, $4. *Home Life.*

Insight, P.O. Box 91022, Washington, DC 20090-1022. 1-800-356-3588. One year (51 issues), $25.50. Glossy secular newsweekly that always covers the issues of most interest to me from a far less obnoxious editorial viewpoint than, say, *Time* or *Newsweek.* A subscription to *Insight* and *World* (see below) will get you all the news you realistically can use.

The Teaching Home, P.O. Box 20219, Portland, OR 97220-0219. Bi-monthly. By far the best Christian home-schooling magazine. Features in-depth articles, interviews, commentary, news, reviews, and advertising covering all aspects of home schooling. State editions are bound inside for subscribers in most states, and even Australia. Subscription (6 issues) $15. All back issues available.

Welcome Home, P.O. Box 2208, Merrifield, VA 22116. "A publication in support of mothers who choose to stay at home." Less confident tone than *HELP*—lots of articles justifying staying home. Problem-solving approach. Secular and Christian contributors. $15/six issues.

World. P.O. Box 2330, Asheville, NC 28802. The best Christian newsmagazine around. A size you can read in one sitting, nice professional colorful layout, straightforward editorial positions, great writing by heavy hitters like Cal Thomas and Russ Pulliam. Plus cartoons, letters to the editor, news shorts, features, analysis, money and economics coverage, and so on. *World* covers the "big" stories—not just religious news. One year (weekly during school year, bi-weekly in December and during the summer months), $18. Sample subscription, 11 weeks for $5 (prepaid). While you're at it, sign up for subscriptions to *God's World* weekly-reader newspapers for your children at the same address ($9.50 per sub). Each age group has its own newspaper during the school year. These great little papers feature news stories, editorials, zany Foto Files and cartoons, and letters to the editor.

Suppliers

Christian Life Workshops
182 S.E. Kane Rd.
Gresham, OR 97030
(503) 667-3942

Gregg Harris's *Family Restoration Workshop* and his *Home Schooling Workshop* are the best workshops you've probably ever attended.Write CLW for a brochure listing workshops for the year. Or do the next best thing and buy each workshop on cassette tapes. Videos are also available for viewing by groups too small to sponsor the whole Workshop. The CLW mail-order bookstore also carries titles of interest to readers of this book. Highly recommended.

Conservative Book Club
15 Oakland Ave.
Harrison, NY 10528

You promise to buy four books over the next two years and are treated to some fabulous offer, like the hardback *McGuffey* readers ($80 value) for $10. CBC offers the latest and greatest books on education, politics, economics, family life, and the like, through its every-six-weeks Bulletin. You return the card or get the Featured Selection.

Great Christian Books (GCB)
1319 Newport Gap Pike
Wilmington, DE 19804-2895
(302) 999-8317 8 AM - 5 PM EST M-Fri for orders.
(302) 999-0595 for information.
Dues: $5/year US, $8 Canada/Mexico, $12 overseas.
Membership automatically renewed each time you order. The very best in current and classic Christian books at great discounts. Wonderful service, great selection. Membership entitles you to the monthly catalogs. Home-schooling books, children's books, music, reference, best-sellers, commentaries, lots more. If you want to build up

your spiritual capital in a hurry, join GCB and read the books they recommend the most. It worked for us!

Home Life
P.O. Box 1250
Fenton, MO 63026

Our home business. Books, videos, and video players. We sell our own books (naturally!) plus all the Don Aslett books and a select line of other titles that enhance fruitful family life. Free catalog.

The New Careers Center
1515 - 23rd St.
P.O. Box 297
Boulder, CO 80306
(303) 447-1087 noon-4 PM Mountain time M-Fri. Credit cards only; minimum $20. Office closed December 21-31.

Send these folks $1 and ask for their "Whole Work Catalog." It offers books, cassette tapes, newsletter subscriptions and other materials in the categories of alternative careers, working from home, self-employment, and "better ways of working." Tom and Sue Ellison, the catalog publishers, have done a great job of bringing together the best secular books on these topics. The catalog emphasis is on finding the calling that is right for you—this goes well with the Christian point of view, even though the books are not Christian. One year money-back guarantee.

Index